physiology
coloring workbook

the **princeton review**

physiology
coloring workbook

Kenneth Axen, Ph.D.
New York University Medical Center

and

Kathleen Vermitsky Axen, Ph.D.
Brooklyn College of CUNY

Random House, Inc.
New York

Princeton Review Publishing, L.L.C.
2315 Broadway
New York, NY 10024
E-mail: info@review.com

ISBN: 0-679-77850-0
ISSN: 1093-9849

Editor: Rachel Warren
Designer: Kirsten Ulve
Production Editor: James Petrozzello
Production Supervisor: Chee Pae
Manufactured in the United States of America on partially recycled paper

9

Dedication

We lovingly dedicate this book to
Laurel, Christine, Marie, and Nils

Acknowledgments

We are deeply grateful to Evan Schnittman, who provided us with the opportunity to create this book, and to Rachel Warren, whose meticulous editing and thoughtful suggestions improved the clarity and readability of the manuscript.

We also thank John Bergdahl, Kirstin Ulve, Meher Khambata, and Evelyn O'Hara for the beautiful layout, and Fernando Galeano for the elegant cover design.

We are particularly indebted to Jessica Zeuli, whose coloring recommendations added to the beauty and informational content of our drawings.

Preface

Our goal was to create a clearly written, beautifully illustrated overview for a one-semester, undergraduate course in human physiology. The text evolved from extensive lecture notes that we each prepared while teaching courses to physical therapy students and health science majors.

Our book contains 250 original, elegant, pen-and-ink illustrations that were drawn by one of the authors. The drawings, which range from simple to complex, are clearly labelled in plain English. More than half of them are completely new and cannot be found in any of the standard physiology text books. The illustrations are related to each other through the use of consistent color symbolism, recurring icons, and extensive cross-referencing. They can also serve as an excellent source of transparencies for lectures.

In accordance with our premise that color contains information that can be used to teach physiology, we developed a consistent coloring scheme in which colors were chosen according to functional, anatomical, or artistic considerations. These colors are indicated on each figure by a simple code that enables you to color the entire illustration without referral to a legend. The act of coloring, according to the color code and the detailed instructions in the caption, guides your study of the figure and helps you understand, and therefore remember, the physiological principles that it presents.

Kenneth Axen, Ph.D.
Associate Professor
Department of Rehabilitation Medicine
New York University Medical Center
400 East 34th Street
New York, NY 10016

Kathleen Vermitsky Axen, Ph.D.
Professor
Department of Health & Nutrition Sciences
Brooklyn College of CUNY
2900 Bedford Avenue
Brooklyn, NY 11210

Coloring Instructions

Colors are coded by a lowercase letter that appears on the figure or as a subscript to a label; a code that is used for a particular shape (icon) in a figure applies to all like icons in that figure. The code for each of the 16 different colors that are used in this book appears at the bottom of the even-numbered pages. The symbol "_" is used to indicate application of the color with light pressure; try using the side of the lead.

We used colored pencils that were purchased in an art supply store. The colors included three blues; azure (sky blue), blue (true blue), and navy (indigo blue), two yellows; canary (canary yellow) and yellow (yellow ochre); and one each of gray (light grey), green (grass green), flesh, black, orange (orange ochre), pink, red (crimson red), sienna (terra cotta or brown), tan (golden brown), violet (or lavender), and white (do not color).

Color each illustration as instructed in the figure caption, which guides you through the processes depicted in the figure in the proper sequence. Use the colors that are indicated, since they have been carefully chosen to convey information.

Some examples of our color scheme are:

* green (meaning "go") is the color of sodium, sodium channels, and excitatory neurotransmitters. Therefore, depolarization, muscle contraction, and the QRS complex of the ECG are also green to indicate that these processes are mediated by an influx of sodium ions into cells.

* red (meaning "stop") is the color of potassium, potassium channels, and inhibitory neurotransmitters. Therefore, repolarization, hyperpolarization, muscle relaxation, and the T wave of the ECG are also red to indicate that these processes are mediated by an efflux of potassium ions out of cells.

* arterial blood is red, capillary blood is violet, and venous blood is blue to indicate the corresponding oxygen content of the blood.

* nerves are yellow; skeletal muscle, cardiac muscle, and gastrointestinal smooth muscle are orange; vascular smooth muscle is red; the liver is sienna; and adipose tissue is canary.

When the book is completely colored, it will serve as a useful study tool for review.

Table of Contents

CHAPTER FIVE: MUSCLE

CHAPTER SIX: CARDIOVASCULAR SYSTEM

chapter **one**
homeostasis

The unicellular organism

Unicellular organisms that live in a pond transport nutrients across their cell membranes and excrete their waste products directly into their environment. Since a single cell is miniscule in relation to a pond, the cellular functions it performs in order to sustain its life do not disturb the quality of the pond in which it lives.

The multicellular organism

The situation is more complex for multicellular organisms. Imagine a human being as a collection of 100 trillion cells packed together in a small pond of extracellular fluid. The viability of this arrangement requires that nutrients and oxygen be transported to cells that are unable to obtain them by simple diffusion. The cellular functions carried out by closely packed cells could also disturb the quality of the extracellular fluid that surrounds them (Fig. 1.1). Waste products of cellular metabolism must therefore be removed before they pollute the extracellular fluid.

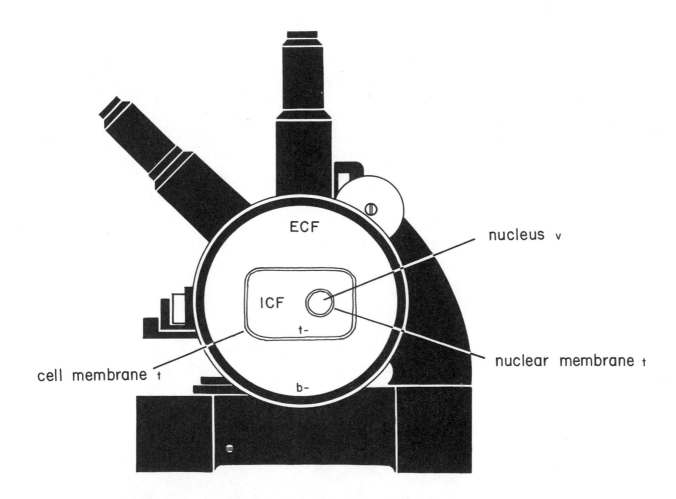

Figure 1.1 *A mammalian cell and its environment. Color the structures, noting that the cell membrane separates the intracellular fluid (ICF) from the extracellular fluid (ECF).*

Homeostasis

Mammalian cells can live, reproduce, and grow only when the extracellular fluid that bathes them has the appropriate concentrations of glucose, oxygen, carbon dioxide, hydrogen ions (acidity), and electrolytes. Mammalian cells thrive when the concentration of glucose in the blood is 80 mg/dL, the oxygen and carbon dioxide tensions are 100 and 40 mmHg, respectively, the pH is 7.4, the concentrations of sodium and potassium in extracellular fluid are 142 and 4 mEq/L, respectively, and the body temperature is 37°C (Fig. 1.2). Homeostasis is the term used to denote this constancy of the body's internal environment.

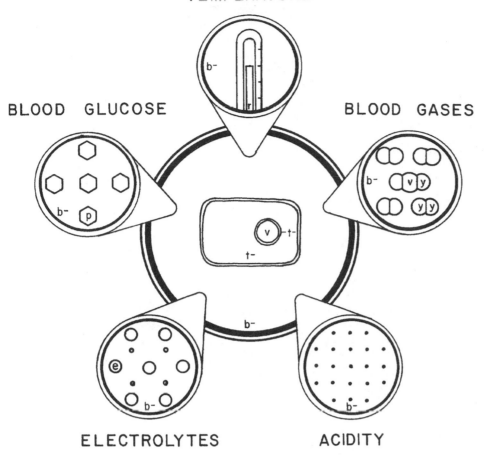

TEMPERATURE

BLOOD GLUCOSE

BLOOD GASES

ELECTROLYTES

ACIDITY

Figure 1.2 *Homeostasis. The fluid that surrounds each mammalian cell is kept at 37°C and has normal concentrations of gases (oxygen and carbon dioxide), hydrogen ions (acidity), electrolytes, and glucose. Each parameter is maintained at its normal level by one or more homeostatic mechanisms, which regulate the actions of specific organ systems. Begin by coloring the interior of the cell and then work outward.*

A variety of physiological mechanisms operate to maintain homeostasis in the face of potentially disruptive external forces (Fig. 1.3). Each of these homeostatic mechanisms works by regulating the actions of specific organ systems.

Figure 1.3 *Naturally occurring factors that can disrupt homeostasis. Homeostatic mechanisms defend the constancy of the extracellular fluid against each of these factors. Begin by coloring the interior of the cell and then work outward. Note that extracellular fluid surrounds the cell and therefore protects it from potentially harmful changes in the external environment.*

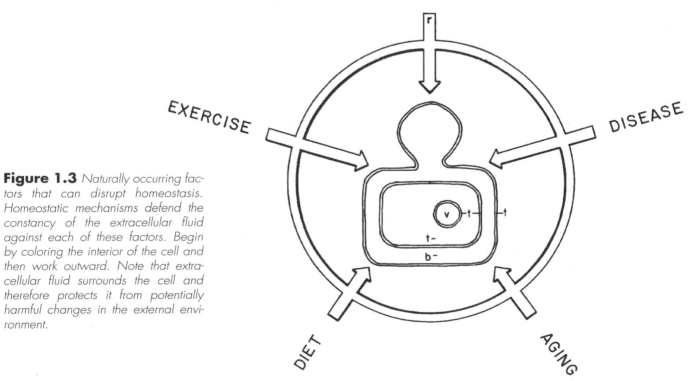

ENVIRONMENT

EXERCISE

DISEASE

DIET

AGING

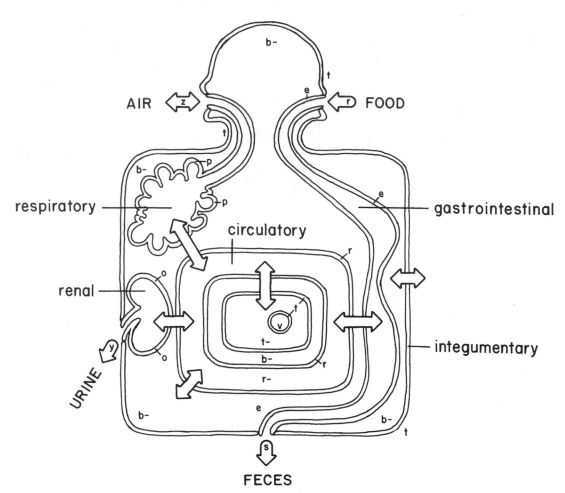

Figure 1.4 *Organ systems that maintain homeostasis. Arrows indicate movement of substances across membranes or between the internal and the external environments. Begin by coloring the interior of the cell and then work outward. Note that the circulatory system is the medium through which the respiratory, gastrointestinal, and renal systems interact with the cell.*

Organ systems

Figure 1.4 illustrates a number of organ systems that work to maintain homeostasis. The circulatory system transports essential substances to cells and removes metabolic waste products from them (Chapter 6). The renal system removes metabolic waste products from the blood and excretes them in the urine; it also regulates the levels of constituents of the body fluids (Chapter 7). The respiratory system supplies oxygen (O_2) to, and removes excess carbon dioxide (CO_2) from, the blood (Chapter 8). The gastrointestinal system digests food and absorbs the products of digestion into the body (Chapter 9). The integumentary system (the skin) protects the body against injury and dehydration.

Not shown in Fig. 1.4 are the musculoskeletal system, which is responsible for locomotion (Chapter 5), the nervous (Chapter 4) and endocrine (Chapter 11) systems, which regulate cell function, and the reproductive system, which is responsible for the perpetuation of the species (Chapter 12).

Specific examples of organ systems that provide homeostasis

The renal and respiratory systems maintain the pH of body fluids (Figs. 8.32, 8.33). The cardiovascular, renal, and nervous systems keep arterial blood pressure at 120/80 mmHg (Fig. 6.31). The digestive and endocrine systems provide normal blood levels of glucose (Fig. 11.15). The respiratory system maintains normal levels of oxygen and carbon dioxide in arterial blood (Fig. 8.29). The renal and endocrine systems maintain normal concentrations of sodium (Fig. 7.26), potassium (Fig. 7.27), and calcium (Fig. 11.13) in extracellular fluid.

Negative feedback control systems

Each of the above homeostatic mechanisms can be described as a negative feedback control system. For this reason, an understanding of negative feedback control systems is extremely useful to an understanding of physiology. One example of a negative feedback control system that you are probably familiar with is a room temperature control system that consists of a thermostat, a furnace, and a thermometer (Fig. 1.5).

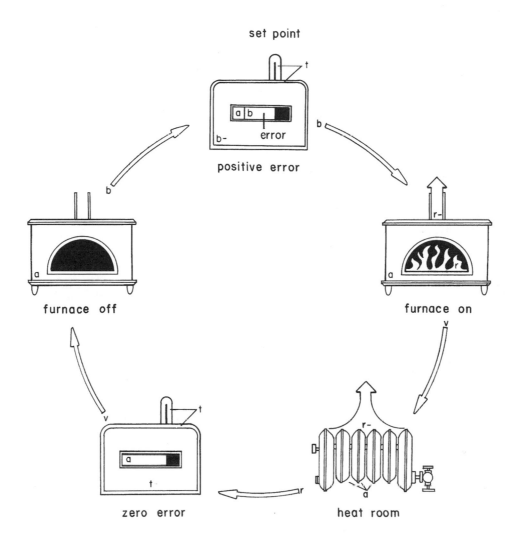

Figure 1.5 *A room temperature control system. Begin by coloring the thermostat at the top and then work clockwise. In this example, the cycle begins when the thermostat set point is moved to a higher temperature. This generates a positive error signal that turns on the furnace and heats the room. When the room temperature rises to the point where it matches the thermostat set point, the error signal becomes zero and the thermostat turns off the furnace. The cycle repeats whenever room temperature falls below the set point again.*

The thermostat compares the desired room temperature (which is indicated by the thermostat setting, or set point) with the actual room temperature (which is indicated by the thermometer). The thermostat uses the difference between the two readings (desired temperature minus actual temperature) to generate an error signal. This enables the signal from the thermometer to form a negative feedback loop that causes the thermostat to shut the furnace off whenever room temperature matches or exceeds the thermostat set point (Fig. 1.6).

This system is designed so that the sign of the error signal is positive when the set point is higher than the actual temperature (the room is colder than desired), and negative when the set point is lower than the actual temperature (the room is hotter than desired). Thus, by using the sign of the error signal to operate the furnace switch, the system maintains room temperature at the desired level by automatically turning on the furnace when the room is too cold and turning it off when the room is too hot.

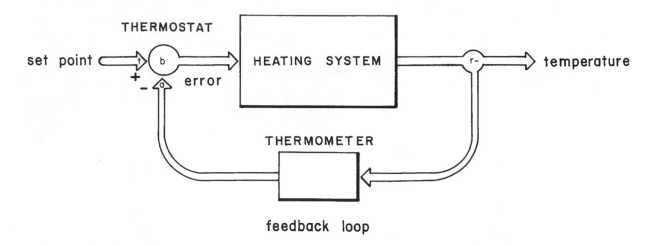

Figure 1.6 *Block diagram of a room temperature control system. By using the sign of the error signal to operate the furnace, this negative feedback control system automatically maintains room temperature at the level dictated by the set point. Begin by coloring the set point and then work clockwise.*

Physiological control systems

Physiological control systems work in a way that is similar to the room temperature control system described above. Physiological control systems employ a sensory receptor (which is analogous to the thermometer), a comparator network (the thermostat), and a physiological system (the furnace) that adjusts the variable that the system is designed to control (Fig. 1.7).

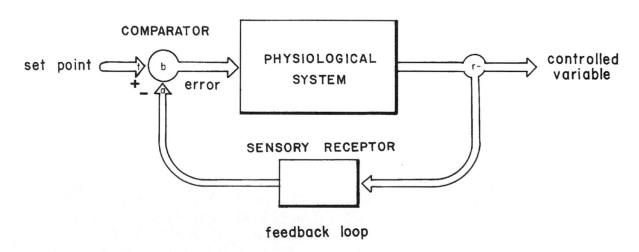

Figure 1.7 *Block diagram of a physiological control system. By using the sign of the error signal to stimulate a physiological system, this system automatically maintains a controlled variable at the level dictated by the set point. Controlled variables, discussed later in more detail, include arterial blood pressure (Fig. 6.31), carbon dioxide tension in arterial blood (Fig. 8.29), and the concentrations of sodium (Fig. 7.26), potassium (Fig. 7.27), calcium (Fig. 11.13), and glucose (Fig. 11.15). Compare this system with the room temperature control system shown in Fig. 1.6. Begin by coloring the set point and then work clockwise.*

Sensory receptors in physiological control systems transmit coded signals to specialized comparator centers that contain internal set points. This arrangement enables the comparator center to generate an error signal that, in turn, stimulates the appropriate organ systems to raise the controlled variable when it is too low and lower it when it is too high. The components of physiological control systems communicate with each other through chemical, neural, or neurochemical pathways (Fig. 1.8).

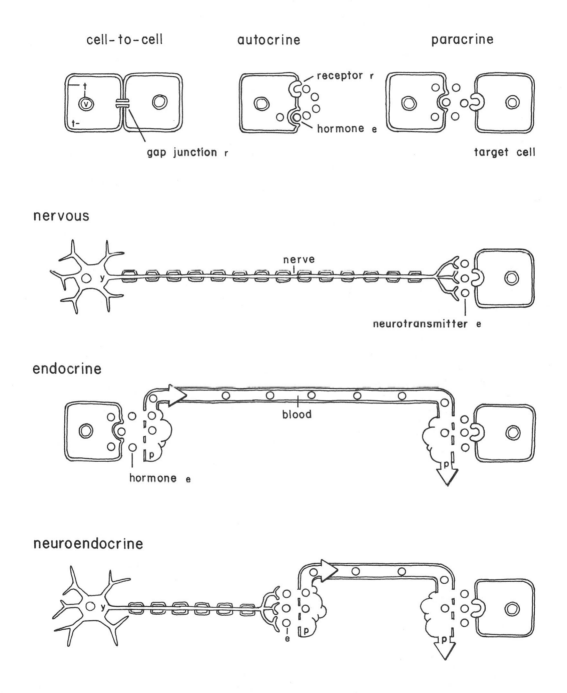

Figure 1.8 *Mechanisms whereby cells can communicate with each other. Color the cells (t-), cell membranes (t), nuclei (v) receptors (r), neurotransmitters (e), and hormones (e) for each method of communication. Begin by coloring the cell-to-cell communication and then color the autocrine and paracrine communications. Color the nervous, endocrine, and neuroendocrine communications from left to right until you reach the target cells. Note that the receptors on target cells can be stimulated by neurotransmitters released by nerve cells or by hormones released by autocrine, paracrine, and endocrine cells.*

The body is equipped with a multitude of sensory receptors that generate signals that are related to the intensity of the mechanical, chemical, or other stimulation that they receive. Sensory receptors, which are described later in more detail, include: muscle spindles (Fig. 4.16), free nerve endings and Pacinian corpuscles (Fig. 4.17), arterial baroreceptors (Fig. 6.28), arterial chemoreceptors (Fig. 8.28) and respiratory mechanoreceptors (Fig. 8.31).

Some physiological control systems employ neural signals that are transmitted along nerve pathways (Fig. 1.9) whereas other systems employ humoral signals that are sent through the blood (Fig. 1.10).

Figure 1.9 *A physiological control system employing neural signals that are transmitted along nerve pathways. Begin at the top by coloring the set point nerve and then work down until you reach the controlled variable. Note that the motor nerve releases neurotransmitters that stimulate the effector organ to adjust the controlled variable, and that the controlled variable is detected by the sensory receptor at the bottom. Now color the feedback loop, which consists of the sensory receptor, its sensory nerve, and the neurotransmitter it releases. In this example, the set point nerve is shown to stimulate the motor nerve (indicated by green neurotransmitter) whereas the sensory nerve is shown to inhibit it (indicated by red neurotransmitter). Thus, the system is a negative feedback control system because the set point nerve and the sensory feedback nerve have opposite effects on the effector organ.*

Fig. 1.10 *A physiological control system employing humoral signals that are sent through the blood. In this example, the controlled variable is detected by an endocrine gland that contains an internal set point. The hormone released by the endocrine gland travels through the blood to stimulate the target organ to adjust the controlled variable. Begin by coloring the endocrine gland and the hormone it releases. Then work clockwise until you reach the controlled variable. Note similarities and differences between this negative feedback control system and that shown in Fig. 1.9.*

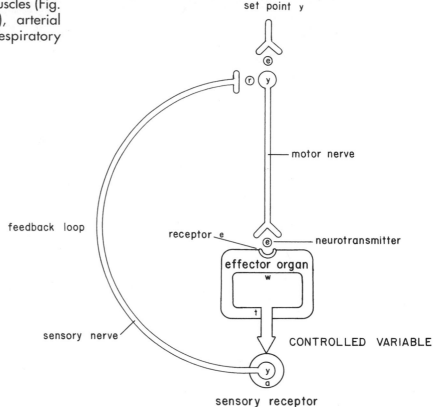

set point y

motor nerve

receptor e — neurotransmitter

effector organ
w
t

feedback loop

sensory nerve

CONTROLLED VARIABLE

sensory receptor

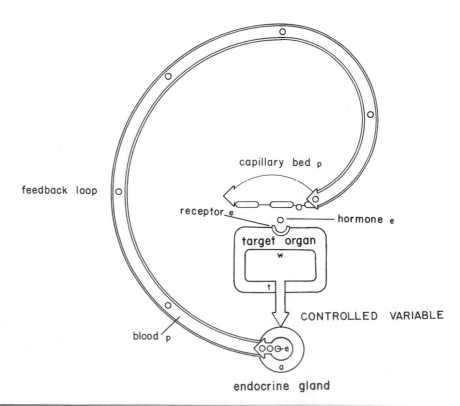

capillary bed p

feedback loop

receptor e — hormone e

target organ
w
t

CONTROLLED VARIABLE

blood p

endocrine gland

chapter **two**
the cell

Anatomy of the cell

Each mammalian cell contains a nucleus that is surrounded by a nuclear membrane and a cytoplasm that is surrounded by a cell membrane (Fig. 1.1). Cells also contain specialized structures called organelles. The major organelles are described below; they are the cell membrane, endoplasmic reticulum, Golgi apparatus, lysosomes, mitochondria, and nucleus (Fig. 2.1).

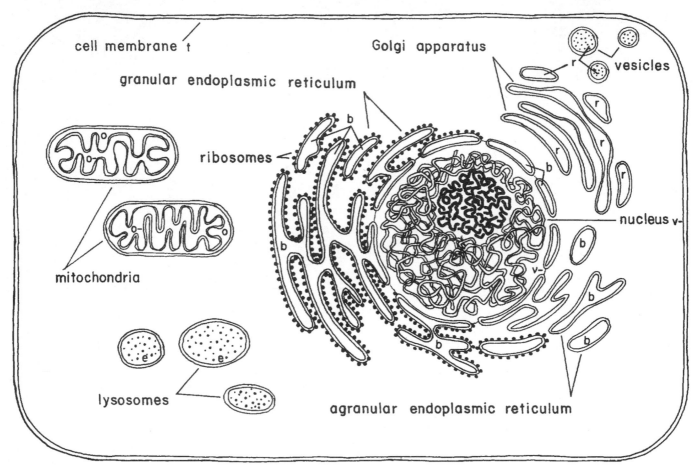

Figure 2.1 *The cell and its organelles. Identify and color each organelle when it first appears in the text.*

The cell membrane

Cell membranes are composed primarily of phospholipid molecules interspersed with large globular protein molecules (Fig. 2.2).

Phospholipid molecules have a phosphate head that is soluble in water (this end is hydrophilic) and a fatty acid tail that is soluble only in fat (this end is hydrophobic). Since fatty acids are repelled by water but attracted to each other, the phospholipid molecules align themselves with their fatty acid tails oriented toward each other. As a result, the cell membrane forms a lipid bilayer that prevents the free movement of water and water-soluble substances across it.

Cell membranes contain integral proteins that span the lipid bilayer and peripheral proteins that are embedded in only one side of the membrane (Fig. 2.2). Some integral proteins provide channels for the passage of specific substances while others serve as carrier proteins in active transport mechanisms (Fig. 3.11). Many peripheral proteins act as enzymes that catalyze intracellular biochemical reactions.

Some integral proteins also combine with carbohydrates to form glycoproteins. In the same way, some membrane lipids combine with carbohydrates to form glycolipids (Fig. 2.2). The binding of circulating hormones to glycoproteins on membrane receptors activates intracellular enzymes that catalyze biochemical reactions (Fig. 11.3).

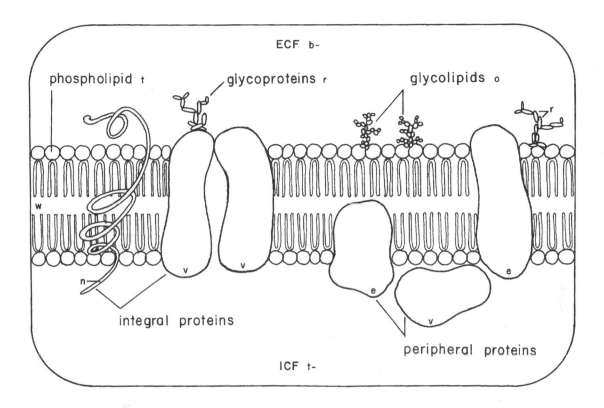

Figure 2.2 *The cell membrane. Identify and color each structure as you see it in the text. Note that the integral proteins penetrate both sides of the membrane whereas the peripheral proteins are embedded in only one side. ECF, extracellular fluid; ICF, intracellular fluid.*

Endoplasmic reticulum

The endoplasmic reticulum is a network of interconnected tubular structures that is enclosed by a lipid bilayer membrane with a large surface area. Granular (rough) endoplasmic reticulum contains ribosomes that are the sites of protein synthesis (Fig. 2.8). Agranular (smooth) endoplasmic reticulum is the site of the synthesis of lipid substances such as cholesterol, steroids, and phospholipids (Fig. 2.1).

Golgi apparatus

The Golgi apparatus is made up of stacked layers of flat vesicles (vesicles are membrane-enclosed sacs) and is located near the nucleus. Substances are transported to the Golgi apparatus from the endoplasmic reticulum by pinocytosis (Fig. 3.2). The Golgi apparatus forms lysosomes, secretory vesicles, and other cytoplasmic components (Fig. 2.1).

Lysosomes

Lysosomes are vesicular organelles that contain hydrolytic enzymes that break molecular bonds (Fig. 9.16). In this way, lysosomes act as an intracellular digestive system that enables the cell to break down a variety of substances, including proteins, lipids, glycogen, nucleic acids, and mucopolysaccharides (Fig. 2.1).

Mitochondria

The mitochondria have an outer and an inner lipid bilayer membrane (Fig. 2.1). The inner membrane has numerous folds called cristae. The inner membrane is the location of the electron transport chain, which captures energy that is released in metabolism and stores it in the high energy bonds of adenosine triphosphate (ATP) (Fig. 10.13). The inner cavity, which is called the matrix, contains oxidative enzymes that catalyze the reactions of the Krebs cycle (Fig. 10.11).

chapter **two**

Nucleus

The nucleus contains large amounts of long, double-stranded molecules of deoxyribonucleic acid (DNA) wound together to form helices. A gene is a specific segment of a DNA molecule that codes for a specific protein. In humans, large numbers of genes are attached end-to-end to form 46 chromosomes that are arranged in 23 pairs (Fig. 12.2). Genes regulate cell function by synthesizing proteins that form cellular structures or act as enzymes or hormones.

The nucleus is surrounded by a nuclear envelope that contains pores that permit the free passage of small molecules. The nuclear envelope is comprised of an inner and an outer lipid bilayer. The outer nuclear membrane is continuous with the endoplasmic reticulum and the space between the inner and outer membranes is continuous with the fluid contained within the endoplasmic reticulum (Fig. 2.1).

Structure of DNA

A strand of DNA is made up of a linear sequence of nucleotides. Each nucleotide consists of a 5-carbon sugar (deoxyribose), a phosphoric acid group, and a nitrogenous base. DNA contains four different bases—two of which are purines (adenine and guanine) and two of which are pyrimidines (thymine and cytosine) (Fig. 2.3).

DNA NUCLEOTIDES

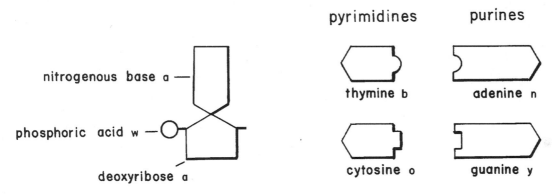

nitrogenous base a

phosphoric acid w

deoxyribose a

pyrimidines

thymine b

cytosine o

purines

adenine n

guanine y

Figure 2.3 *DNA nucleotides. Color each structure. Note that adenine always bonds with thymine and guanine always bonds with cytosine. These combinations form the complementary base pairs in DNA.*

The backbone of each of the two DNA strands is made up of alternating molecules of deoxyribose and phosphoric acid. A base is attached to each of the deoxyribose molecules and the two DNA strands are held together by weak hydrogen bonds between the bases.

The purine base adenine always bonds with the pyrimidine base thymine, and guanine always bonds with cytosine. (Fig. 2.4) Bases that always bond with each other form what is called a complementary pair.

DNA strand

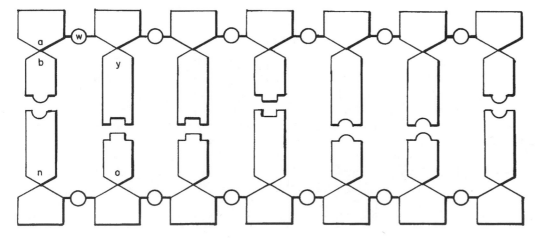

complementary DNA strand

Figure 2.4 *Complementary base pairing in DNA. Begin by coloring the deoxyribose and phosphate groups that form the backbone of each of the DNA strands; note that the two backbones are parallel and identical. Identify and color the nitrogenous bases in each DNA strand (refer to Fig. 2.3). Note that the base sequence in one DNA strand determines the base sequence in the complementary DNA strand.*

gray **b**lue **c**anary gr**ee**n fl**e**sh blac**k** **n**avy **o**range **p**ink **r**ed **s**ienna **t**an **v**iolet **w**hite **y**ellow **a**zure [-] means use light pressure

Structure of RNA

Since DNA does not leave the nucleus, it controls biochemical reactions in the cell by directing the assembly of another nucleic acid, called messenger ribonucleic acid (mRNA), which passes through the nuclear membrane into the cytoplasm.

RNA is similar to DNA in that it also consists of a linear sequence of nucleotides. Each RNA nucleotide is made up of a 5-carbon sugar (ribose), a phosphoric acid group, and a nitrogenous base. The backbone of an RNA molecule is formed by alternating molecules of ribose and phosphoric acid. RNA has uracil in place of thymine, and in RNA adenine always bonds with uracil (Fig. 2.5).

RNA NUCLEOTIDES

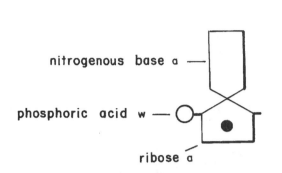

nitrogenous base a —

phosphoric acid w —

ribose a

pyrimidines   purines

uracil v   adenine n

cytosine o   guanine y

Figure 2.5 *RNA nucleotides. Color each structure as you see it in the text. Note that adenine always bonds with uracil and guanine always bonds with cytosine. These combinations form the complementary base pairs in RNA.*

Protein synthesis

Proteins are made up of specific sequences of amino acids linked together by peptide bonds (Fig. 9.32). Since each group of three successive bases in a DNA strand (codon) codes for a specific amino acid, each strand of DNA contains the instructions needed to assemble a specific protein. The process by which the information contained in a sequence of DNA nucleotides is transferred to a complementary sequence of RNA nucleotides is called transcription.

Transcription begins in the nucleus of a cell when an enzyme called RNA polymerase recognizes and binds to a sequence of nucleotides in the DNA strand called a promoter sequence. The attachment of RNA polymerase to the promoter sequence unwinds about two turns of the DNA helix (about 20 nucleotides). The polymerase then moves along the DNA strand and links together RNA nucleotides that are complementary to the DNA nucleotides. This process yields a strand of messenger RNA (mRNA) that contains a transcribed version of the DNA codons (Fig. 2.6). When the polymerase reaches what is called a chain terminating sequence in DNA, it breaks away from the DNA strand and releases the newly-formed strand of mRNA into the cytoplasm.

DNA strand

Figure 2.6 *Complementary base pairing in RNA. Color the nitrogenous bases in the DNA strand and the complementary RNA strand as indicated. Identify each of the bases by referring to Fig. 2.5. Note that the base sequence in the DNA strand determines a unique base sequence in the complementary RNA strand. Finish the picture by coloring the deoxyribose and ribose molecules and the phosphate groups. Note that the backbones of the DNA and RNA strands are similar but not identical.*

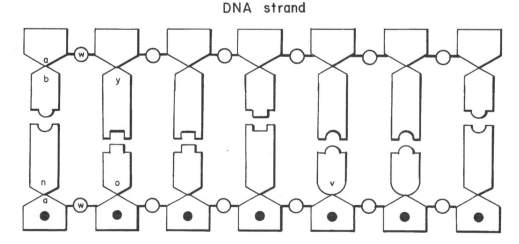

complementary RNA strand

Messenger RNA carries the code for the specific protein to the ribosomes, where protein synthesis takes place. A specific transfer RNA (tRNA) exists for each of the 20 different amino acids found in the body. Each tRNA transports its particular amino acid to the ribosomes where tRNA matches its exposed codon to the complementary codon on the mRNA molecule, thereby lining up the amino acids according to the instructions contained in the mRNA (Fig. 2.7). The process whereby ribosomes read the code of the mRNA and assemble the corresponding protein is called translation (Fig. 2.8).

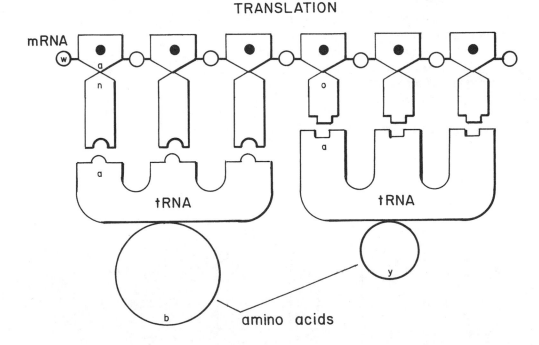

Figure 2.7 *Transcription and translation. Begin with transcription; color the backbones of the DNA and the mRNA strands. Note that the two backbones are parallel but not identical because DNA contains deoxyribose while RNA contains ribose. Identify and color the nitrogenous base pairs in the DNA and mRNA strands (refer to Figs. 2.3 and 2.5). Note that the base sequence of the DNA strand determines the base sequence of the complementary mRNA strand. Move on to translation; color the mRNA strand. Note that this mRNA strand is identical to the one shown for transcription. Color the tRNA molecules and the amino acids that are attached to them. Note that the exposed codons of tRNA complement those of the mRNA strand. Also note that the tRNA codons are similar to those contained in the DNA molecule at top. This result is to be expected, since the complement of a complement yields the original codon.*

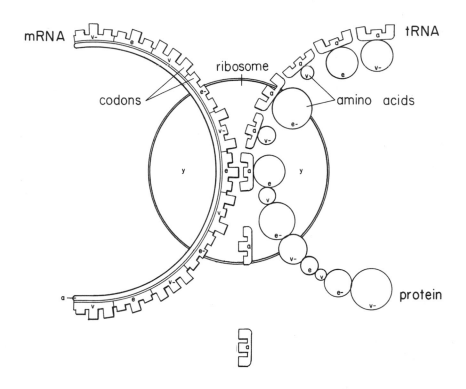

Figure 2.8 *Protein synthesis. Begin by coloring the backbone of mRNA and the individual tRNAs. Examine the shapes of the tRNA and mRNA codons and note that tRNA and mRNA codons form complementary pairs. Color the mRNA codons, the amino acids, and the ribosome as indicated. Note that the color sequence of the mRNA codons is identical to that of the amino acid sequence of the protein synthesized in the process. This shows that the mRNA codons contain the information necessary to synthesize a specific protein.*

chapter **three**
transport mechanisms

A number of transport mechanisms enable cells to move substances across their membranes, which creates a difference in the chemical composition of the intracellular and extracellular fluids.

The transport mechanisms discussed below include the processes of endocytosis, exocytosis, diffusion, filtration, osmosis, conduction, facilitated diffusion, and active transport (Fig. 3.1).

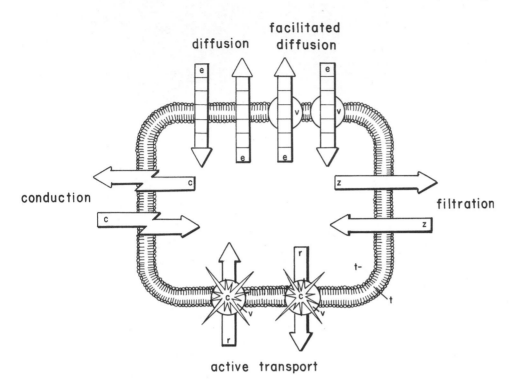

Figure 3.1 *Membrane transport mechanisms. Color the cell, cell membrane, and arrows for each transport mechanism shown. Hatched arrows indicate diffusion (ignore cross hatches when coloring), jagged arrows indicate conduction, and straight unmarked arrows indicate filtration. Note that facilitated diffusion and active transport both require carrier molecules in the cell membrane (indicated by circles in the bilayer membrane). Note also that active transport mechanisms require energy supplied by ATP (indicated by flash*

Endocytosis and exocytosis

Endocytosis is a process in which extracellular substances are ingested by the cell and enclosed in a vesicle derived from the cell membrane. One of the two types of endocytosis is called pinocytosis, which is the ingestion of extracellular fluid; the other is phagocytosis, which is the ingestion of large particles from the extracellular fluid. Phagocytosis begins with the attachment of the particle to specific receptors on the cell membrane. This causes the membrane to invaginate and surround the particle, forming an internal vesicle that pinches off from the membrane (Fig. 3.2). Exocytosis is essentially the reverse of endocytosis.

Figure 3.2 *Endocytosis and exocytosis. Begin with endocytosis by coloring the extracellular fluid (ECF), the particles indicated by circles and triangles within the ECF, and the receptors on the cell membrane indicated by small circles. Color the arrow that points down. Note that the particles that bind to membrane receptors become internalized by the cell through the formation of a vesicle. Color the vesicle and compare its contents with the ECF. Move on to exocytosis by coloring the vesicle shown at the right. Work upward, coloring its arrow and the release of its contents into the ECF. Finish the picture by coloring the intracellular fluid (ICF).*

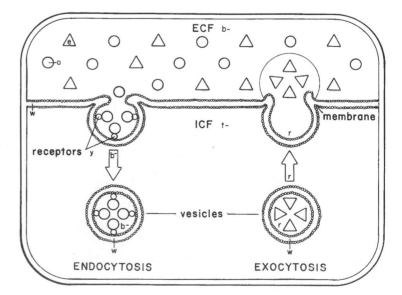

Diffusion

Diffusion is the movement of molecules of gas or dis-solved substances from regions in which they are more concentrated to ones in which they are less concentrated, i.e., down their concentration gradients (Fig. 3.3).

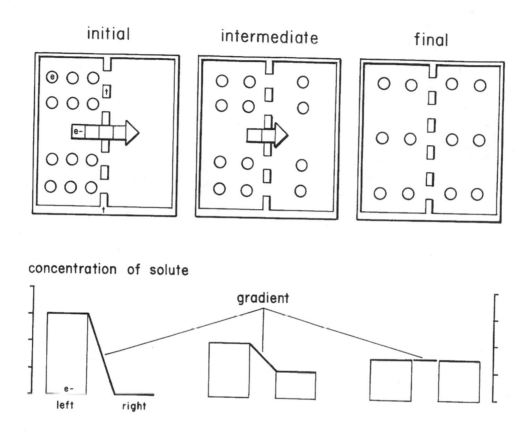

Figure 3.3 *Diffusion. Color the outer walls and the permeable membrane that partitions each of the three boxes into two chambers. Note that the molecules indicated by circles are small enough to pass through the pores of the membrane. Color and count the molecules on each side of the membrane as you move from left (initial state) to right (final state). Color the bar graph below, noting that the height of each bar represents the number of molecules that you just counted in the chamber directly above it. The bar graph enables the concentration gradient for each condition to be visualized from the steepness of the lines that connect the bars. Color the arrows that indicate the rate at which molecules pass through the membrane by diffusion. Note that the rate of diffusion (indicated by the length of the arrow) in each box reflects the magnitude of the concentration gradient (indicated by the slope of the line in the bar graph beneath the box). The horizontal (zero slope) line in the final state shows that the concentration gradient vanishes when molecules appear in equal concentrations on both sides of the membrane.*

The rate of diffusion of any given substance through a membrane depends on three factors: 1) the permeability of the membrane, which is a measure of how easily a particular substance can pass through it (Fig. 3.4); 2) the area and thickness of the membrane (Fig. 3.5); and 3) the concentration gradient (the amount by which the concentration of a substance on one side of the membrane exceeds its concentration on the other) (Fig. 3.3).

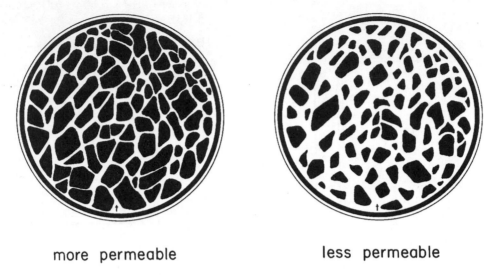

more permeable   less permeable

Figure 3.4 *Effect of pore size on membrane permeability. Color the membrane in each circle; the filled in areas are pores. Note that larger and more numerous pores increase membrane permeability. The permeability of cell membranes for specific substances also depends on the solubility of the substance in the membrane and on whatever electrical charges might also be present.*

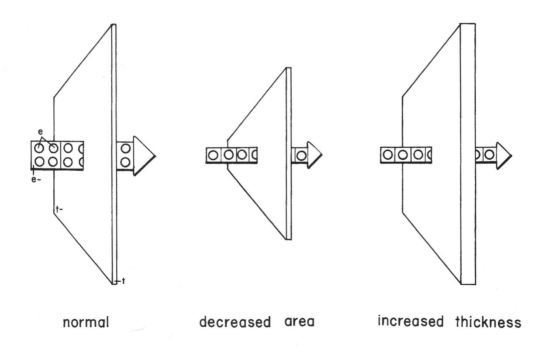

normal   decreased area   increased thickness

Figure 3.5 *Effect of membrane geometry on diffusion. Color the membranes and the diffusion arrows for each of the conditions shown. The size of each arrow indicates the diffusion rate associated with a given concentration gradient. Note that the rate at which molecules diffuse through a membrane (indicated by the size of the arrow) decreases when the membrane has a smaller area and/or a greater width.*

Diffusion is an important process in the transmission of signals from one nerve cell to another (Fig. 4.10), the generation of action potentials in nerve (Fig. 4.7) and muscle (Fig. 5.8) cells, and the movement of oxygen and carbon dioxide across the pulmonary membrane in the lung (Fig. 8.3).

Filtration

Filtration is another transport mechanism in which gas or fluid moves from a region of higher pressure to one of lower pressure. Since the driving force for filtration is a difference in hydrostatic pressure between two regions, filtration is said to occur down a pressure gradient. The hydrostatic pressures that exist in the body are usually measured in terms of the height of a column of fluid and expressed in units of mmHg or cmH_2O (Figs. 3.6, 3.7).

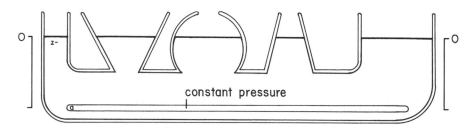

Figure 3.6 *Hydrostatic pressure. The hydrostatic pressure measured at any point in the system shown depends on the vertical distance between that point and the fluid surface, and not on the shape of the vessels that contain the fluid. For this reason, hydrostatic pressures are measured in terms of the height of a column of fluid and expressed in units of cmH_2O or mmHg. By convention, this method considers the pressure at the fluid surface (atmospheric pressure) to be zero. Color the water and note that it fills each container to the same height. Note that the pressure at every point on a given horizontal line is the same.*

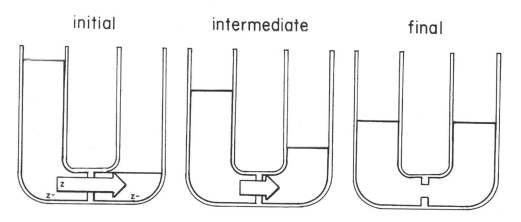

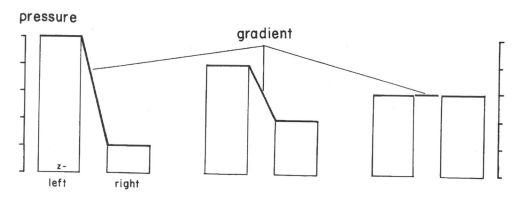

Figure 3.7 *Filtration. Color the water in each of the U-tubes as you move from left (initial state) to right (final state). Color the bar graph below, noting that the height of each bar represents the height of the water in the side of the U-tube directly above it. The bar graph enables the pressure gradient within each U-tube to be visualized from the steepness of the line that connects the bars. Color the arrows that indicate the rate at which water flows from left to right. Note that the rate at which water flows by filtration (indicated by the length of each arrow) reflects the magnitude of the pressure gradient (indicated by the slope of the line in the bar graph beneath it). The horizontal (zero slope) line in the final state indicates that the pressure gradient vanishes when the pressures on both sides of the U-tube are equal. Note the similarities between this bar graph and that shown in Fig. 3.3.*

Filtration occurs when blood flows from the aorta, where blood is at high pressure, to the vena cava, where blood is at low pressure (Fig. 6.1). Filtration also occurs in the kidney and is involved in the production of glomelular filtrate and the movement of fluid through the kidney tubules (Fig. 7.7).

Osmosis

Osmosis is a special case of diffusion; it refers to the dif-

fusion of water or any solvent down its concentration gradient. Concentration gradients for water arise whenever unequal concentrations of particles occur across a membrane that is permeable to water but not to the particle. Such membranes are called semipermeable membranes. Nondiffusible particles exert an osmotic pull on water that can be quantified in terms of an osmotic pressure (π) (Fig. 3.8).

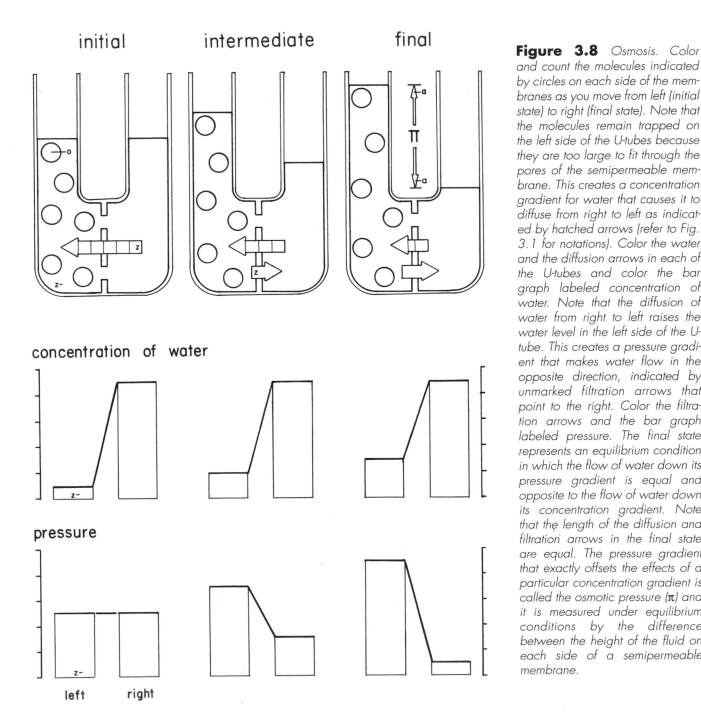

Figure 3.8 *Osmosis. Color and count the molecules indicated by circles on each side of the membranes as you move from left (initial state) to right (final state). Note that the molecules remain trapped on the left side of the U-tubes because they are too large to fit through the pores of the semipermeable membrane. This creates a concentration gradient for water that causes it to diffuse from right to left as indicated by hatched arrows (refer to Fig. 3.1 for notations). Color the water and the diffusion arrows in each of the U-tubes and color the bar graph labeled concentration of water. Note that the diffusion of water from right to left raises the water level in the left side of the U-tube. This creates a pressure gradient that makes water flow in the opposite direction, indicated by unmarked filtration arrows that point to the right. Color the filtration arrows and the bar graph labeled pressure. The final state represents an equilibrium condition in which the flow of water down its pressure gradient is equal and opposite to the flow of water down its concentration gradient. Note that the length of the diffusion and filtration arrows in the final state are equal. The pressure gradient that exactly offsets the effects of a particular concentration gradient is called the osmotic pressure (π) and it is measured under equilibrium conditions by the difference between the height of the fluid on each side of a semipermeable membrane.*

Osmosis plays an important role in the removal of water from tubular fluid so that the kidney can make highly concentrated urine (Fig. 7.25). Since nondiffusible plasma proteins exert an osmotic pull on water, osmosis also plays an important role in preventing excess fluid from leaking out of the capillaries and causing edema (excess fluid in the interstitial space) (Fig. 6.22).

Conduction

Conduction is the movement of ions due to electrical fields, which are produced by unequal distributions of positive and/or negative charges. Since like charges repel one another and unlike charges attract one another, positively charged ions will move from a region of higher concentration to one of lower concentration. Since voltage is a measure of charge density (Fig. 3.9), conduction occurs from a region of higher voltage to one of lower voltage, i.e., down a voltage gradient. Unequal distributions of charges are responsible for the voltage gradients that exist across the membrane of every cell in the body.

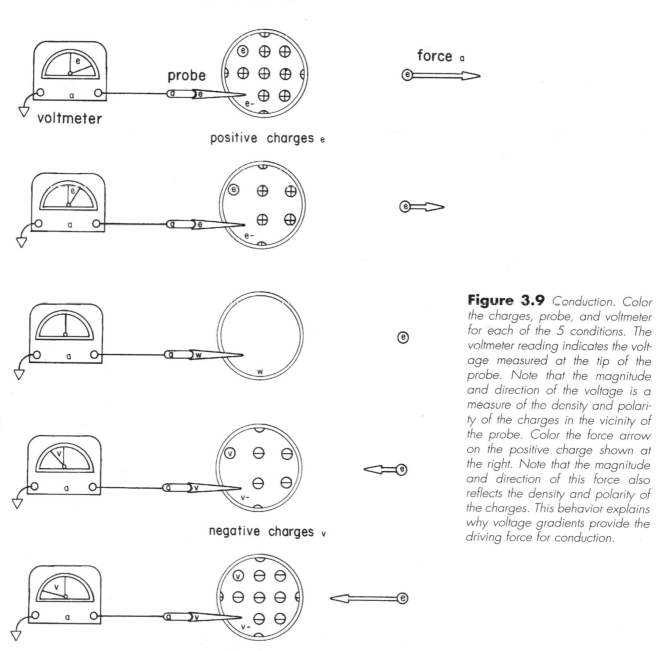

Figure 3.9 *Conduction. Color the charges, probe, and voltmeter for each of the 5 conditions. The voltmeter reading indicates the voltage measured at the tip of the probe. Note that the magnitude and direction of the voltage is a measure of the density and polarity of the charges in the vicinity of the probe. Color the force arrow on the positive charge shown at the right. Note that the magnitude and direction of this force also reflects the density and polarity of the charges. This behavior explains why voltage gradients provide the driving force for conduction.*

Conduction is an important process in the maintenance of the resting membrane potentials (Fig. 4.6), as well as in the generation (Figs. 4.7 and 5.8) and propagation (Fig. 4.9) of action potentials in nerve and muscle cells.

Summary

Table 3.1 compares the driving force for each of the passive transport mechanisms described above.

Table 3.1 Passive Transport Mechanisms	
Mechanism	**Driving force**
diffusion	concentration gradient for gas or solute
filtration	hydrostatic pressure gradient
osmosis	concentration gradient for water or solvent
conduction	voltage gradient

Facilitated Diffusion

Facilitated diffusion mechanisms employ carrier proteins that span the membrane (Fig. 2.2) and provide channels through which certain substances can diffuse (Fig. 3.10). Facilitated diffusion enables substances that bind to specific transmembrane proteins to diffuse more rapidly down their concentration gradients than they would by simple diffusion alone. Facilitated diffusion is a passive process because it requires a concentration gradient and will cease when the concentrations of a substance on both sides of the membrane are equal. Facilitated diffusion is the main mechanism for the entry of glucose into cells (Fig. 10.3).

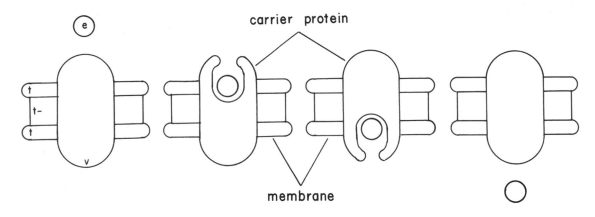

Figure 3.10 *Facilitated diffusion. Move from left to right as you color the membrane, the transmembrane carrier protein, and the molecule that passes through it by facilitated diffusion. Note that the carrier protein undergoes conformational changes as it transports the molecule across the membrane.*

Active Transport

Active transport mechanisms employ transmembrane proteins that transport substances against concentration and/or voltage gradients. Active transport mechanisms require the input of energy from an external source.

Primary active transport mechanisms include ion pumps that derive their energy from the breakdown of ATP (Fig. 3.11). The two types of secondary active transport are co-transport and counter-transport, both of which derive their energy from the electrochemical gradient that is set up by a primary active transport mechanism (Fig. 3.12). For example, the movement of sodium ions down the concentration and voltage gradients that are established by the sodium-potassium pump can be used to pull another substance along with it in a process called sodium co-transport (Fig. 7.5). In sodium counter-transport, the substance is transported in the direction opposite to that of sodium.

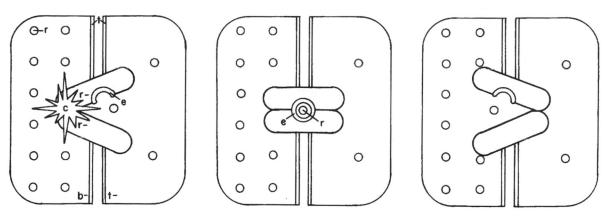

Figure 3.11 *Primary active transport. Color the membrane, carrier protein, and receptor in each panel. Color the flash in the left panel to indicate that the breakdown of ATP provides the energy for primary active transport mechanisms. Color and count the molecules (circles) on each side of the membrane as you move from left to right. Finish the picture by coloring the background areas on both sides of the membrane. Note that active transport mechanisms can move molecules against their concentration gradient.*

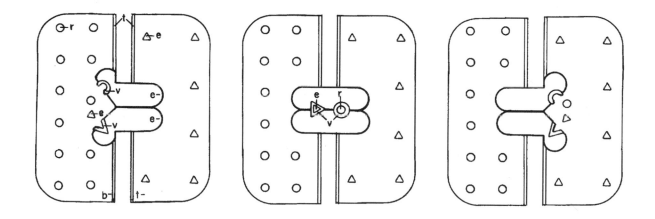

Figure 3.12 *Secondary active transport. Color the membrane, carrier protein, and receptors in each panel. Color and count the circles and triangles on each side of the membrane as you move from left to right. Finish the picture by coloring the background areas on both sides of the membrane. Note that the transport of a circular molecule from left to right (down its concentration gradient) is accompanied by the co-transport of a triangular molecule against its concentration gradient.*

Primary active transport mechanisms are important in the generation of membrane potentials in nerve cells (Fig. 4.4), the operation of the calcium reuptake pump in contracting muscle (Fig. 5.8), and the maintenance of a proton gradient across the inner mitochondrial membrane (Fig. 10.13). Secondary active transport mechanisms are important in the reabsorption of glucose in the kidney tubules (Fig. 7.15), and the absorption of glucose in the intestine (Fig. 9.24).

Rate limitations of transport mechanisms

Facilitated diffusion and active transport mechanisms differ from passive diffusion in that the action of their carrier proteins can become the rate-limiting step. Because of this, both facilitated diffusion and active transport mechanisms exhibit a maximum rate at which they can operate (Fig. 3.13).

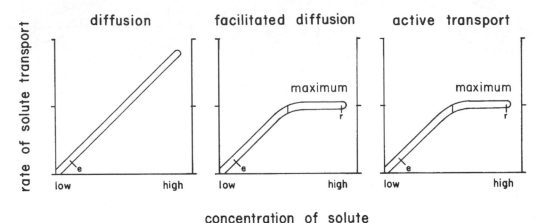

Figure 3.13 *Rates of transport mechanisms. The rate at which molecules are transported across a membrane by diffusion, facilitated diffusion, and active transport are each plotted against the concentration of molecules that appear on one side of the membrane. Color each line and note that the steep (green) portion indicates a range in which a higher concentration of molecules on one side of the membrane yields a proportional increase in their transport through the membrane. Note that the lines for facilitated diffusion and active transport both have a flat (red) portion that indicates a range in which the rate of transport remains the same regardless of the concentration gradient. This shows that facilitated diffusion and active transport mechanisms both exhibit rate limitations whereas passive diffusion does not.*

Composition of intracellular and extracellular fluids

Transport mechanisms create differences in the chemical composition of intracellular and extracellular fluids that are important to the normal function of the cell.

Some substances that are found in higher concentrations in extracellular fluid are sodium ions, calcium ions, and glucose. Other substances that are more concentrated in intracellular fluid are potassium ions, magnesium ions and amino acids (Fig. 3.14).

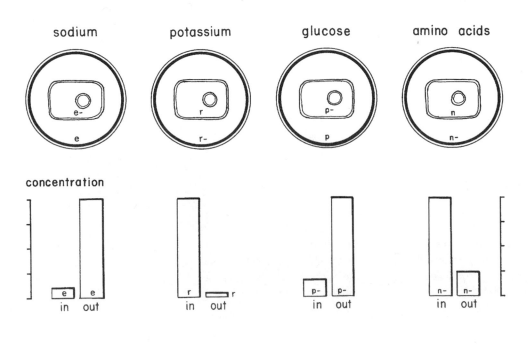

Figure 3.14 *Composition of intracellular and extracellular fluids. Color the cell, its surrounding fluid, and the bar graph directly beneath it for each electrolyte (sodium and potassium) and each nutrient (glucose and amino acids). The height of each bar depicts the relative concentrations of each substance as it normally appears in intracellular and extracellular fluids. Note that sodium and glucose are more concentrated outside the cell, while potassium and amino acids are more concentrated inside the cell. In fact, there are 10 sodium ions outside the cell for each one that is inside, and there are 35 potassium ions inside the cell for each one that is outside. The physiological significance of these concentration ratios are discussed in Fig. 4.5.*

Body fluid compartments

The total body water, representing about 70% of the body weight, can be partitioned into an intracellular and an extracellular compartment (Fig. 1.1). The concentration (c) of any substance in any compartment is determined by the total number of molecules (n) divided by the volume of water in the compartment (V), i.e., $c = n/V$.

The volumes of specific body fluid compartments can be measured experimentally using the indicator-dilution method. In this method, a known amount (n) of dye or radioactive substance (known as an indicator) is introduced into a compartment, and its concentration (c) is measured after it distributes itself uniformly throughout the compartment (Fig. 3.15). Under these conditions, larger fluid compartments yield more dilute concentrations of indicator substances. Since indicator substances that are used in practice do not leave the compartment (i.e., n remains constant), the final concentration of indicator (c) can be used to calculate the volume of water (V) into which it was mixed, i.e., $V = n/c$.

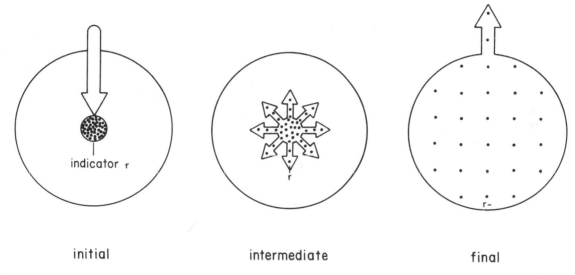

initial   intermediate   final

Figure 3.15 *The indicator-dilution principle. Color the panels from left to right. Note that the final concentration of indicator is determined by the number of molecules that were introduced and the volume of water in the compartment.*

The intracellular and extracellular fluid compartments refer to the fluid contained inside (28 liters in the adult male) and outside (14 L) the cells, respectively. Extracellular fluid is made up primarily of interstitial fluid (11.5 L) and blood plasma (2.5 L) (Fig. 3.16) plus comparatively small amounts of cerebrospinal fluid in the brain, intraocular fluid in the eye, and fluid in the joints.

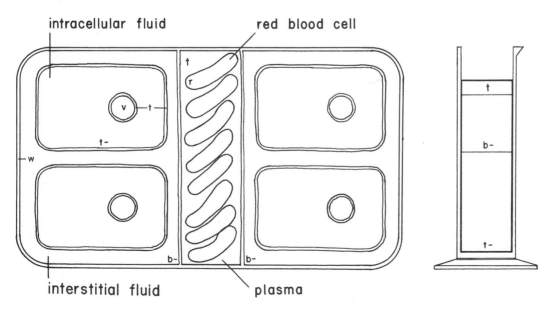

intracellular fluid   red blood cell

interstitial fluid   plasma

Figure 3.16 *Body fluid compartments. Color the cell membranes, the intracellular and interstitial fluids, and the blood. Color the graduated cylinder at right and note the relative contributions of intracellular fluid, interstitial fluid, and plasma to the total body fluids.*

Blood

Whole blood is actually a mixture of red blood cells, white blood cells and platelets that are suspended in plasma. Whole blood therefore separates into three distinct layers when it is spun at high speed in a centrifuge.

The greater density of red blood cells causes them to pack tightly in the bottom of the tube. The white blood cells and platelets appear as a buffy coat in the middle of the tube, and blood plasma appears as a clear layer on top (Fig. 3.17).

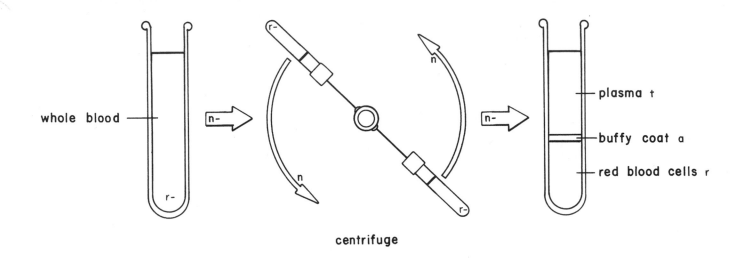

Figure 3.17 *Constituents of blood. Whole blood can be separated into three distinct layers by spinning it at high speed in a centrifuge. The layers correspond to the red blood cells, white blood cells (buffy coat), and plasma.*

Red blood cells

The red blood cells, also called erythrocytes, are biconcave discs that contain the hemoglobin molecules, which carry oxygen in the blood (Fig. 8.10). Since the mean diameter of red blood cells is comparable to that of capillaries (about 8 microns), red blood cells pass single-file through capillaries. This aids in the delivery of oxygen from the blood to the tissues because it minimizes the distance that oxygen must diffuse in the process (Fig. 3.5).

White blood cells

Six different types of white blood cells, also called leukocytes, are found in the blood. White blood cells are: polymorphonuclear neutrophils, polymorphonuclear eosinophils, polymorphonuclear basophils, monocytes, lymphocytes, and occasional plasma cells. There are also large numbers of platelets that are fragments of another type of white blood cell called megakaryocytes. Neutrophils, eosinophils and basophils are collectively termed granulocytes because of their granular appearance. The granulocytes, monocytes and a few lymphocytes are formed in bone marrow while lymphocytes and plasma cells are formed in the lymph tissue.

Neutrophils and lymphocytes normally comprise around 90% of the white blood cells. The remaining fraction is made up of a combination of monocytes, eosinophils and basophils (Fig. 3.18). Neutrophils and macrophages that are derived from monocytes attack and destroy bacteria and viruses by phagocytosis (Fig. 3.2). Monocytes that enter cells are transformed into macrophages when they grow in size and develop large numbers of lysosomes that contain hydrolytic enzymes (Fig. 2.1).

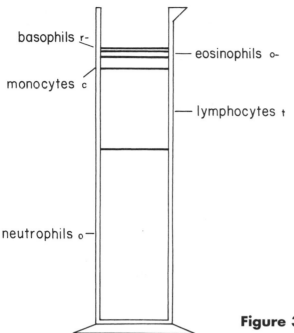

basophils r-

monocytes c

— eosinophils o-

— lymphocytes t

neutrophils o—

Figure 3.18 *Relative concentrations of white blood cells.*

Anemia

Anemia is a deficiency of hemoglobin in the blood that can be due to a reduced number of red blood cells, or a low concentration of hemoglobin in the red blood cells. A number of anemias have been categorized, including: 1) hemorrhagic anemia, which occurs after blood loss or during a parasitic infection; 2) aplastic anemia, which is due to a dysfunction in the bone marrow, where red blood cells are made; 3) megaloblastic anemia, which is caused by an inadequate supply of the vitamins B_{12} and folic acid; 4) microcytic anemia, which is due to lack of iron, protein, or vitamin B_6 necessary for the synthesis of hemoglobin; 5) hemolytic anemia, which stems from abnormalities that make the red blood cells fragile and have a shortened life span; and 6) sickle cell anemia, which is due to an abnormal form of hemoglobin called hemoglobin S that precipitates into elongated crystals when it is exposed to low concentrations of oxygen. This precipitation changes the shape of the red blood cell from that of a biconcave disc to that of a sickle, thereby impeding the flow of blood to the tissues.

Hematocrit

The hematocrit is the percentage of the blood volume that is occupied by red blood cells. The hematocrits of normal adult males and females are around 42 and 38, respectively. The hematocrit is decreased in anemia (low number or smaller size of red blood cells) and increased in polycythemia (high number of red blood cells, a normal adaptation to living at high altitude) (Fig. 3.19). Since the viscosity of blood (viscosity is a measure of its lack of slipperiness) depends on the hematocrit, it follows that blood viscosity is low in anemia and high in polycythemia. The hematocrit therefore influences the ease with which blood can be pumped through the circulation (Fig. 6.19).

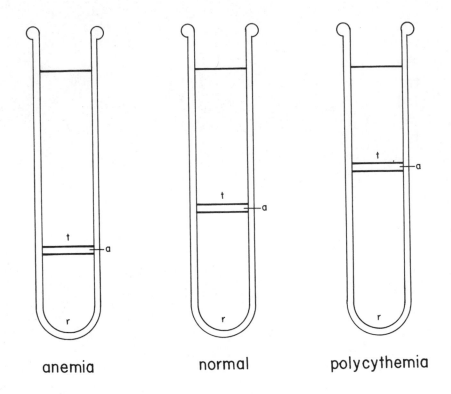

anemia   normal   polycythemia

Figure 3.19 *Hematocrit. The hematocrit is the percentage of the blood volume that is occupied by red blood cells. Color each tube of centrifuged blood and note that the hematocrit is decreased in anemia and increased in polycythemia.*

chapter **four**
nervous system

The nervous system receives, processes, and transmits information in the form of neural signals.

Organization of the nervous system

The nervous system is organized into two main parts: the central nervous system (CNS), which consists of the brain and spinal cord, and the peripheral nervous system (PNS), which consists of nerves that transmit impulses to and from the CNS. Afferent (sensory) nerve fibers are part of the PNS and carry impulses from peripheral sensory receptors to the CNS and efferent (motor) nerve fibers carry impulses from the CNS to peripheral effector organs such as muscles or glands (Fig. 4.1).

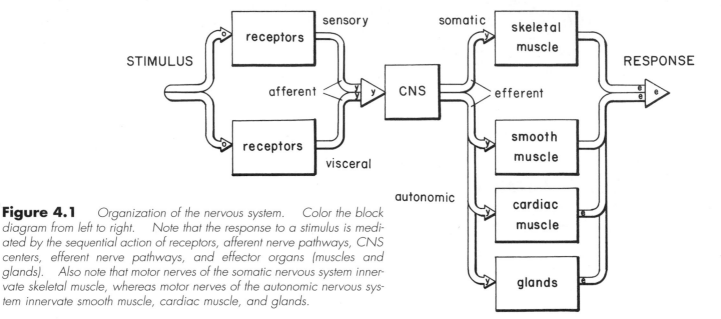

Figure 4.1 *Organization of the nervous system. Color the block diagram from left to right. Note that the response to a stimulus is mediated by the sequential action of receptors, afferent nerve pathways, CNS centers, efferent nerve pathways, and effector organs (muscles and glands). Also note that motor nerves of the somatic nervous system innervate skeletal muscle, whereas motor nerves of the autonomic nervous system innervate smooth muscle, cardiac muscle, and glands.*

Some efferent nerve fibers belong to the somatic nervous system, which is comprised of motor neurons that control skeletal muscle, while others belong to the autonomic nervous system, which controls smooth muscle, cardiac muscle, and glands (Fig. 4.1). The autonomic nervous system is subdivided into a parasympathetic division and a sympathetic division.

Structure of nerves

The nervous system contains a variety of nerve cells (Fig. 4.2) that are arranged in different ways, including

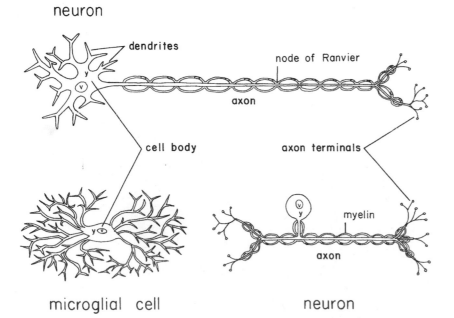

Figure 4.2 *Structure of nerve cells. Color the nerve cells and identify the structures described in the text. Note similarities and differences between the cell types.*

diverging, converging, and reverberating networks (Fig. 4.3). The CNS contains interneurons and glial cells that support them. Types of glial cells include astrocytes, oligodendrocytes, and microglia (Fig. 4.2).

Neurons consist of a cell body, an axon that transmits electrical impulses called action potentials, and dendrites that respond to chemical, mechanical, or other stimuli. The axons have terminals that release chemical

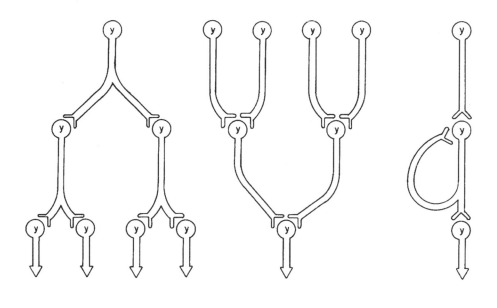

diverging   converging   reverberating

Figure 4.3   *Neural circuits.   Color each of the neural circuits from top to bottom. Note that signals from one nerve excite many nerves in a diverging network and signals from many nerves excite one nerve in a converging network. Note also that the reverberating network has a positive feedback loop within it that re-excites the nerve and enables it to   discharge for a longer time.*

messengers called neurotransmitters. Some axons are insulated by myelin sheaths that are separated by short unmyelinated segments called nodes of Ranvier (Fig. 4.2). In myelinated nerve fibers, the nerve impulse jumps from one unmyelinated node to the next in a process called saltatory conduction. Two benefits of myelin are that it increases the speed at which impulses are transmitted along nerves and it reduces the energy expended in their transmission.

Resting membrane potentials of nerves
There is a primary active transport mechanism in the

nerve cell membrane that pumps 3 sodium ions (Na^+) out of the cell for every 2 potassium ions (K^+) that enter the cell (Fig. 3.11). Since sodium and potassium ions are both positively charged, the sodium-potassium pump removes an excess of positive charges from the interior of the cell so that the inside of the nerve fiber becomes negatively charged with respect to the outside. This polarization of charges across the membrane causes the membrane potentials of large motor neurons to be around −90 mV (Fig. 4.4).

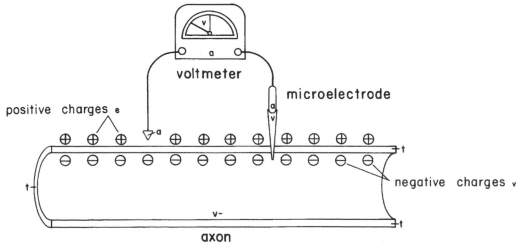

Figure 4.4   *Membrane potentials.   Color the membrane and the charges on each side.   Color the microelectrode and the voltmeter.   Note that the voltmeter reading reflects the degree to which the inside of the nerve cell is charged negatively with respect to the outside. Finish the picture by coloring the inside of the axon.*

Electrochemical gradients for sodium and potassium

The operation of the sodium-potassium pump establishes an electrical gradient across the nerve cell membrane that attracts positively charged sodium and potassium ions to the negatively charged interior of the cell (down their voltage gradient, Fig. 3.9). The pump also establishes concentration gradients for Na^+ and K^+. Sodium is more concentrated outside the cell but potassium is more concentrated inside the cell (Fig. 3.14). Since diffusion occurs from a region of higher concentration to one of lower concentration (Fig. 3.3), these concentration gradients pull sodium into the cell and push potassium out.

In summary, the combined forces on the sodium and potassium ions are such that: 1) sodium is pulled to the inside of the cell by both its voltage gradient and concentration gradient; and 2) potassium is pulled to the inside of the cell by its voltage gradient but pushed to the outside of the cell by its concentration gradient. The relative effects of these particular voltage and concentration gradients on sodium and potassium are considered below.

The Nernst equation

A state of equilibrium exists when the flow of an ion down its voltage gradient is equal and opposite to the flow of the same ion down its concentration gradient. Under these conditions, the Nernst equation can be used to calculate the voltage gradient (E) that is needed to exactly counterbalance the effect of a specific concentration gradient, i.e.,

$$E = -60 \log [C_{in}]/[C_{out}]$$

where $[C_{in}]$ and $[C_{out}]$ represent the concentrations of a freely diffusible positive ion at the inside and outside of the membrane, respectively.

As an example, assume that the concentration of a positive ion inside the cell happened to be 10 times its concentration outside the cell. Under these conditions, $[C_{in}]$ = 10 $[C_{out}]$, or $[C_{in}]/[C_{out}]$ = 10. Since log (10) = 1, the substitution of the assumed concentrations into the Nernst equation yields a membrane potential of -60 mV.

This theoretical result means that the transmembrane potential would have to be −60 mV in order to sustain

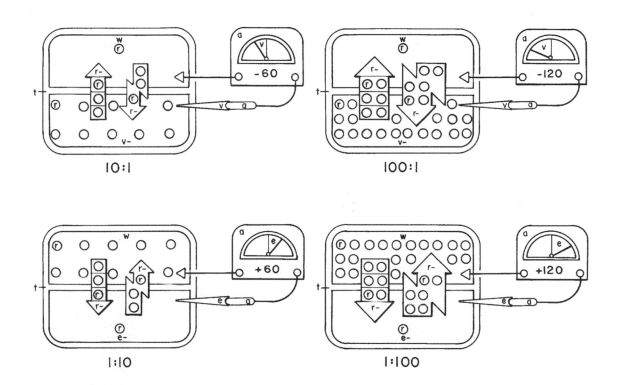

Figure 4.5 *Nernst equation. For each panel, color the membrane and background areas. Color and count the number of positive ions that cross the membrane by diffusion (hatched arrow) and conduction (jagged arrow). Note that the flow of ions across the membrane by diffusion is equal and opposite to the flow by conduction. Color the probes and voltmeters. Note that each concentration gradient has a corresponding voltage gradient. Note also that −60mV can sustain a 10:1 concentration ratio and −120mV can sustain a 100:1 concentration ratio. Compare this figure with Fig. 3.9.*

the assumed concentration gradient. In other words, the rate at which a positive ion enters the cell down a 60 mV voltage gradient is exactly equal to the rate at which it exits the cell down a 10:1 concentration gradient.

The sodium and potassium potentials

Since every concentration gradient has a corresponding voltage gradient, the Nernst equation can also be used to calculate the voltage gradients that correspond to the concentration gradients for sodium and potassium. The substitution of the normal intracellular and extracellular concentrations of sodium and potassium (Fig. 3.14) into the Nernst equation yields a sodium potential (E_{Na}) of +60 mV and a potassium potential (E_K) of −90 mV. The outcome of these considerations is

that the membrane potential of a nerve cell should be around −90 mV when the membrane is permeable to potassium and around +60 mV when it is permeable to sodium. Thus, the membrane potential exhibited by a nerve cell depends both on the concentration gradients of sodium and potassium across the membrane and on the membrane's permeability to the two ions.

Resting membrane potential of nerve cells

At rest, the membranes of nerve cells are permeable to potassium but not to sodium, and the resting membrane potential turns out to be −90 mV, a value that closely matches the calculated potassium potential. This result means that the rate at which potassium leaves the cell down its concentration gradient is equal to the rate at which it enters the cell down its voltage gradient (Fig. 4.6).

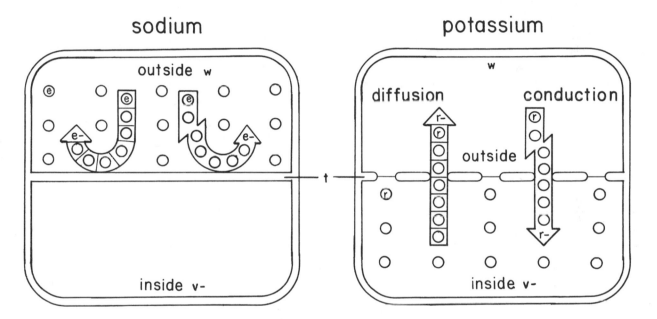

Figure 4.6 *Permeability of nerve cell membrane at rest. In this book, sodium ions are always green and potassium ions are always red. Color and count the sodium (left panel) and potassium (right panel) molecules in the hatched diffusion arrows and the jagged conduction arrows. Finish the picture by coloring the arrows, the membranes, and the areas labeled inside and outside. Note that the rate at which potassium exits the cell by diffusion is equal to the rate at which it enters the cell by conduction. Note also that sodium remains outside the cell because the resting cell membrane is impermeable to it.*

Generation of the action potential

Nerve signals are transmitted by action potentials, which are rapid changes in membrane potential that occur whenever the membrane potential attains a criti-

cal threshold level (typically −65 mV). Action potentials are characterized by an initial rapid rise in membrane potential (depolarization) followed by a return to the baseline level (repolarization) (Fig. 4.7).

Depolarization is caused by a brief opening of sodium channels that allows sodium ions to flow rapidly down their concentration and voltage gradients into the cell (Fig. 4.8). Sodium channels can be activated by electrical (voltage-gated), chemical (ligand-gated) or mechanical stimuli. This influx of positively charged sodium ions to the interior of the cell causes the membrane potential to rise rapidly from the resting level of −90 mV to around +40 mV; a value that approaches the calculated sodium potential (Fig. 4.7).

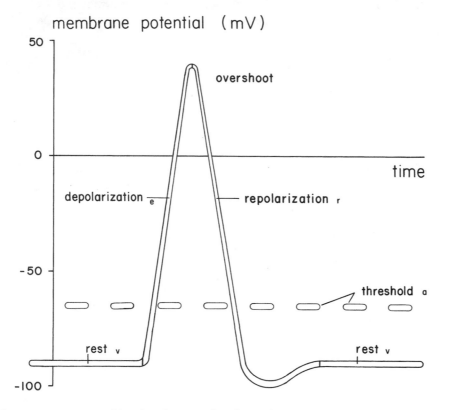

Figure 4.7 *The action potential. Color the threshold and the action potential from left to right. Color the depolarization phase green because it is due to the influx of sodium and color the repolarization phase red because it is due to an efflux of potassium. The overshoot corresponds to that portion of the action potential that appears above the abscissa (x-axis). The concentrations of potassium on both sides of the membrane determine the resting membrane potential, and the concentrations of sodium on both sides of the membrane determine the overshoot potential.*

Repolarization is caused by the closing of sodium channels and the opening of potassium channels that enable potassium to diffuse more rapidly out of the nerve cell, down its concentration gradient (Fig. 4.8). This efflux of potassium ions removes positive charges from the interior of the cell and causes the membrane potential to return to its resting level of −90 mV.

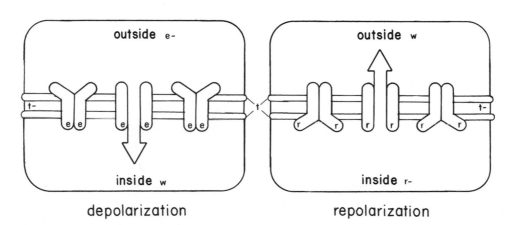

Figure 4.8 *Ion fluxes during an action potential. Color the membranes, their channels, and the background areas on both sides of the membranes. Note that depolarization is due to a flow of positively charged, green sodium ions to the inside of the nerve cell (left panel) and that repolarization is due to a flow of positively charged, red potassium ions to the outside of the nerve cell (right panel).*

gray **b**lue **c**anary green flesh blac**k** **n**avy **o**range **p**ink **r**ed **s**ienna **t**an **v**iolet **w**hite **y**ellow a**z**ure [-] means use light pressure

Propagation of the action potential

Depolarization at one point on a nerve fiber creates local currents that depolarize adjacent points. As a result, an action potential at any point is propagated as a wave of depolarization that travels the entire length of the nerve fiber (Fig. 4.9). The speed at which an action potential travels along a nerve fiber is determined by the diameter of the nerve fiber and its myelination (Fig. 4.2). Nerve conduction velocities vary from 0.25 m/s in narrow, unmyelinated fibers to 100 m/s in wide, myelinated fibers.

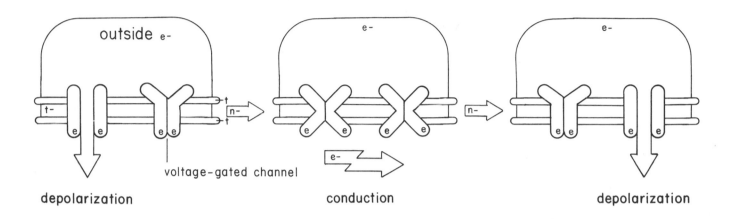

Figure 4.9 *Propagation of an action potential. Color the membrane, the sodium channels, and the background area in the left panel. Note that the left channel is open while the right one is closed. Color the middle panel, where the flow of current opens the voltage-gated channel in the membrane. Finish the picture by coloring the right panel, in which the left channel is closed while the right one is open. The sequential opening and closing of voltage-gated channels enables the action potential to be propagated as a wave of depolarization that moves from left to right.*

Synaptic transmission

Signals are transmitted from a presynaptic neuron to a postsynaptic neuron by chemicals called neurotransmitters that diffuse across the synapse between the presynaptic terminal and the postsynaptic neuron (Fig. 4.10). The four phases of synaptic transmission are: 1) the synthesis and storage of neurotransmitter; 2) the release of neurotransmitter; 3) the interaction between the neurotransmitter and the postsynaptic receptor; and 4) the termination of synaptic transmission.

The spread of an action potential over the presynaptic terminal opens voltage-gated calcium channels in this section of the nerve cell membrane. Calcium enters the presynaptic terminal, and some of the vesicles that store molecules of neurotransmitter undergo exocytosis and release their contents into the synapse (Fig. 4.10).

The neurotransmitter molecules diffuse across the synapse and combine with receptor proteins on the postsynaptic neuron; this alters the permeability of the postsynaptic membrane. Depending on the particular neurotransmitter and type of receptor, this change in permeability might excite the postsynaptic neuron by opening sodium channels or inhibit the postsynaptic neuron by opening potassium or chloride channels (Fig. 4.11). A given synapse is always excitatory or inhibitory and always uses the same neurotransmitter.

Neurotransmitters

There are two classes of neurotransmitters; low molecular weight neurotransmitters are derived from single amino acids, and neuropeptides consist of chains of amino acids.

Low molecular weight neurotransmitters are synthesized in the presynaptic terminals. The vesicles that contain them are refilled after each discharge. Some low molecular weight neurotransmitters that are used by the central nervous system are acetylcholine (ACh), norepinephrine (NE), dopamine, serotonin, glutamate, and gamma-aminobutyric acid (GABA). Acetylcholine and norepinephrine are also found in the peripheral nervous system. Acetylcholine is the neurotransmitter used by motor neurons that control skeletal muscle and by

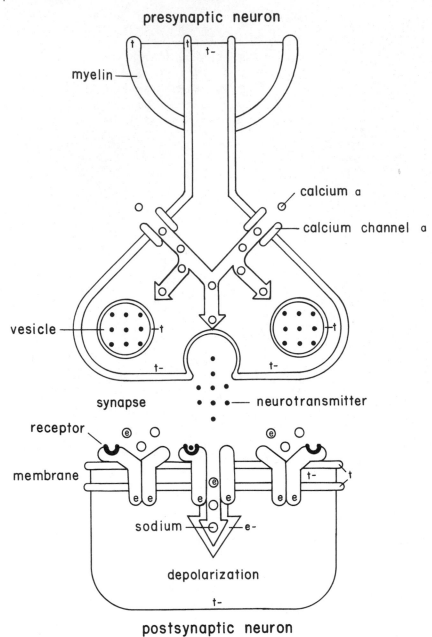

presynaptic neuron

myelin

calcium a

calcium channel a

vesicle

synapse — neurotransmitter

receptor

membrane

sodium

depolarization

postsynaptic neuron

Figure 4.10 *Synaptic transmission. Begin by coloring the myelin sheath, the membrane, and the calcium channels of the presynaptic neuron. Color the calcium molecules as they flow inward to make contact with the middle vesicle and cause it to undergo exocytosis. Color the vesicular membranes and identify the released molecules of neurotransmitter. Color the membrane, sodium channels, and the background area of the postsynaptic neuron. Note that only the channel with neurotransmitter in its receptor is open. Color the sodium ions that remain in the synapse above the closed channels; then color the ones that pass through the open channel to enter the postsynaptic neuron. Color the arrow, which shows that depolarization is due to an influx of positively charged sodium ions.*

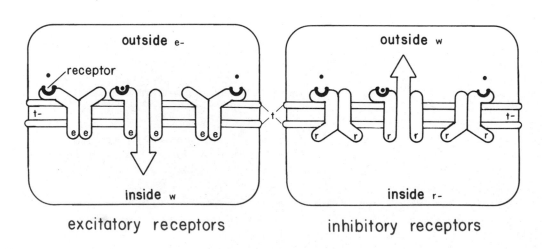

outside e-

receptor

inside w

excitatory receptors

outside w

inside r-

inhibitory receptors

Figure 4.11 *Excitatory and inhibitory receptors. Color the membranes, their channels, and the background area on both sides. Identify the receptors and the molecules of neurotransmitter. Note that excitatory receptors depolarize the membrane by opening sodium channels (left panel) whereas inhibitory receptors hyperpolarize the membrane by opening potassium channels (right panel). Compare this figure with Fig. 4.8.*

parasympathetic nerve fibers that control smooth muscle, cardiac muscle, and glands. Norepinephrine is the neurotransmitter used by sympathetic nerve fibers, which also control smooth muscle, cardiac muscle and glands (Fig. 4.1).

Neuropeptides, the high molecular weight neurotransmitters, are manufactured in the cell body of the neuron, which is also where new secretory vesicles are formed. Neuropeptides include hypothalamic releasing hormones, pituitary peptides, and sleep peptides.

Postsynaptic receptors

Postsynaptic receptors for acetylcholine are called cholinergic receptors. Postsynaptic receptors for norepinephrine (a neurotransmitter released by the sympathetic nervous system) or epinephrine (a hormone released by the adrenal medulla) are called adrenergic recep-

tors. The two types of adrenergic receptors are the alpha receptors and the beta receptors. Alpha receptors are more sensitive to norepinephrine than epinephrine, whereas beta receptors are equally sensitive to norepinephrine and epinephrine.

Excitatory and inhibitory postsynaptic potentials

The transient depolarization of a postsynaptic neuron, caused by the release of excitatory neurotransmitters, is called an excitatory post-synaptic potential, or EPSP. EPSPs are caused by the opening of sodium channels, which allows sodium to enter the cell and depolarize the membrane. Depolarization brings the membrane potential closer to threshold so that a smaller than normal stimulus can initiate an action potential. Under these conditions, the neuron is said to be facilitated (Fig. 4.12).

Figure 4.12 EPSPs and IPSPs. Begin at the left by coloring the nerve stimulators, the electric shocks they produce, and the neurons they stimulate. Color the neurotransmitters and the postsynaptic neuron. Color the microelectrode that has been placed in the postsynaptic neuron to record its membrane potential. Color the polygraph recorder, which amplifies and displays the voltage at the tip of the microelectrode. Color the nerve stimulators and their shocks beneath the polygraph tracing. Color the threshold and the polygraph tracing of the membrane potential. Note that the stimulation of an excitatory nerve depolarizes the postsynaptic neuron and produces an EPSP. Note also that the stimulation of an inhibitory nerve hyperpolarizes the postsynaptic neuron and produces an IPSP.

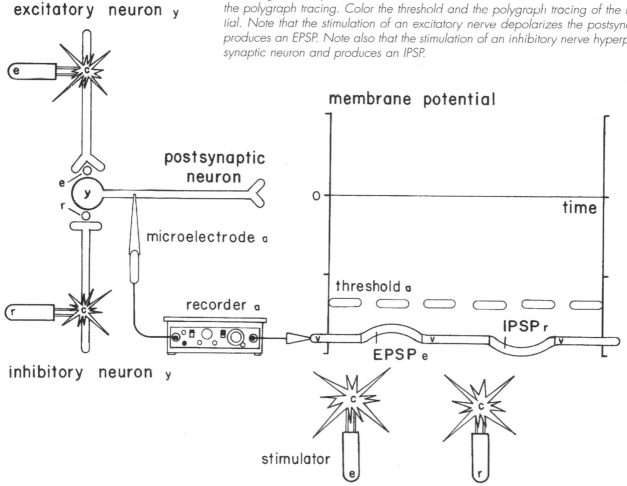

Similarly, the transient hyperpolarization caused by the release of inhibitory neurotransmitters is called an inhibitory post-synaptic potential, or IPSP. IPSPs are due to the opening of potassium and/or chloride channels that hyperpolarize the membrane. Hyperpolarization brings the membrane potential farther away from threshold so that a larger than normal stimulus is required to initiate an action potential. Under these conditions, the neuron is said to be inhibited (Fig. 4.12).

Spatial and temporal summation

When a single action potential is delivered to one presynaptic terminal there is usually not enough neuro-

transmitter released into the synapse to initiate an action potential in the postsynaptic neuron.

The amount of excitatory neurotransmitter that is needed to initiate an action potential is usually provided by the combined action of two different mechanisms; spatial summation and temporal summation. Spatial summation occurs when additional presynaptic terminals are recruited to release their neurotransmitter into the synapse (Fig. 4.13). Temporal summation occurs when the same number of presynaptic terminals are stimulated more frequently so that they each release more neurotransmitter into the synapse (Fig. 4.14).

Figure 4.13 *Spatial summation. Begin at the left by coloring the nerve stimulators, the electric shocks they produce, and the excitatory neurons they stimulate. Color the excitatory neurotransmitter, the postsynaptic neuron, the microelectrode and the recorder. Color the nerve stimulators and their shocks beneath the polygraph tracing. Move from left to right as you color the recording of the membrane potential and the threshold. Note that a single shock does not depolarize the postsynaptic membrane to the threshold level so no action potential is generated. Note also that two shocks in rapid succession—one from each stimulator—depolarize the postsynaptic neuron to the threshold level and an action potential is generated. This process is called spatial summation. Compare this with Fig. 4.7.*

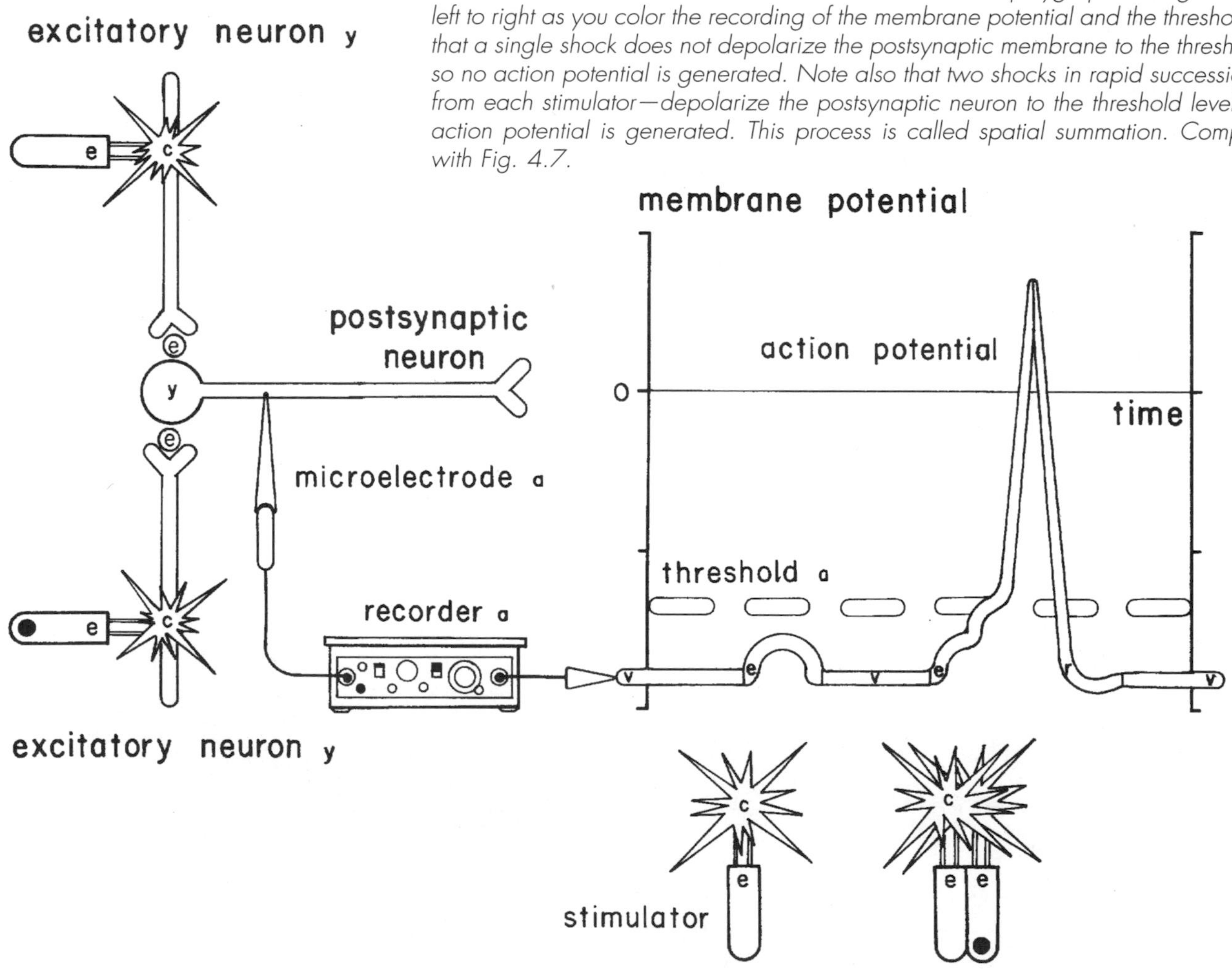

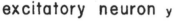

excitatory neuron y

postsynaptic neuron

microelectrode a

recorder a

excitatory neuron y

membrane potential

action potential

0

time

threshold a

stimulator

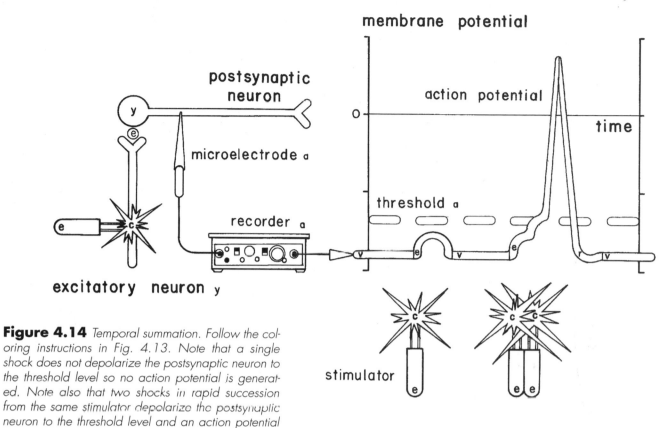

Figure 4.14 *Temporal summation. Follow the coloring instructions in Fig. 4.13. Note that a single shock does not depolarize the postsynaptic neuron to the threshold level so no action potential is generated. Note also that two shocks in rapid succession from the same stimulator depolarize the postsynaptic neuron to the threshold level and an action potential is generated. This process is called temporal summation. Compare this figure with Fig. 4.13.*

Components of a reflex arc

A reflex arc can be viewed as a physiological system that responds automatically to a stimulus (Fig. 4.15). One of the components of a reflex system is a sensory receptor that translates the stimulus into a coded neural signal, which is transmitted along afferent (sensory) pathways to a coordinating center in the CNS. The neural output from the coordinating center is then transmitted along efferent (motor) pathways to an effector organ (muscle or gland). The resultant action of the effector organ constitutes the response.

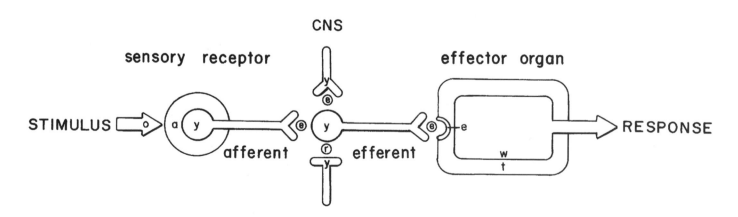

Figure 4.15 *Reflex arc. Color the components of the reflex arc from left to right. Identify the sensory receptor, afferent pathway, coordinating center, efferent pathway, and effector organ. Note that the coordinating center also receives excitatory and inhibitory inputs from other nerve fibers in the CNS. Compare this figure with Figs. 1.9 and 4.1.*

Stretch reflex

The knee-jerk reflex is a well-known example of a reflex arc. In this reflex, a sudden stretch of a muscle (stimulus) causes the muscle to contract (response) and thereby oppose its stretch (Fig. 4.16). The stretch reflex originates in muscle spindles that are sensory receptors connected in parallel with the fibers of the muscle in which they reside. Muscle spindles generate action potentials when they are stretched. These action potentials are transmitted along a sensory nerve (afferent pathway) to the spinal cord. The afferent neuron makes a monosynaptic connection (CNS coordinating center) with the motor neuron (efferent pathway) that causes contraction of the muscle (effector organ) (Fig. 4.16).

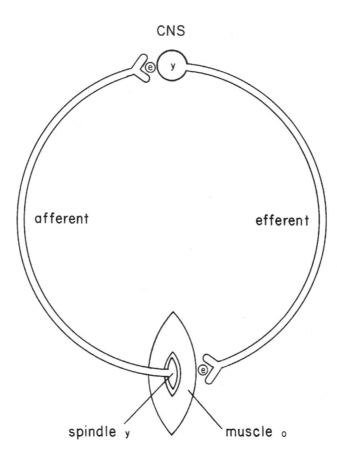

Figure 4.16 *Stretch reflex. Color the muscle spindle and work clockwise until you finish the picture. Identify the sensory receptor, afferent pathway, coordinating center, efferent pathway, and effector organ. Note the similarities and differences between this figure and those shown in Figs. 1.9 and 4.15.*

Sensory receptors

The body contains a multitude of receptors that detect a variety of stimuli, including mechanical (mechanorecep- tors), chemical (chemoreceptors), thermal (thermore- ceptors), osmotic (osmoreceptors), and visual (photore- ceptors) sensations (Fig. 4.17).

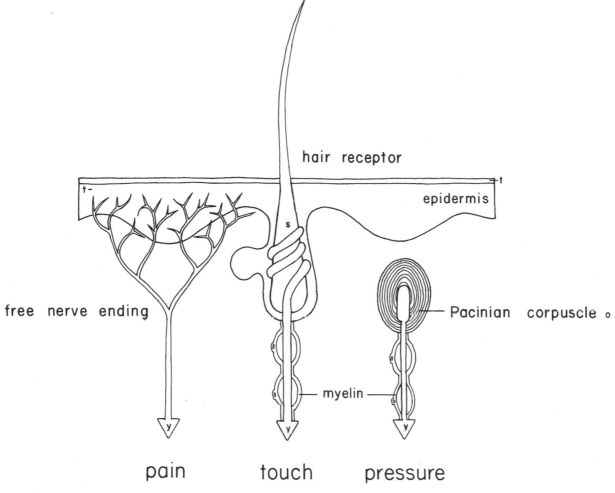

hair receptor

epidermis

free nerve ending

Pacinian corpuscle o

myelin

pain   touch   pressure

Figure 4.17 *Sensory receptors. Color the epidermis and each sensory receptor, noting similarities and differences between them. Compare these structures with those shown in Fig. 4.2.*

Sensory receptors behave as transducers, which are devices that convert one form of energy to another. Sensory receptors encode the intensity of their stimula- tion in terms of the frequency with which they generate and transmit action potentials. Thus, a weak stimulus produces a low frequency train of action potentials and a strong stimulus produces a high frequency train of action potentials.

Transduction characteristics of sensory receptors

The transduction characteristics of a sensory receptor refers to the relationship between the stimulus intensity and the frequency of action potentials. It can be studied by recording the neural output from a sensory receptor that receives a range of stimulus intensities that are grad- ually incremented. Under these conditions, slowly- adapting receptors continue to generate action poten- tials when their stimulus is maintained at a constant level (Fig 4.18). The transduction characteristics of slowly- adapting sensory receptors can therefore be visualized by plotting the frequency of its action potentials against the magnitude of the applied stimulus (Fig. 4.19).

In contrast, the discharge from rapidly-adapting receptors diminishes rapidly with time even though their stimulation is maintained at a steady level (Fig. 4.18). Thus, rapidly-adapting sensory receptors discharge mostly during periods in which their level of stimulation changes; this behavior is called rate-sensitivity.

slowly adapting sensory receptor

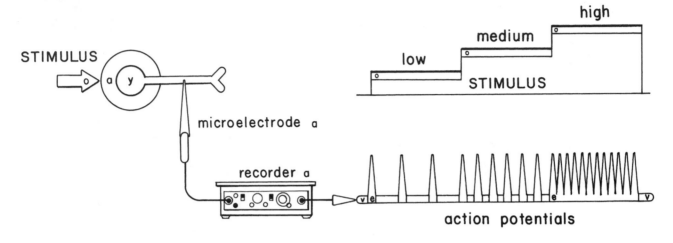

rapidly adapting sensory receptor

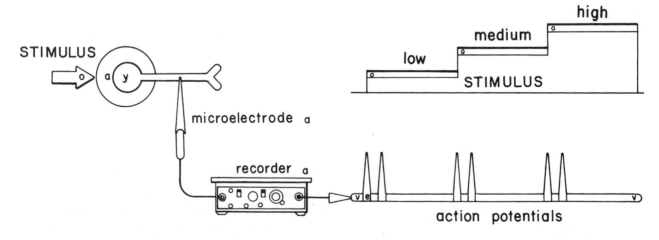

Figure 4.18 *Transduction characteristics of sensory receptors. Begin at the left by coloring the stimulus arrow applied to the slowly-adapting sensory receptor. Color the receptor, its sensory nerve fiber, the microelectrode, and the recorder. Color the bar graph, which indicates the applied stimulus, and the corresponding action potentials. Note that the frequency of action potentials reflects the magnitude of the stimulus. Color the stimulus arrow, sensory receptor, sensory nerve, microelectrode, and recorder for the rapidly adapting sensory receptor. Color the bar graph that indicates stimulus intensity and note that it is identical to the one in the top panel. Color the membrane potentials at each level of stimulus intensity. Note that the rapidly-adapting sensory receptor generates action potentials only when the level of stimulation changes.*

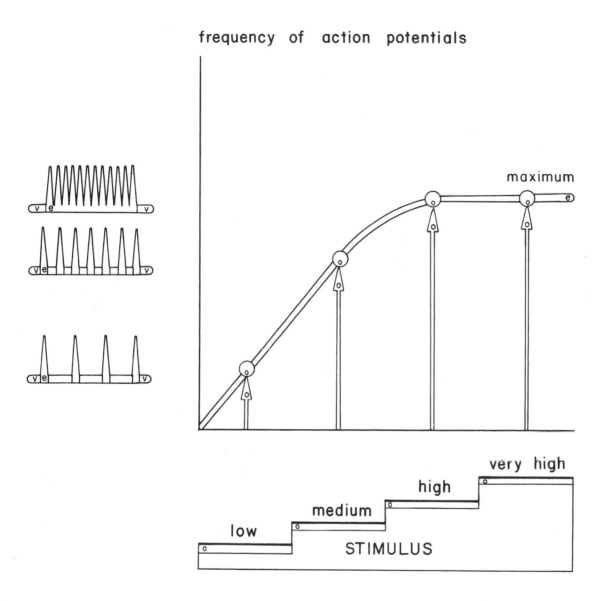

Figure 4.19 *Transduction characteristics of slowly-adapting sensory receptors. Color the bar graph of the stimulus, the vertical arrows, and their points on the graph. Color the action potentials that correspond to each level of stimulation. Finish the picture by coloring the line that connects the 4 points. The steep portion of the line indicates a range in which the frequency of action potentials reflects the stimulus intensity and the flat portion indicates a range in which the frequency remains the same, regardless of the stimulus. Note that the sensory receptor produces the same frequency of action potentials during high and very high levels of stimulation. For this reason, the sensory receptor cannot distinguish between different stimulus intensities within this range.*

chapter **five**
muscle

Skeletal muscles are responsible for voluntary movement.

Structure of skeletal muscle
Skeletal muscles are made up of bundles of long fibers that extend the entire length of the muscle. These fibers are formed from bundles of myofibrils, which, in turn, are made up of thick (myosin) and thin (actin) filaments that are connected to each other by cross bridges (Fig. 5.1).

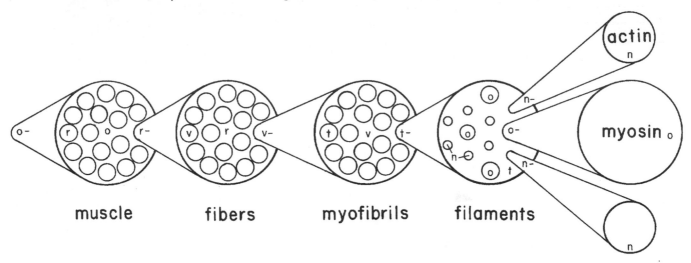

muscle   fibers   myofibrils   filaments

Figure 5.1 *Structure of skeletal muscle.   Color the picture from left to right.   Note that the actin filaments form a hexagon that surrounds the myosin filament.*

The sarcomere
The sarcomere is the functional unit of skeletal muscle; it is the shortening of the sarcomere that causes the muscle to contract.

Each sarcomere consists of actin and myosin filaments that are connected by cross bridges (Fig. 5.2). This arrangement of the filaments causes the myofibril to appear striped, with alternating dark and light bands. The darker A, or anisotropic, bands contain myosin filaments, whereas the light I, or isotropic, bands do not contain myosin filaments (Fig. 5.3). One end of each actin filament attaches to a structure called a Z disc. The sarcomere is that portion of the myofibril between two successive Z lines.

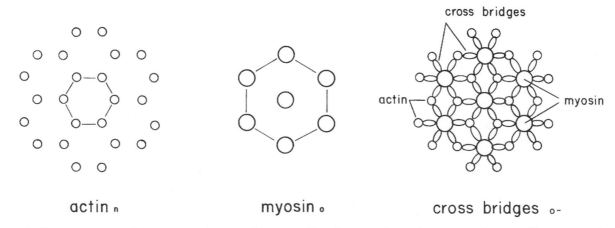

actin   myosin   cross bridges

Figure 5.2 *Arrangement of the actin and myosin filaments. This diagram shows the actin and myosin filaments as they would appear in a cross section of a sarcomere. Color the actin filaments in the left and right panels. Color the myosin filaments in the middle and right panels. Note that the right panel shows the actin filaments from the left panel superimposed on the myosin filaments from the middle panel. Note also that the actin and myosin filaments are oriented in such a way that they form hexagons. Finish the picture by coloring the cross bridges that connect the actin and myosin filaments.*

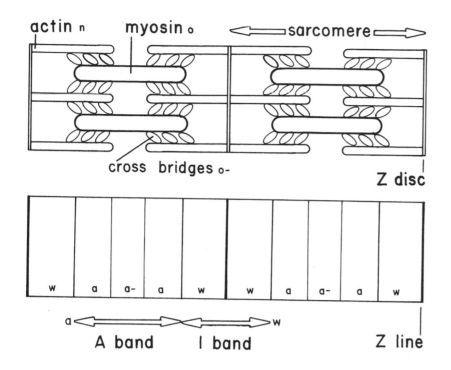

actin n   myosin o   ⟵ sarcomere ⟶

cross bridges o-

Z disc

w a a- a w   w a a- a w

a ⟵⟶ ⟵⟶ w

A band   I band

Z line

Figure 5.3 *The sarcomere.   Identify two sarcomeres and three Z discs in the figure. Color the actin and myosin filaments and the cross bridges that connect them. Color the A and I bands in the lower panel, noting that the color of the bands reflects the density of the filaments that are contained in it. Note also that the Z line corresponds to the Z disc.*

Structure of actin and myosin filaments

A myosin filament is composed of numerous myosin molecules that are bundled together with their globular protein heads protruding. Each individual myosin molecule is made up of two heavy meromyosin chains and four light meromyosin chains. The two heavy chains are wound around each other to form two heads at one end and a tail at the other. Each myosin head also contains two of the four light chains and makes up part of a cross bridge (Fig. 5.4).

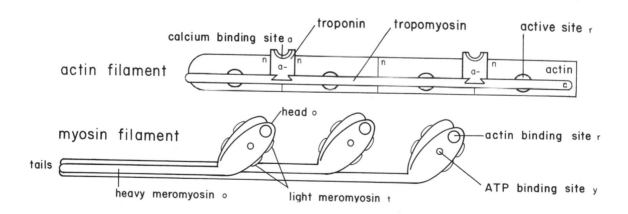

calcium binding site a   troponin   tropomyosin   active site r

actin filament   actin

myosin filament   head o

tails   actin binding site r

heavy meromyosin o   light meromyosin t   ATP binding site y

Figure 5.4 *Structure of actin and myosin filaments. Identify and color each of the structures as it appears in the text. Note that the tropomyosin strand covers the active sites on the actin strand and prevents actin from binding with myosin.*

The actin filament contains three proteins—actin, tropomyosin, and troponin. It is made up of two helical strands that are loosely connected; one strand is composed of actin molecules, and the other strand is composed of tropomyosin molecules. The tropomyosin strand covers the active sites on the actin strand and thereby prevents actin from binding with myosin (Fig. 5.4).

A troponin molecule is attached to each tropomyosin molecule (Fig. 5.4). Troponin is made up of three protein subunits—troponin A has an affinity for actin, troponin T has an affinity for tropomyosin, and troponin C has an affinity for calcium ions.

Interaction between actin and myosin filaments

At rest, there are no chemical reactions between the actin and myosin filaments and the muscle can be stretched without much resistance. In the presence of calcium ions, however, actin and myosin bind strongly to one another. It is believed that the binding of calcium ions to troponin physically moves the troponin-tropomyosin complex so that the active sites on the actin filaments are exposed and the myosin heads can attach to them. This attachment causes the myosin head to tilt in a power stroke that pulls the actin filament across the myosin filament (Fig. 5.5). The energy for this process is provided by the breakdown of ATP into ADP, a chemical reaction that is catalyzed by the enzymatic properties (ATPase activity) of the myosin heads (Fig. 5.4).

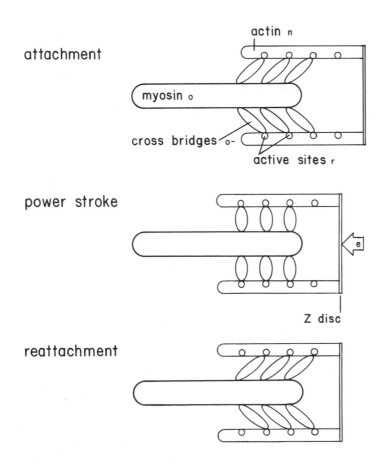

Figure 5.5 *Interaction between actin and myosin filaments. This figure shows how the actin and myosin filaments interact with each other when the active sites on the actin molecules are uncovered by the displacement of tropomyosin. Color the actin and myosin filaments, the cross bridges, and the active sites on the actin filaments in each panel. Note that the rotation of the cross bridges to a vertical position during the power stroke pulls the actin filaments to the left and thereby shortens the sarcomere. Color the arrow that indicates the resultant displacement of the Z disc. Compare this figure with Fig. 5.3.*

Following the power stroke, the head breaks away from the active site, returns to its normal configuration, and attaches itself to the next active site farther down the actin filament. This bending back and forth of the myosin heads causes the actin filaments to be pulled across the myosin filaments and brings the Z discs closer together. The resultant shortening of the sarcomere causes the muscle to shorten (Fig. 5.5).

The length-tension relationship of skeletal muscle

The length of the sarcomere determines the amount of overlap between the actin and myosin filaments and thus, the number of cross-bridges that participate in a given contraction. Since each cross bridge contributes to the contraction, sarcomeres generate their maximal force when their contraction employs the maximal number of cross-bridges between the actin and myosin filaments. The length of the sarcomere that provides the maximum number of cross bridges is its optimal length (Fig. 5.6).

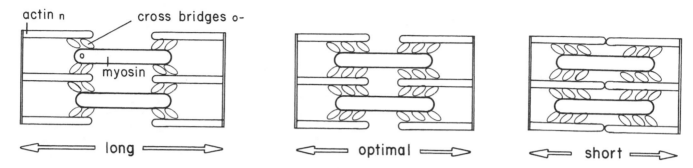

actin n   cross bridges o-

myosin

long   optimal   short

Figure 5.6 *Effect of sarcomere length on filament interaction. Color the actin and myosin filaments in each panel. Color and count the cross bridges in each panel. Note that the long sarcomere generates less force than the optimal length sarcomere because it has fewer cross bridges available to participate in the contraction. Note also that the short sarcomere generates less force than the optimal length sarcomere because the actin filaments abut each other and interfere with the contraction.*

Stretching a sarcomere to make it contract from a longer than optimal length decreases its contractile force by reducing the number of activated cross-bridges. Shortening a sarcomere to make it contract from a less than optimal length also decreases its con-tractile force, but for different reasons. In a short sarcomere, force is reduced because the ends of actin filaments overlap each other. In a very short sarcomere, force is further reduced because the Z discs abut the ends of the myosin filaments (Fig. 5.7).

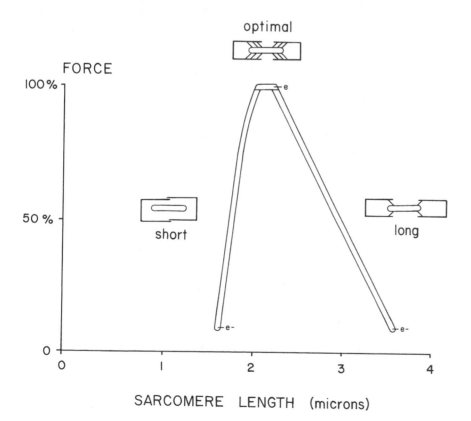

Figure 5.7 *The length-tension relationship of skeletal muscle. The length-tension relationship of skeletal muscle describes how the fiber length of a muscle prior to its contraction influences the maximal force that the muscle generates during its contraction. A wide range of resting sarcomere lengths are obtained by compressing or stretching the muscle prior to its contraction. Muscle force is measured during the subsequent isometric contraction, in which the muscle is not permitted to shorten (Fig. 5.18). Color the length-tension curve that shows how muscle force (expressed as a percentage of its maximal value) varies with sarcomere length (measured in microns). Note that the muscle generates its maximal force when it contracts from an optimal sarcomere length (from 2.0 to 2.2 microns) and that force decreases considerably when it contracts from a sarcomere length that is either too short or too long. Compare this figure with Fig. 5.6.*

Neuromuscular junction

Motor neurons control the contraction of skeletal muscle by releasing molecules of acetylcholine at the neuromuscular junction. The terminals of the nerve fibers at the neuromuscular junction are separated from the membranes of the muscle fibers by a space called the synaptic cleft. The nerve terminals have vesicles that contain acetylcholine molecules. The spread of an action potential over the nerve terminal opens voltage-gated calcium channels in the nerve membrane, and the resultant influx of calcium ions causes a number of vesicles to undergo exocytosis and discharge their acetylcholine molecules into the synapse (Fig. 5.8).

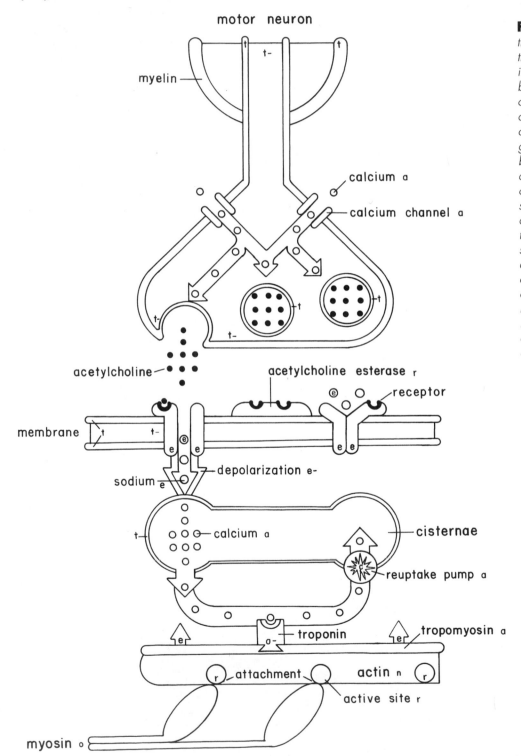

motor neuron

myelin

calcium a

calcium channel a

acetylcholine

acetylcholine esterase r

receptor

membrane

depolarization e-

sodium

calcium a

cisternae

reuptake pump a

troponin

tropomyosin a

attachment

actin n

active site r

myosin o

Figure 5.8 *Neuromuscular transmission and excitation-contraction coupling. Begin by coloring the myelin sheath, the membrane, and the calcium channels of the motor neuron. Color the calcium ions and note how they make contact with the vesicle that undergoes exocytosis. Color the membranes of the vesicles, identify the acetylcholine molecules, noting the ones that are released into the synapse between the motor nerve and the muscle membrane. Color the membrane of the muscle, the sodium channels that span it, and the enzyme, acetylcholine esterase, that breaks down acetylcholine. Color the sodium ions that remain in the synapse, then color the ones that pass through the open channel to enter the muscle cell and depolarize it. Note that the receptor in the open channel contains acetylcholine. Color the depolarization arrow and note that it stimulates the release of calcium ions from the cisternae. Color the membrane of the cisternae and the calcium ions. Note that the calcium ions are returned to the cisternae by a reuptake pump after they bind with troponin. Color the reuptake pump and the flash that indicates that it is a primary active transport mechanism that uses energy derived from the breakdown of ATP. Color the troponin molecule and the tropomyosin strand and the vertical arrows that indicate that it has been displaced from its resting position, shown in Fig. 5.4. Finish the picture by coloring the actin filament, the active sites that are uncovered, and the myosin filaments that attach to them as shown in Fig. 5.5.*

The acetylcholine molecules diffuse across the synaptic cleft to combine with receptor proteins that open ligand-gated channels on the muscle membrane. These open channels allow sodium ions to flow down their concentration and voltage gradients and enter the muscle cell. The sudden influx of positive charges depolarizes the cell and produces an action potential that spreads rapidly over the entire surface of the muscle membrane (Fig. 5.8). Action potentials in muscle are characterized by an initial rapid rise in membrane potential (depolarization) followed by a return to the baseline level of around −80 mV (repolarization).

Excitation-contraction coupling

The action potential spreads rapidly to the central por-tions of the muscle through fast-conducting transverse tubules (T tubules) that penetrate the entire muscle fiber. The conduction of an action potential through the T tubules stimulates the release of calcium ions that are stored in closed sacs (cisternae) located within the sarcoplasmic reticulum, a specialized version of the endoplasmic reticulum (Fig. 2.1). The released calcium ions bind troponin to uncover the active sites on the actin filament and thereby permit the muscle fiber to contract. The contraction ends when the calcium ions are returned to the cisternae by an active transport mechanism called a calcium reuptake pump (Fig. 5.8). This removal of calcium ions presumably allows the troponin-tropomyosin complexes to return to their resting positions, where they cover the active sites on the actin filaments.

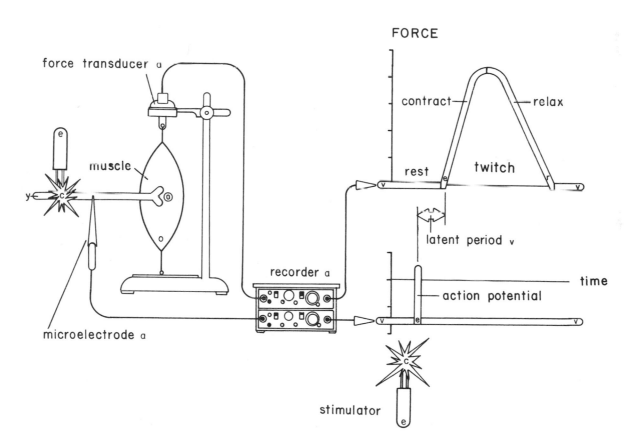

Figure 5.9 *Muscle twitch. This figure describes how the tension generated by a muscle during an isometric twitch is recorded by a polygraph. In this experiment, a nerve stimulator delivers a single shock to the motor nerve that produces an action potential in each of the nerve fibers simultaneously. Action potentials are recorded by a polygraph using the methods described in Fig. 4.12. The muscle is connected to an apparatus containing a force transducer, a device that converts muscle tension into an electrical signal that can be amplified and displayed by a polygraph recorder. Begin at the left by coloring the nerve stimulator and its electric shock, the motor nerve, the neurotransmitter, and the body of the muscle. Color the microelectrode, the force transducer and the recorders. Color the stimulator, its shock, and the polygraph tracings of the action potential in the nerve and the twitch tension in the muscle. Note that the twitch is characterized by a period of contraction during which muscle tension rises to its peak and a period of relaxation during which muscle tension returns to the baseline level. Color the arrow labeled latent period and note that it corresponds to the time delay between the onset of the action potential in the nerve and the onset of the twitch in the muscle. Note also that the duration of the action potential is short in comparison to the duration of the twitch.*

Twitch

The twitch is the fundamental unit of muscle contraction. It is the contraction that is produced by a single action potential in a muscle fiber. It is characterized by a short delay called a latent period, a contraction time in which muscle tension rises to its peak, and a relaxation time during which tension returns to the baseline level (Fig. 5.9). The duration of the action potential is short in comparison to the duration of the twitch it produces.

Muscle fiber types

Two distinct muscle fiber types have been identified on the basis of their speed of contraction and their meta-bolic characteristics (Fig. 5.10). Type I fibers are slow-twitch, fatigue-resistant fibers that derive most of their energy from the aerobic pathways of the Krebs cycle and the electron transport chain, both of which require a continuous supply of oxygen (Fig. 10.13). Type I fibers are adapted for activities that require endurance (e.g., marathon running). Type II fibers are fast-twitch, fatigable fibers that derive most of their energy from anaerobic sources, including the energy stored in the bonds of ATP and creatine phosphate as well as the pathway of glycolysis (Fig. 10.14). Type II fibers are well adapted for activities that require short bursts of high-power output (e.g., sprinting).

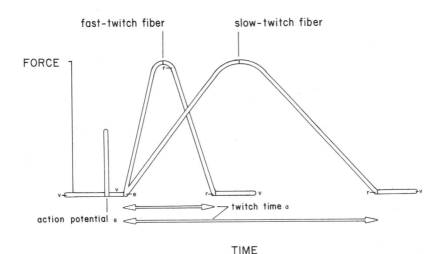

Figure 5.10 *Effect of muscle fiber type on twitch time. Color the action potential, the contraction phase, the relaxation phase, and the twitch time for each fiber. Note that the fast-twitch fiber has a shorter twitch time than the slow-twitch fiber. Compare this figure with Fig. 5.9.*

Muscle biopsies performed on the leg muscles of elite racing cyclists and sprint swimmers reveal considerable differences between the relative distributions of slow-twitch and fast-twitch fibers (Fig. 5.11). As would be expected, slow-twitch fibers predominate in highly-trained cyclists and fast-twitch fibers predominate in highly-trained sprinters.

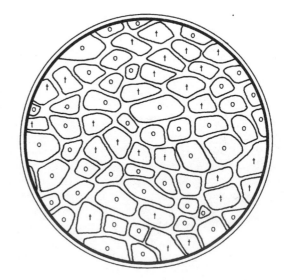

Figure 5.11 *Distribution of muscle fiber types. Color the individual muscle fibers in this cross section and note the relative distributions of fast-twitch (tan) and slow-twitch (orange) fibers.*

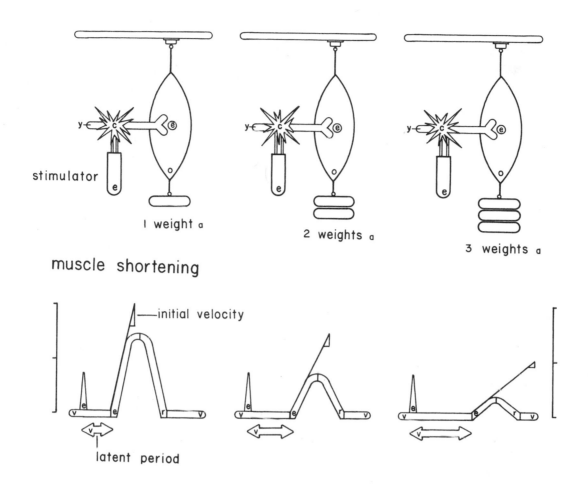

stimulator

1 weight a

2 weights a

3 weights a

muscle shortening

initial velocity

latent period

Figure 5.12 *Effect of load on twitch. This figure describes how muscle contracts when it lifts three different weights. Color the nerve stimulator, its shock, the motor nerve, and the muscle in each panel. Note that the stimulus to the nerve and the resting length of the muscle are the same in all three cases. Color and count the weights. Color the action potential, the latent period, and the polygraph tracings that show how the muscle shortens over time against each weight. The peak values indicate the maximum distance that the muscle shortens (in mm). Since the slope of a line in a graph of distance (in mm) vs. time (in sec) has the units of velocity (in mm/sec), it follows that the slope of each tracing indicates the initial velocity of muscle shortening. Note that heavier weights, which require the muscle to generate more force to lift them, also prolong the latent period, reduce the maximal amount of shortening, and decrease the initial velocity of shortening.*

The force-velocity characteristic of skeletal muscle

The force generated by a muscle depends on the resistance against which the muscle contracts. Heavier weights prolong the latent period, decrease the initial velocity of shortening, and increase the maximal muscle tension (Fig. 5.12). Depending on the load, therefore, the twitch produced by a muscle can range from a high force, low velocity contraction against a heavy weight to a low force, high velocity contraction against a light weight. The force generated by a muscle is maximal when it contracts against a load that is too heavy for it to lift, i.e., an isometric contraction, and the velocity of shortening is maximal when it contracts against no load. The spectrum of all possible combinations of force and velocity, obtained using a range of weights, describes the force-velocity characteristic of a muscle (Fig. 5.13).

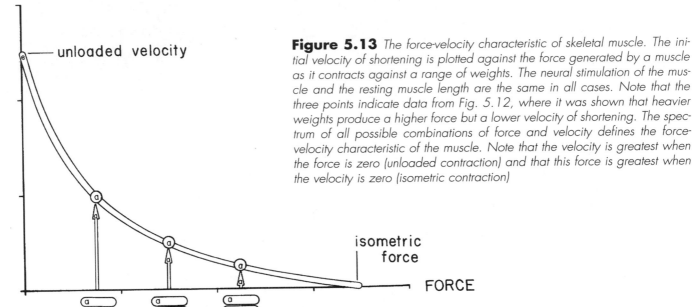

INITIAL VELOCITY

— unloaded velocity

isometric force

FORCE

1 weight

2 weights

3 weights

Figure 5.13 *The force-velocity characteristic of skeletal muscle. The initial velocity of shortening is plotted against the force generated by a muscle as it contracts against a range of weights. The neural stimulation of the muscle and the resting muscle length are the same in all cases. Note that the three points indicate data from Fig. 5.12, where it was shown that heavier weights produce a higher force but a lower velocity of shortening. The spectrum of all possible combinations of force and velocity defines the force-velocity characteristic of the muscle. Note that the velocity is greatest when the force is zero (unloaded contraction) and that this force is greatest when the velocity is zero (isometric contraction)*

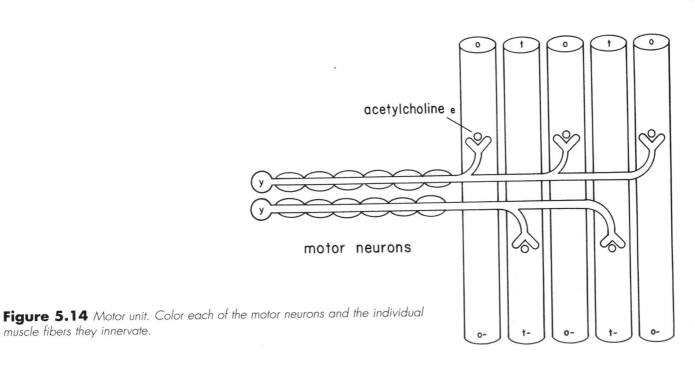

acetylcholine e

motor neurons

muscle fibers

Figure 5.14 *Motor unit. Color each of the motor neurons and the individual muscle fibers they innervate.*

gray blue canary green flesh black navy orange pink red sienna tan violet white yellow azure [–] means use light pressure

Motor unit

A motor unit is a single nerve fiber plus all of the muscle fibers it innervates (Fig. 5.14). Motor units of muscles involved in fine control (e.g., laryngeal muscles) have few muscle fibers per nerve fiber whereas motor units of muscles involved in gross control (e.g., leg muscles) have many muscle fibers per nerve fiber.

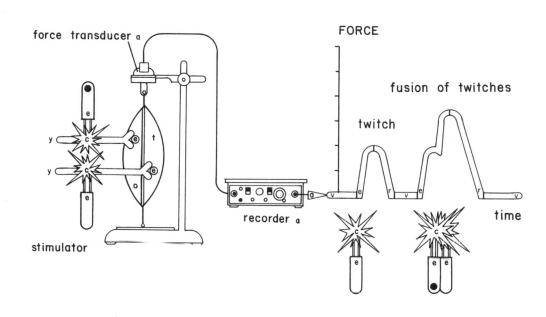

Figure 5.15 *Spatial summation. Begin at the left by coloring the nerve stimulators, their shocks, the motor nerves and the muscle fibers they innervate. Color the force transducer and recorder. Color the stimulators, their shocks, and the polygraph tracings that indicate the force generated by the muscle during an isometric twitch. Note that a single shock produces a twitch similar to that shown in Fig. 5.9. Note also that two shocks applied in rapid succession produce twitches that fuse to yield a stronger contraction. This summation of twitches due to the recruitment of motor units is called spatial summation. Compare this figure with Fig. 4.13.*

Spatial and temporal summation

Spatial and temporal summation are two different mechanisms that enable muscle to adjust the strength of its contraction. In spatial summation, an increase in muscle force is due to an increase in the number of motor units that are recruited to produce a contraction. Thus, weak contractions employ few motor units while strong contractions employ many motor units (Fig. 5.15).

Figure 5.16 *Temporal summation. Color the nerve stimulator, its shock, the motor nerve, and the muscle. Color the force transducer and recorder. Color the stimulator, its shocks, and the polygraph tracing that indicates the force generated by the muscle during an isometric twitch. Note that a single shock produces a single twitch similar to that shown in Fig. 5.9 and that two shocks applied in rapid succession produces twitches that fuse to yield a stronger contraction. The summation of twitches that is due to more rapid stimulation of a given motor unit is called temporal summation. Compare this figure with Figs. 4.14 and 5.15.*

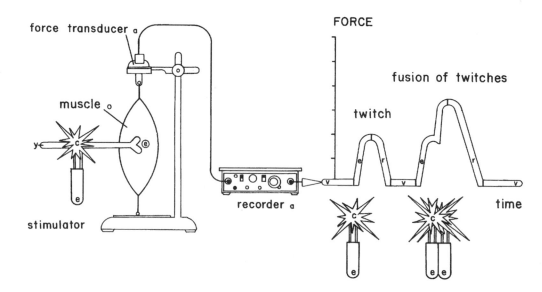

Temporal summation occurs when an increase in muscle force is due to an increase in the neural drive that is delivered to the same number of motor units. Since one action potential produces a twitch (Fig. 5.9), frequent action potentials generate sequential twitches that fuse to produce a stronger contraction. Thus, weak contractions employ trains of low-frequency action potentials whereas strong contractions employ trains of higher-frequency action potentials (Fig. 5.16). Tetanus occurs when the frequency of muscle stimulation is so high that there is no time for relaxation between successive stimuli. Under these conditions, the individual twitches fuse to produce a steady contraction of maximal force (Fig. 5.17).

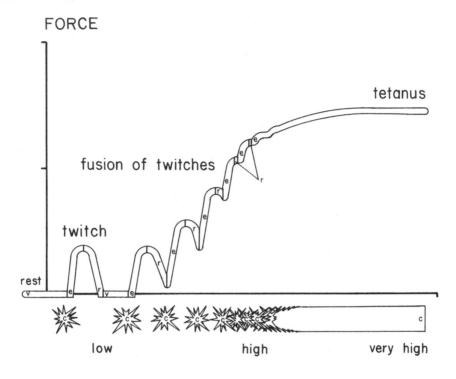

Figure 5.17 *Tetanus. Color the shocks and the graph, which shows the force developed by a skeletal muscle in response to repetitive stimulation at gradually increasing frequencies. As the frequency of stimulation increases, note that the twitches begin to fuse, the period of relaxation between successive contractions begins to decrease and, at very high frequencies, the contraction becomes a complete or fused tetanus with no periods of relaxation. Note also that the muscle generates its maximal force during a tetanic contraction.*

concentric   isometric   eccentric

Figure 5.18 *Types of muscle contraction. Color the panels from left to right. Note that lifting a weight against gravity is a concentric contraction because muscle length decreases during tension development, holding a weight is an isometric contraction because muscle length remains constant during tension development, and lowering a weight slowly is an eccentric contraction because muscle length increases during tension development.*

Types of muscle contraction

Types of muscle contractions include: 1) concentric contraction, in which muscle length decreases during tension development; 2) isometric contraction, in which muscle length remains constant during tension development; and 3) eccentric contraction, in which muscle length increases during tension development (Fig. 5.18).

Because the ability of skeletal muscle to generate tension decreases as the muscle shortens (Fig. 5.7), the maximal force that a muscle can generate depends on the type of contraction; it is highest in an eccentric contraction, intermediate in an isometric contraction, and lowest in a concentric contraction.

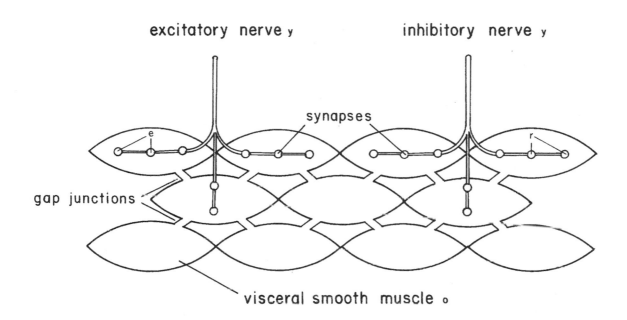

Figure 5.19 *Smooth muscle. Color the excitatory and inhibitory nerves, their synapses, and the smooth muscle cells. Note that gap junctions provide connections between individual smooth muscle cells that enable action potentials to travel from one fiber to the next.*

Smooth muscle

Smooth muscle fibers are smaller than skeletal muscle fibers, they also have longer contraction times and consume less energy. The resting membrane potential of smooth muscle is −60 to −50 mV. The actin and myosin filaments of smooth and skeletal muscle have similar chemical composition but are arranged differently so that smooth muscle lacks the characteristic striations, or stripes, of skeletal muscle (Fig. 5.3).

The two types of smooth muscle are the multi-unit smooth muscle and the visceral (single-unit) smooth muscle. Multi-unit smooth muscle contains discrete fibers that are each innervated by a single nerve ending. Multi-unit smooth muscle is controlled mainly by motor nerves of the autonomic nervous system (Fig. 4.1). This type of smooth muscle, which rarely exhibits spontaneous contraction, is found in the ciliary muscle and the iris of the eye.

Visceral smooth muscle differs from multi-unit smooth muscle in that the fibers are attached to each other to form sheets, bundles, and tubes. Visceral smooth muscle is found in the walls of the the blood vessels (Fig. 6.17), the intestine (Fig. 9.4), and the urinary bladder.

The individual muscle fibers are also connected by gap junctions that enable action potentials to spread from one fiber to another so that the entire muscle contracts as a unit (Fig. 5.19).

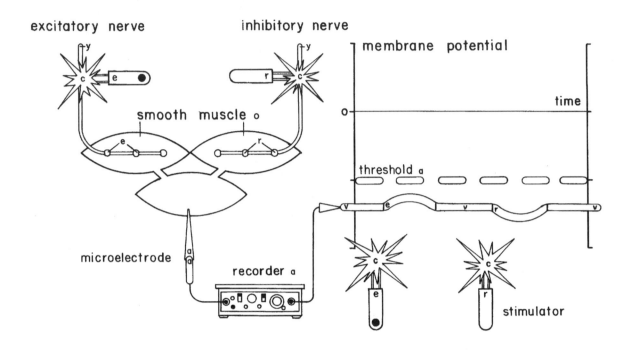

Figure 5.20 *Autonomic control of smooth muscle. Color the nerve stimulators, their shocks, the autonomic nerves, and the smooth muscle fibers. Color the microelectrode and the recorder. Color the stimulators, their shocks, and the polygraph tracing of the membrane potential recorded in a smooth muscle cell. Note that the stimulation of an excitatory nerve causes depolarization of the muscle cell whereas the stimulation of an inhibitory nerve causes hyperpolarization. Compare this figure with Fig. 4.12.*

Regulation of smooth muscle contraction

In contrast to skeletal muscle, which is controlled entirely by neural stimuli, smooth muscle is controlled by a variety of stimuli, including neural, hormonal, chemical, and mechanical signals. The difference between skeletal and smooth muscle is due to receptor proteins that are specific to the membranes of smooth muscle.

The autonomic nervous system regulates smooth muscle contraction through the action of the parasympathetic and sympathetic nerves (Fig. 4.1). The parasympathetic and sympathetic nerves release acetylcholine and norepinephrine, respectively, into diffuse junctions between the nerve endings and the outer layer of the smooth muscle cells. Acetylcholine excites the smooth muscle of some organs but inhibits it in others. Norepinephrine usually has an effect that is opposite to that of acetylcholine.

These neurotransmitters exert their effects by binding to membrane receptors that control the opening and/or closing of specific ion channels which, in turn, determines whether the smooth muscle will be excited or inhibited. Excitation is due to an opening of sodium channels that depolarizes the membrane. Inhibition is due to an opening of potassium channels that hyperpolarizes the membrane (Fig. 5.20). The regulation of smooth muscle contraction by hormonal, chemical, and mechanical stimuli are discussed as they arise in other parts of this book (Figs. 6.21, 7.14, 9.6, 9.7, and 9.8).

chapter **six**
cardiovascular system

The cardiovascular system transports essential substances to cells, removes metabolic waste products from cells, and helps regulate body temperature.

Anatomy of the cardiovascular system

The cardiovascular system contains two pumps; the right and left heart, and two circulations; the pulmonary and systemic circuits, which are connected in series.

Each side of the heart consists of a thin-walled atrium that serves as a reservoir for blood and a thick-walled ventricle that pumps blood through its circuit (Fig. 6.1). The right ventricle pumps mixed venous blood into the pulmonary capillaries where oxygen (O_2) is added to, and excess carbon dioxide (CO_2) is removed from, the blood. The left ventricle pumps oxygenated blood into the systemic capillaries where O_2 is delivered to, and CO_2 is picked up from, the tissues (Fig. 8.1).

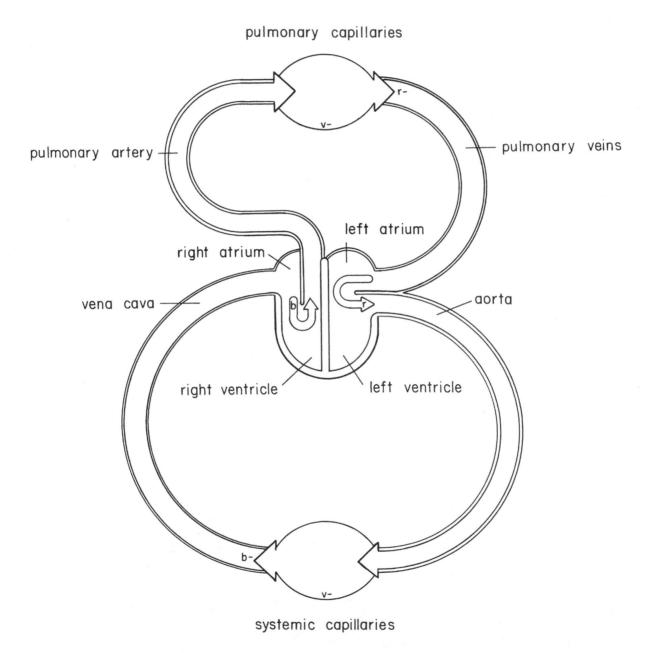

pulmonary capillaries

pulmonary artery

pulmonary veins

right atrium

left atrium

vena cava

aorta

right ventricle

left ventricle

systemic capillaries

Figure 6.1 *The cardiovascular system. Begin at the top by coloring the blood in the pulmonary veins red, to indicate that it is fully oxygenated. Continue coloring clockwise from this point; identify the left heart chambers and the aorta. Oxygen is removed from the blood in the systemic capillaries. Color these capillaries and the venous blood that leaves them; identify the right heart chambers and the pulmonary artery. Finish the picture by coloring the pulmonary capillaries; the site at which oxygen is added to the blood.*

gray **blue** canary green flesh black navy orange pink red sienna tan violet white yellow azure [-] means use light pressure

Electrical activity of the heart

The action potentials of cardiac muscle fibers differ from those of skeletal muscle. Fibers of the SA node, in the right atrium, exhibit spontaneous depolarization and fibers of the ventricles exhibit a long plateau phase in which they remain completely depolarized (Fig. 6.2). Since ventricular fibers cannot be restimulated during the plateau phase, this prevents the heart from being tetanized, which would render the heart incapable of pumping blood (Fig. 5.17).

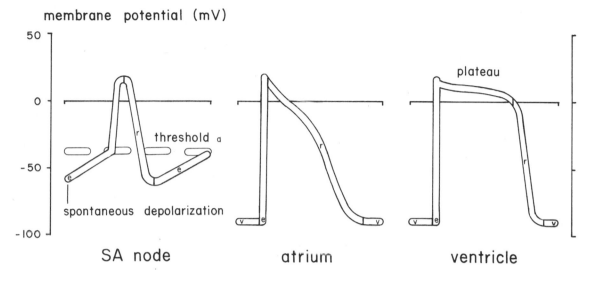

Figure 6.2 Action potentials in cardiac muscle. Color the action potentials of the cardiac muscle fibers, noting that they can be characterized as a green period of depolarization followed by a red period of repolarization. Identify the prolonged plateau phase of the ventricular fiber and the resting membrane potentials of the atrial and ventricular fibers. Color the threshold and note that the SA node cells differ from the atrial and ventricular cells in that they do not exhibit a stable resting membrane potential. Compare this figure with Fig. 4.7.

Also unlike skeletal muscle, cardiac muscle fibers are connected to each other by intercalated discs, which are highly permeable cell membranes that function as gap junctions between adjacent fibers (Fig. 5.19). This feature of cardiac muscle permits an action potential that is initiated in one cell to spread throughout the muscle, thereby enabling the heart to contract as a single unit (Fig. 6.3). These action potentials normally originate in the pacemaker cells, which are spontaneously depolarizing cells that are located in the sinoatrial (SA) node of the right atrium (Fig. 6.2).

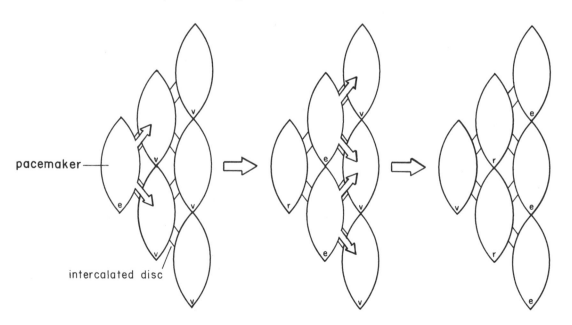

Figure 6.3 Spread of action potentials in cardiac muscle. Color the cardiac muscle fibers from left to right, noting the intercalated discs. Note that the spread of the action potential in cardiac muscle can be viewed as a green wave of depolarization followed by a red wave of repolarization. Compare this figure with Figs. 4.8 and 6.2.

Conduction system of the heart

The heart also contains a specialized conduction system that helps synchronize the contraction of its muscle fibers. The conduction system consists of internodal fibers, the atrioventricular (AV) node, the bundle of His, the right and left bundle branches, and the Purkinje fibers (Fig. 6.4).

The spontaneous depolarization of pacemaker cells initiates a wave of depolarization that spreads over the atria and through the internodal pathways to the AV node (Fig.6.5), which is the only pathway that conducts impulses from the atria to the ventricles. The impulse travels slowly through the narrow fibers of the AV node. This provides time for the atria to contract before the impulse is delivered to the fast-conducting fibers of the bundle of His, the right and left bundle branches, and the Purkinje fibers. The fast-conducting fibers enable all of the ventricular fibers to depolarize and therefore contract simultaneously. This synchrony among the ventricular fibers makes the heart an effective pump.

Figure 6.4 *Conduction system of the heart. Color the SA node, the internodal pathways, and the AV node. Note that the impulse originates in the SA node and that the fibers of the AV node are the only connection between the atria and ventricles. Color the bundle of His, the right and left bundle branches, and the Purkinje fibers. Finish the picture by coloring the cardiac muscle and its chambers.*

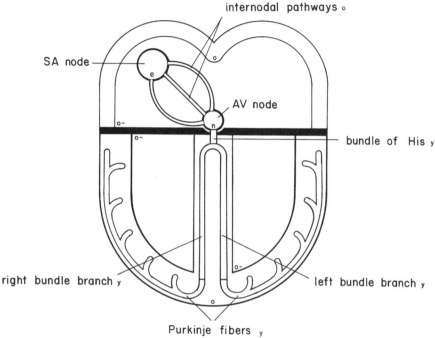

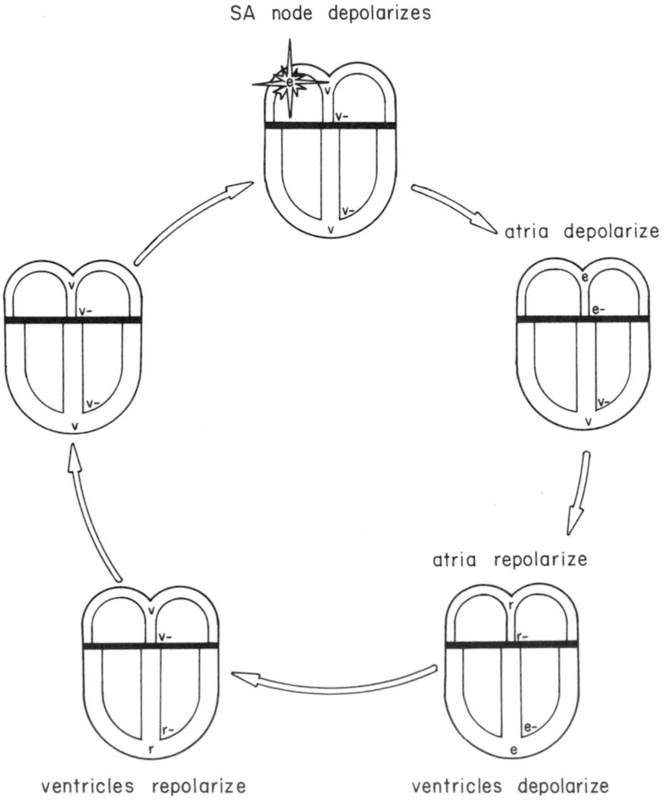

Figure 6.5 *Electrical activity of the heart. Begin coloring at the top, noting that the cycle begins when the pacemaker cells of the SA node depolarize while the atria and ventricles are in their resting state. Continue coloring clockwise, noting that the spread of the action potential through the atria causes them to depolarize before the ventricles. Continue clockwise, noting that atria repolarize when the ventricles depolarize, and that the atria are in their resting state when the ventricles repolarize. Thus, the electrical activity of the heart can also be viewed as a green wave of depolarization followed by a red wave of repolarization.   Compare this figure with Fig. 6.3.*

SA node depolarizes

atria depolarize

atria repolarize

ventricles depolarize

ventricles repolarize

gray **b**lue **c**anary gr**ee**n **f**lesh blac**k** **n**avy **o**range **p**ink **r**ed **s**ienna **t**an **v**iolet **w**hite **y**ellow a**z**ure [-] means use light pressure

Effect of the autonomic nervous system on heart rate

The autonomic nervous system controls the heart rate by releasing neurotransmitters that alter the pattern of spontaneous depolarization exhibited by the pacemaker cells. Parasympathetic fibers in the vagus nerve, release acetylcholine at the SA node, while sympathetic fibers release norepinephrine (Fig. 6.6). The two neurotransmitters have an opposite effect on heart rate. Parasympathetic stimulation decreases the heart rate by prolonging the period between successive action potentials of the pacemaker cells, and sympathetic stimulation increases the heart rate by shortening the period between successive action potentials (Fig. 6.7).

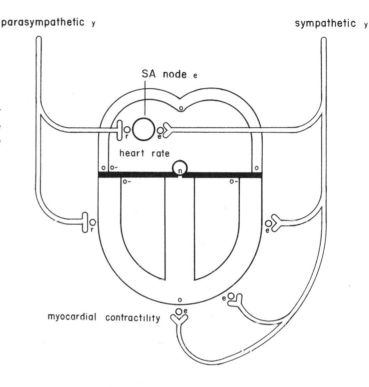

Figure 6.6 *Autonomic innervation of the heart. Color the heart and the autonomic nerves that innervate it. Note that the parasympathetic nerves inhibit the heart while the sympathetic nerves stimulate the heart.*

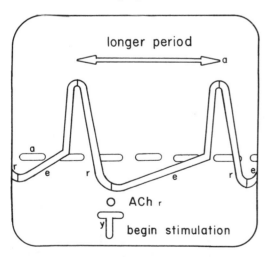

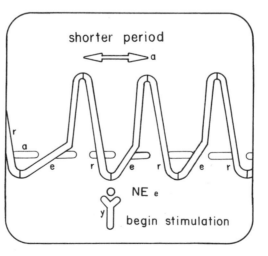

Figure 6.7 *Autonomic control of heart rate. Color the threshold and the membrane potentials from the pacemaker cells of the SA node, noting that they are similar to those shown in Fig. 6.2. Note that acetylcholine (ACh), released by parasympathetic stimulation, decreases the rate of spontaneous depolarization and prolongs the period between successive action potentials. Note also that norepinephrine, released by sympathetic stimulation, increases the rate of spontaneous depolarization and shortens the period between successive action potentials. Thus, parasympathetic stimulation decreases heart rate and sympathetic stimulation increases heart rate.*

The normal electrocardiogram

An electrocardiogram (ECG) is a recording of the electrical activity of the heart that is obtained by measuring the voltage between surface electrodes that are placed on the skin (Fig. 6.8). The normal ECG is characterized by a P wave, a QRS complex, and a T wave. The P wave corresponds to atrial depolarization, the QRS complex corresponds to ventricular depolarization, and the T wave corresponds to ventricular repolarization. The wave that corresponds to atrial repolarization is normally obscured by the large QRS complex.

Abnormal electrocardiograms

Abnormal electrocardiograms are due to cardiac arrhythmias.

One example of a cardiac arrhythmia is complete atrioventricular block, a condition in which the impulse from the SA node is not conducted to the ventricles; this results in an abnormal ECG recording. In complete atrioventricular block, the atria and the ventricles beat at their own rate, and the QRS complexes become dissociated from the P waves (Fig. 6.9). Another cardiac arrhythmia is ventricular fibrillation, a condition in which the individual ventricular fibers depolarize asynchronously and produce an ECG that lacks a QRS complex and T wave (Fig. 6.9). Abnormal ECGs are also found in bradycardia (abnormally slow heart rate), tachycardia (abnormally fast heart rate), atrial fibrillation, and many other arrhythmias.

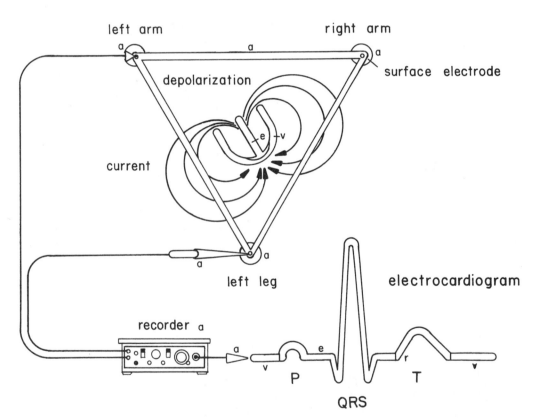

Figure 6.8 *The electrocardiogram. Begin by coloring the heart, noting that it is in a phase in which only a portion of it is depolarized. Identify the current that flows from the depolarized fibers to the resting fibers, noting that the voltage it creates in the body can be recorded by the surface electrodes. Identify and color the surface electrodes, the recorder and its probe, and the electrocardiogram. Note that the ventricle remains completely depolarized during the S-T segment, the period between the end of the QRS complex and the beginning of the T wave. This segment of the ECG corresponds to the plateau phase of the ventricular fibers (Fig. 6.2). Identify the parts in Fig. 6.5 that correspond to the P wave, the QRS complex, and the T wave.*

Cardiac cycle

One-way valves between the atria and ventricles and between the ventricles and arteries prevent the retrograde (backward) flow of blood when pressure builds up in the chambers of the contracting heart (Fig. 6.10). Cardiac valves contain cusps that open and close in accordance with the pressures that develop across them. Since open valves do not normally constitute an impediment to blood flow, the pressures on the two sides of an open valve are essentially equal. However, the pressure on one side of a closed valve exceeds that on the other (Fig. 6.11).

complete atrioventricular block

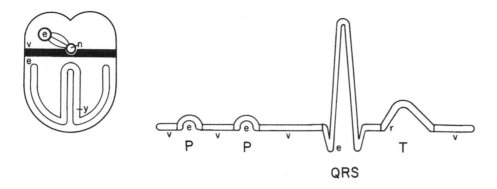

QRS

ventricular fibrillation

Figure 6.9 *Abnormal electrocardiograms. Begin at the top by coloring the SA node, AV node, bundle branches, and Purkinje fibers. Compare this conduction system with the one shown in Fig. 6.4, noting that fibers from the AV node are disconnected from the bundle branches. Color the electrocardiogram, noting that the QRS complex is dissociated from the P waves. Color the heart in the bottom panel, noting that the fibrillating ventricle has regions in which the cells are depolarized, repolarized, and at rest. Color the electrocardiogram, noting that its lack of distinguishable features reflects the asynchronous electrical activity of the ventricle.*

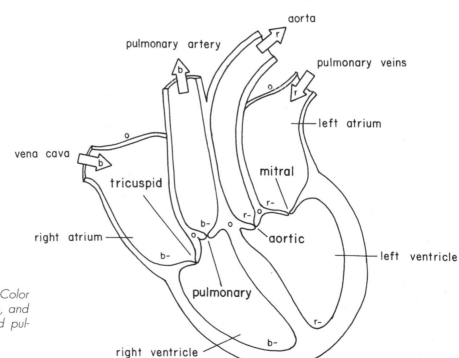

Figure 6.10 *Valves of the heart. Color and identify the valves, cardiac muscle, and chambers of the heart. The aorta and pulmonary artery are shown displaced.*

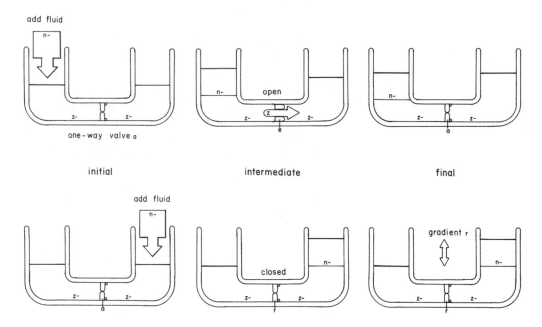

Figure 6.11 *Function of one-way valves. Color each panel from left to right. Note that the addition of fluid to the left side transiently increases the pressure, opens the valve, and permits fluid to flow from left to right until both sides are filled to the same level. In contrast, the addition of fluid to the right side closes the valve so that fluid cannot flow through it. Thus, the one-way valve permits fluid to flow in only one direction and supports a pressure gradient only when it is closed.*

Phases of the cardiac cycle

The cardiac cycle consists of a period of diastole, during which the heart relaxes, and a period of systole, during which the heart contracts. The opening and closing of the heart valves further divides the cardiac cycle into four distinct phases: 1) filling, 2) isovolumetric contraction, 3) ejection, and 4) isovolumetric relaxation (Fig. 6.12). Note that diastole corresponds to the entire period in which isovolumetric relaxation and filling occur, and that systole corresponds to the entire period of isovolumetric contraction and ejection.

Figure 6.12 *Phases of the cardiac cycle. Begin coloring at the top and work clockwise, noting the flow of blood and the opening and closing of the valves. Color a valve green when it is open and red when it is closed. Note that the stroke volume reflects the change in ventricular volume that occurs during ejection. Note also that two valves are never open at the same time, and that this figure depicts events at only one side of the heart.*

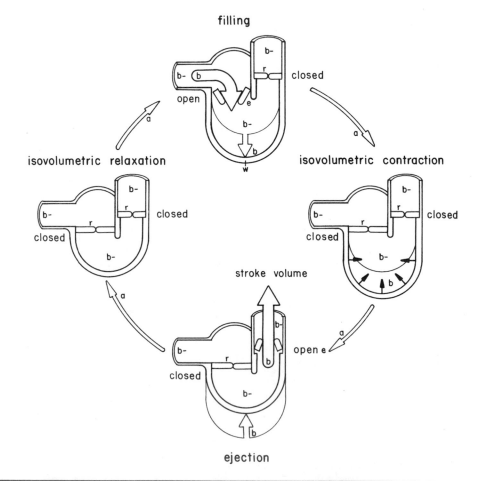

Pressure and volume changes during the cardiac cycle

The pressure and volume changes during the phases of the cardiac cycle are similar in the right and left sides of the heart; only the events in the left heart are described below.

During the filling phase, the mitral valve is open and blood flows from the left atrium into the left ventricle (Fig. 6.13), thereby increasing ventricular volume. Atrial pressure and ventricular pressure are essentially the same when the mitral valve is open (Fig. 6.11). The aortic valve is closed during this phase because arterial pressure exceeds ventricular pressure (Fig. 6.13).

During isovolumetric contraction, the mitral valve closes when the pressure in the contracting ventricle exceeds the pressure in the atrium. Throughout this phase, ventricular pressure is higher than atrial pressure but lower than arterial pressure. Consequently, both the mitral and aortic valves are closed and blood can neither enter nor leave the ventricle. This rise in ventricular pressure occurs at a constant ventricular volume (an isometric contraction) (Fig. 6.13).

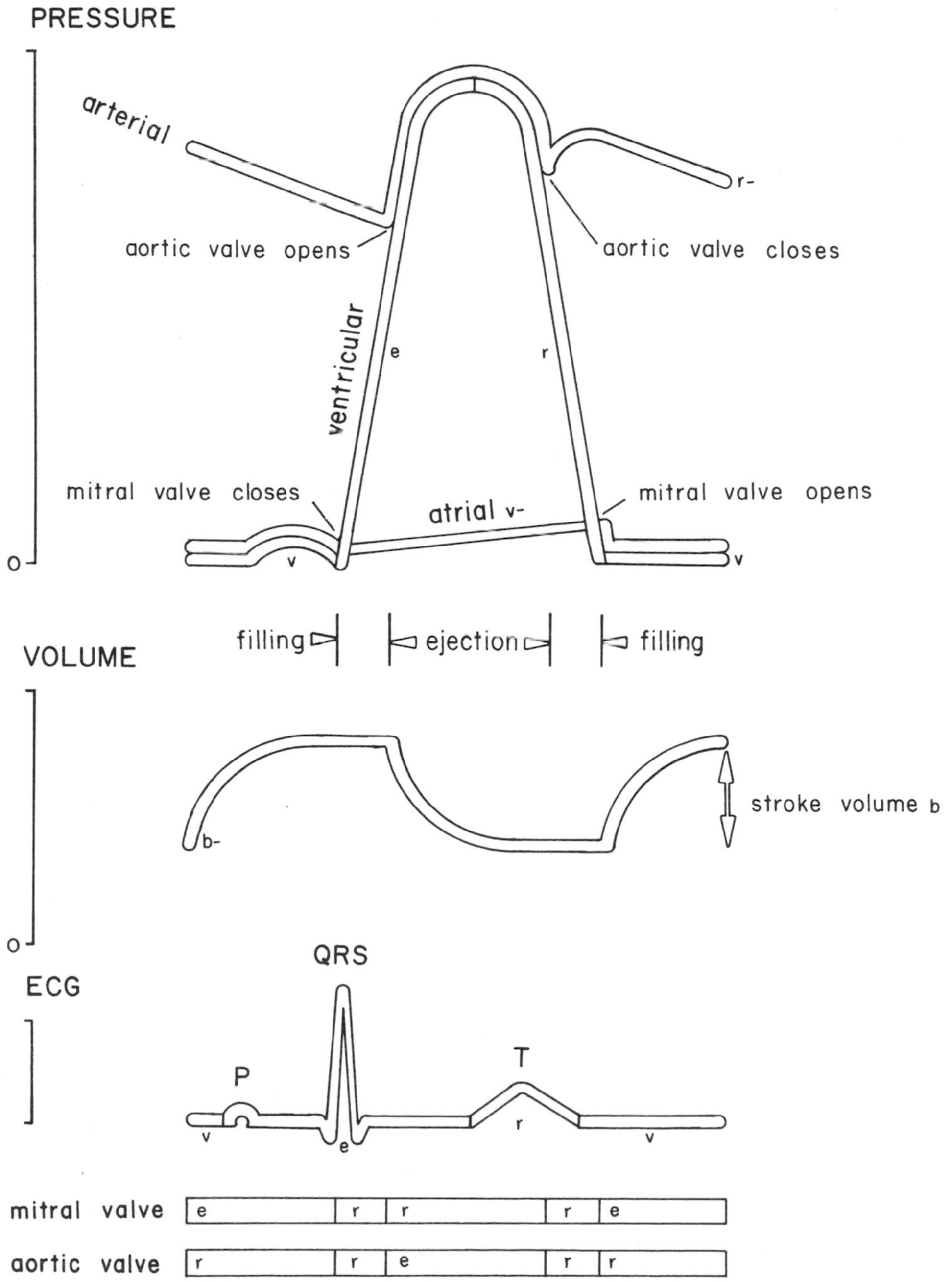

PRESSURE

arterial

aortic valve opens   aortic valve closes

r-

ventricular   e   r

mitral valve closes   mitral valve opens

atrial v-

0   v   v

| filling |⊳ |◁ ejection ⊳| |◁ filling |

VOLUME

b-   stroke volume b

0

ECG

QRS

P   T

v   e   r   v

| mitral valve | e | | | r | r | | | r | e | |
| aortic valve | r | | | r | e | | | r | r | |

Figure 6.13 *Pressure and volume changes during the cardiac cycle. Begin by coloring the ventricular pressure tracing. Identify the contraction and relaxation phases of the ventricle and compare them with those shown in Fig. 5.9. Color the arterial pressure tracing and note that it coincides with the ventricular pressure tracing when the aortic valve is open (during the ejection phase). Color the atrial pressure tracing and note that it coincides with the ventricular pressure tracing when the mitral valve is open (during the filling phase). Color the ventricular volume tracing, noting that volume increases during filling and decreases during ejection. Note also that the stroke volume is determined by the difference between the volume in the ventricle at the end of the filling phase and the end of the ejection phase. Color the ECG, noting its relationship to the ventricular pressure tracing. Finish the picture by coloring the horizontal bars that indicate the periods in which the mitral and aortic valves are open (green) and closed (red).*

During ejection, the propulsion of blood by the ventricle into the aorta decreases ventricular volume. Throughout this phase, ventricular pressure and arterial pressure are the same because the aortic valve is open. The volume of blood ejected by the ventricle is called the stroke volume; it is determined by the difference between the volume of blood in the ventricle at the end of the filling phase (called the end-diastolic volume) and at the end of the ejection phase (called the end-systolic volume) (Fig. 6.13).

The phase of isovolumetric relaxation begins when the aortic valve closes. Throughout this phase, both the aortic and mitral valves are closed because the pressure in the relaxing ventricle is lower than arterial pressure but higher than atrial pressure. The fall in ventricular pressure therefore occurs at a constant ventricular volume (an isometric relaxation). When ventricular pressure falls to the point where it matches the rising atrial pressure, the mitral valve opens and the next filling phase begins (Fig. 6.13).

The relationship between ECG and ventricular pressure

Cardiac muscle is similar to skeletal muscle in that an action potential triggers the release of calcium ions into the sarcoplasmic reticulum, which, in turn, bind troponin and initiate a muscle contraction. The duration of the action potential is very short in comparison to the twitch it produces in skeletal muscle (Fig. 5. 9), but this is not the case in cardiac muscle (Fig. 6.14).

A comparison between the timing of an action potential and the twitch it produces in a ventricular muscle fiber shows that muscle tension begins to develop at the onset of depolarization and that the maximum tension developed by the muscle fiber occurs during the phase of repolarization (Fig. 6.14).

This relationship between the electrical (action potential) and mechanical (muscle tension) events in a single fiber explains why the QRS complex, which corresponds to the onset of ventricular depolarization, coincides with the initial rise in ventricular pressure. It also explains why the T wave, which corresponds to ventricular repolarization, coincides with the maximum pressure attained by the ventricle during systole (Fig. 6.13).

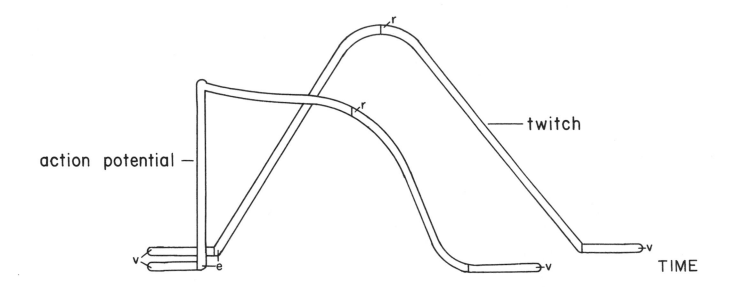

action potential

twitch

TIME

Figure 6.14 *Relationship between the action potential and twitch tension in cardiac muscle. Color the action potential, which is a measure of the changes in voltage across the membrane of the muscle, and identify the depolarization and repolarization phases. Color the twitch tension, which is a measure of the force generated by the contracting sarcomeres, and identify the contraction and relaxation phases. Note that the onset of depolarization coincides with the beginning of tension development, and that maximal tension occurs during repolarization. Compare this figure with Fig. 5.9.*

Measurement of blood pressure

The pulsatile nature of blood flow causes arterial blood pressure to rise during systole and fall during diastole. Arterial blood pressure is therefore expressed in terms of its maximum systolic and minimum diastolic values. For example, normal arterial blood pressure is said to be 120/80, where 120 and 80 are the systolic and diastolic pressures in mmHg, respectively (Fig. 6.15, upper panel).

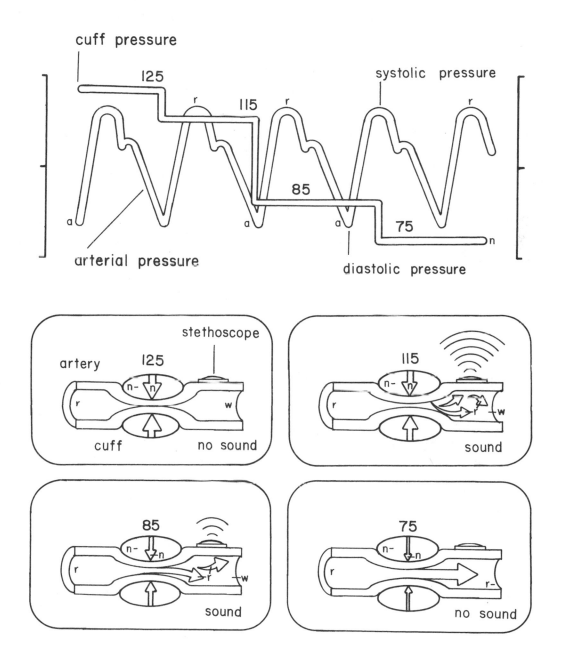

Figure 6.15 *Measurement of arterial blood pressure. Color the cuff pressure and arterial blood pressure tracings. Color the panels, noting the changes in blood flow that occur when the pressure in the cuff is slowly reduced. Note that sound occurs only when cuff pressure interrupts the blood flow for some portion of the cycle.*

Blood pressure in the brachial artery can be measured by sphygmomanometry, a method that employs an inflatable pressure cuff that is wrapped around the arm and connected to a mercury manometer. When the cuff is inflated to a pressure that exceeds systolic pressure, the cuff occludes (collapses) the artery, blood flow stops, and a brachial pulse cannot be felt (palpated) or heard (auscultated) downstream from the occlusion. The pressure in the cuff is then reduced slowly until the first faint sounds of turbulent blood flow can be heard. Cuff pressure at this point is taken as systolic pressure. Cuff pressure is reduced further until the muffled sounds of interrupted blood flow just disappear. Cuff pressure at this point is taken as diastolic pressure (Fig. 6.15, lower panels).

The systemic circulation

Arterial blood pressure is the driving force that pumps blood through the vascular beds, which are networks of blood vessels that perfuse the tissues of the body. The vascular beds of different tissues in the systemic circulation are arranged in parallel. This arrangement enables the pressure gradient across each vascular bed to be the same (Fig. 6.16). The magnitude of this pressure gradient is determined by the amount by which arterial pressure exceeds venous pressure, which is small by comparison. Thus, arterial pressure must be maintained in order to provide an adequate perfusion of blood to the tissues.

Types of blood vessels

The four different types of blood vessels that are found in the vascular beds are: 1) arteries, which transport blood at high pressure; 2) arterioles, which regulate the amount of blood that flows through them: 3) capillaries, which exchange substances between the blood and the surrounding cells; and 4) venules and veins, which not only conduct blood back to the heart but also serve as a reservoir for blood (Fig. 6.16).

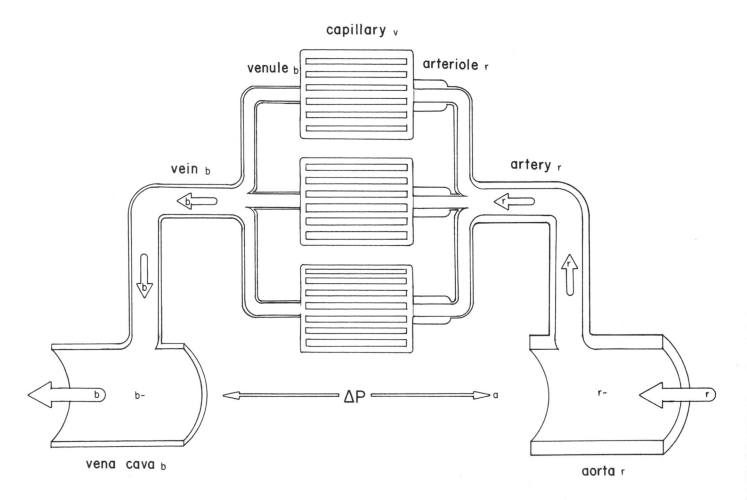

Figure 6.16 *The vascular bed. Color the blood and the blood vessels from right to left. Note the relative numbers, sizes, and shapes of the different types of blood vessels. Note also that the pressure gradient across the vascular bed (ΔP) is determined by the amount by which the blood pressure in the aorta exceeeds that in the vena cava. Compare this with Fig. 6.1.*

The types of blood vessels differ in terms of their relative amounts of endothelium, smooth muscle, elastic tissue, and fibrous tissue. Arteries have a high percentage of elastic tissue, arterioles are made primarily of smooth muscle, and capillaries are made entirely of endothelial cells. The types of blood vessels also differ in terms of their numbers, their internal diameters, and the relative thickness of their walls (Fig. 6.17).

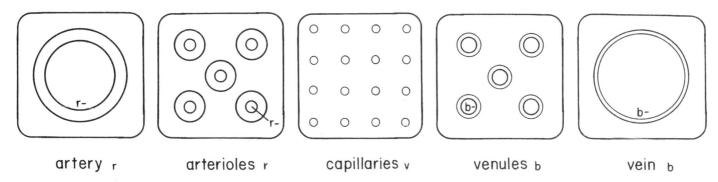

artery r   arterioles r   capillaries v   venules b   vein b

Figure 6.17 *Morphology of the blood vessels. Color each of the blood vessels and the blood it contains; noting their numbers and shapes. Compare these vessels with those shown in Fig. 6.16.*

Functional differences between types of blood vessels

The anatomical and structural differences between the types of blood vessels give rise to their functional differences. The major functional differences between the vessel types are that: 1) the blood pressure is highest in the arteries; 2) the resistance to blood flow is greatest in the arterioles; 3) the velocity of blood flow is slowest in the capillaries; and 4) the volume of blood is largest in the veins.

Model of the systemic circuit

A simple but useful model of the systemic circuit is a thin cylindrical reservoir that is connected by a narrow bore tube to a wide cylindrical reservoir. The thin cylinder represents the arteries, the narrow bore tube represents the arterioles, and the wide cylinder represents the veins (Fig. 6.18). The blood pressures in the arteries and veins can be visualized from the height of the fluid in their respective reservoirs. Similarly, the volumes of blood stored in the arteries and veins can be visualized from the volumes of fluid in their respective reservoirs.

The flow of blood into the model is the cardiac output, and the flow of blood out of the model is the venous return. These flows are analogous to those in the actual circulation, where cardiac output is defined as the rate at which the left ventricle pumps blood into the aorta. Cardiac output (CO), in L/min, is determined by the product of heart rate (HR, in beats/min) and stroke volume (SV, the volume of blood ejected per beat, in ml), i.e., $CO = HR \cdot SV$. Venous return is defined as the rate at which the systemic circuit delivers blood to the right atrium. Cardiac output and venous return are normally equal because blood flows into and out of the systemic circulation at the same average rate.

This model embodies the main features of the systemic circulation—pressure is highest in the arteries, resistance is greatest in the arterioles, and volume is largest in the veins. The value of this model is that the relationships among pressure, flow, and volume in the model are the same as those in the actual circulation.

Factors that determine arterial blood pressure

The model shows that pressure gradient (ΔP) across the arterioles is given by the difference between arterial blood pressure (P_A) and venous blood pressure (P_V), i.e., $\Delta P = P_A - P_V$. Physical principles dictate that this pressure gradient (ΔP) is determined by the flow of blood through the arterioles (CO) and by the resistance of the arterioles (TPR), i.e., $\Delta P = CO \cdot TPR$. Since arterial pressure is by far the major determinant of ΔP, it follows that arterial pressure can be raised by increases in cardiac output and/or increases in total peripheral resistance.

The model also shows that the level of arterial pressure depends on the volume of blood that is stored in the arteries; blood pressure is lowered by a decrease in blood volume and raised by an increase in blood volume.

In summary, the above considerations explain why arterial blood pressure can be regulated by mechanisms and/or control systems that adjust cardiac output, total peripheral resistance, and blood volume. (Fig. 6.18).

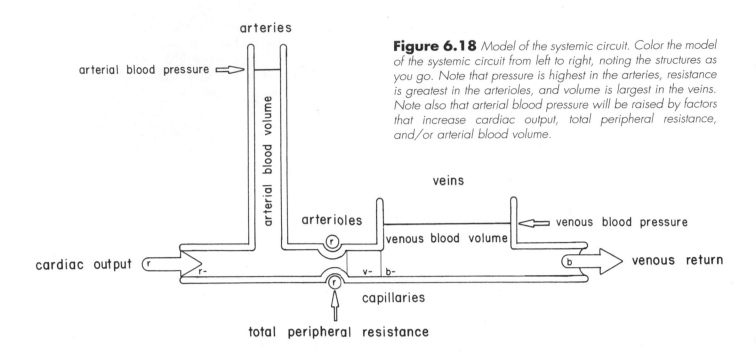

Figure 6.18 *Model of the systemic circuit. Color the model of the systemic circuit from left to right, noting the structures as you go. Note that pressure is highest in the arteries, resistance is greatest in the arterioles, and volume is largest in the veins. Note also that arterial blood pressure will be raised by factors that increase cardiac output, total peripheral resistance, and/or arterial blood volume.*

Factors that determine the resistance to blood flow

The resistance to blood flow in any particular vascular bed depends both on the hematocrit of the blood that perfuses it and on the diameter of its arterioles, which are the major site of resistance.

The hematocrit determines the viscosity of blood, which, in turn, influences the ease with which it flows through narrow vessels (Fig. 6.19). The work that the heart performs in order to pump a given cardiac output is therefore decreased in anemia and increased in polycythemia (Fig. 3.19).

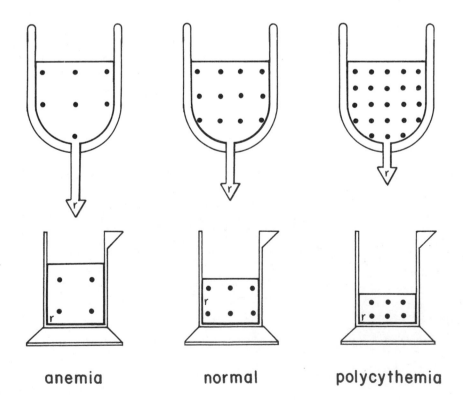

anemia   **normal**   **polycythemia**

Figure 6.19 *Effect of hematocrit on resistance. Color the blood in each reservoir, noting that the geometry of the reservoirs and the extent to which they are filled are identical in each case. Note that the flow rate, indicated by the length of the arrow, is highest in anemia and lowest in polycythemia. Color and note the volumes of blood contained in each of the graduated cylinders. Since the pressures are the same, these differences in flow reflect corresponding differences in resistance. Thus, the hematocrit influences the resistance to blood flow.*

In theory, the resistance of a cylinder varies inversely with the fourth power of its radius. For a given pressure gradient, therefore, halving the radius of a cylinder would reduce the flow to 1/16 its initial value, and doubling the radius would increase its flow 16-fold (Fig. 6.20). Since the arterioles are the major site of resistance, the blood flow to individual vascular beds is regulated by adjustments in the diameter of its arterioles.

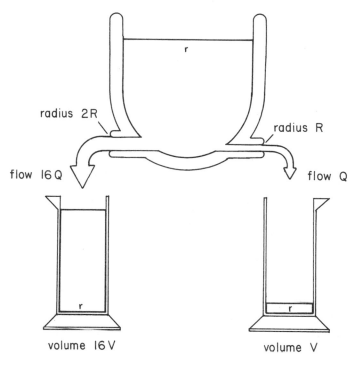

Figure 6.20 *Effect of radius on resistance. Color the fluid in the reservoir. Note that the port at the left has a radius (2R) that is twice that of the port at the right (R), and that the pressure of the fluid at each of the ports is the same (Fig. 3.6). Note also that the rate at which blood flows through the big port is 16 times that through the small port. Finish the picture by coloring and comparing the volume of fluid contained in each of the graduated cylinders.*

Factors that influence the diameter of arterioles

The diameter of the arterioles depends on the combined effects of a number of mechanical, neural, and chemical factors (Fig. 6.21).

A mechanical factor that influences the caliber of a blood vessel is its transmural pressure, which is the amount by which the pressure inside a vessel exceeds the pressure outside. Because of their elasticity, blood vessels dilate, or widen, when their transmural pressures increase and constrict when it decreases.

Neural factors that influence the diameter of arterioles can be attributed to the effects of sympathetic stimulation on the contraction of vascular smooth muscle. The norepinephrine released by sympathetic nerve endings combines with alpha receptors in the smooth muscle of the blood vessels and causes constriction of both the arterioles (called vasoconstriction) and the veins (called venoconstriction).

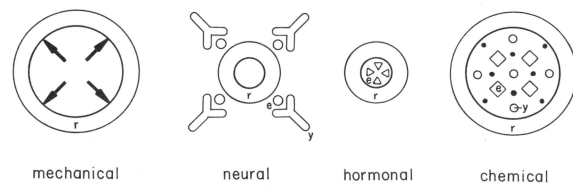

mechanical   neural   hormonal   chemical

Figure 6.21 *Factors that influence the radius of an arteriole. Color the panels from left to right. Note that the diameter of arterioles depends on the competition between mechanical, neural, and chemical factors. Since the arterioles are the major site of resistance in a vascular bed, the blood flow to individual vascular beds can be regulated by one or more of these factors.*

Some chemical factors that regulate the contraction of vascular smooth muscle are hormones that circulate in the blood. These hormones include epinephrine, which is secreted by the adrenal medulla (Fig. 11.9), angiotensin, a hormone whose formation in the blood is stimulated by renin, which is a protein released by the kidney (Fig. 7.14), and antidiuretic hormone (ADH), a hormone that is released by the posterior pituitary gland (Fig. 11.8).

Other chemical factors that influence the contraction of vascular smooth muscle are the levels of oxygen, carbon dioxide, and acidity (pH) of the local blood supply. Arterioles in the systemic circulation dilate when exposed to blood with a low level of oxygen (hypoxemia), a high level of carbon dioxide (hypercarbia), or a low pH (acidosis).

Autoregulation

Autoregulation is the process whereby vascular beds regulate their blood flow in accordance with the metabolism of the tissues they supply. When blood flow is insufficient to meet the metabolic needs of a tissue, the tissue removes more oxygen from the blood and hypoxemia occurs. For the same reasons, the tissues add more carbon dioxide to the blood and hypercarbia also occurs. These local changes in blood chemistry dilate the arterioles and thereby increase blood flow. The increased blood flow

supplies more oxygen to and removes more carbon dioxide from the tissues, thereby restoring the normal levels of oxygen and carbon dioxide in the tissues.

Capillary fluid shift mechanism

The flow of water across a capillary wall (Q, in ml/min), is determined by the permeability of its membrane for water (K) and the balance between the hydrostatic and osmotic pressures within the capillary itself and in the interstitial space just outside the capillary, i.e.,

$$Q = K [(P_c - P_i) - (\pi_c - \pi_i)]$$

where P_c and P_i are the hydrostatic pressures inside and outside the capillary and π_c and π_i are the osmotic pressures inside and outside the capillary, respectively.

The direction of the flow of water across a capillary membrane therefore depends on the relative magnitudes of each of the inward and outward forces. In theory, capillary pressure (P_c) is an outward force while interstitial fluid pressure (P_i) is an inward force; plasma osmotic pressure (π_c) is an inward force and interstitial fluid osmotic pressure (π_i) is an outward force (Fig. 6.22). These osmotic pressures are due to the presence of nondiffusible particles, such as proteins (Fig. 3.8).

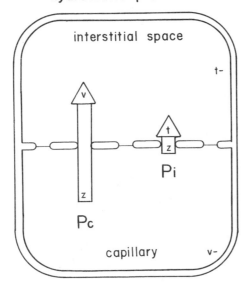

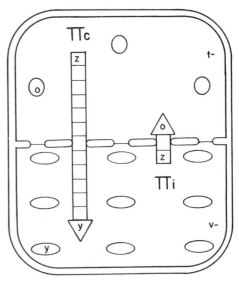

Figure 6.22 *Effects of pressures on fluid balance at the capillaries. Color the arrows that depict the rate at which water flows across the membrane by filtration (unmarked arrows) and osmosis (hatched arrows). Note the magnitude and direction of each arrow and identify its corresponding hydrostatic or osmotic pressure. Finish the picture by coloring the background areas on both sides of the membrane. Plasma osmotic pressure, a major inward force, is due to nondiffusible plasma proteins, such as serum albumin (mw about 69,000). Interstitial hydrostatic pressure is shown as an outward force because it is normally negative (subatmospheric).*

The algebraic sum of these forces is close to zero (actually 0.3 mmHg net outward force) so that only a small amount of fluid leaves the capillaries and flows into the interstitial space. This flow can change markedly when one or more of the individual forces changes. For example, an increase in an outward force and/or a decrease in an inward force will increase the rate at which fluid filters out of the capillary. Increased capillary pressure (as can occur in heart failure) or decreased plasma osmotic pressure (as can occur when plasma proteins decrease due to malnutrition) causes excessive filtration of fluid from the capillaries which can lead to the development of edema (excess interstitial fluid) (Fig. 6.23).

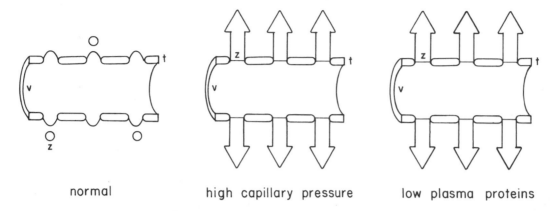

normal   high capillary pressure   low plasma proteins

Figure 6.23 *Factors that predispose to edema. Color the panels from left to right, comparing the normal condition with those that correspond to a high capillary pressure and a low plasma osmotic pressure. Note that excessive filtration of fluid from the capillaries into the interstitial spaces could be due to an increase in an outward force or a decrease in an inward force (Fig. 6.22). Thus, high capillary pressures and/or a loss of plasma proteins can lead to excessive filtration of fluid from the capillaries.*

Lymphatic system

The lymphatic circulation is made up of a system of vessels that transports lymph, which is a fluid derived from interstitial fluid. The lymphatic system picks up fluid and protein molecules that leak out of the capillaries into the interstitial spaces and returns them to the blood (Fig. 6.24).

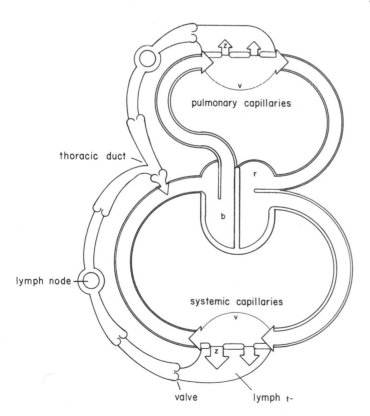

Figure 6.24 *The lymphatic system. Color the circulation as in Fig. 6.1. Color the water that filters out of the pulmonary and systemic capillaries. Color the lymph as it travels from the capillaries to the thoracic duct where it is returned to the general circulation. Note that the lymphatic circulation has one-way valves, which prevent the backward flow of lymph, and lymph nodes, which contain cells of the immune system called lymphocytes.*

The lymph from the lower part and left side of the body flows through the thoracic duct to enter the general circulation at the left subclavian vein. Lymph from the right side of the upper body flows into the right lymph duct and enters the circulation at the right subclavian vein.

The flow of lymph depends on the pressure in the interstitial fluid and on the activity of the lymphatic pump. The lymphatic pump works because the smooth muscle in the wall of a lymphatic vessel contracts whenever it is stretched by entering fluid. The contraction of smooth muscle in one segment propels lymph through a one-way valve into the next segment. This smooth muscle action is supplemented by the external compression of lymphatic vessels by skeletal muscles.

The lymphatic system plays important roles in regulating the protein concentration in interstitial fluid and in transporting absorbed fats from the gastrointestinal tract (Fig. 9.30).

Frank-Starling mechanism

A fundamental property of cardiac muscle is that it contracts more forcefully if it is stretched prior to its contraction. This property explains Starling's original observation that a denervated heart can pump more blood and do more work when it operates from a longer initial fiber length (Fig. 6.25).

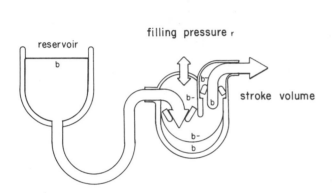
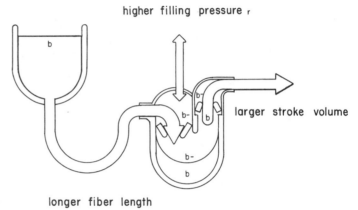

Figure 6.25 *The Frank-Starling mechanism. Color each panel from left to right. Color the vertical arrows that indicate the filling pressure. Note that a higher filling pressure results in a larger stroke volume. Note also that the stroke volume is determined by the volume of blood displaced by ventricular contraction.*

This behavior can be expressed graphically by a cardiac function curve in which cardiac output is plotted against filling pressure, which determines the initial fiber length. Cardiac function curves are characterized by a steep portion and a flat, or horizontal, portion (Fig. 6.26). The steep portion of the cardiac function curve corresponds to the range of fiber lengths over which higher filling pressures yield higher cardiac outputs. Over this range, the heart pumps all of the blood

it receives from the veins. The flat portion of the cardiac function curve corresponds to a range of filling pressures over which the cardiac output remains constant, at its maximum value. An important implication of these considerations is that at rest and during mild exercise, cardiac output is determined by peripheral factors that limit venous return, whereas during strenuous exercise, cardiac output is limited by cardiac factors that limit the ability of the heart to pump blood.

Figure 6.26 *The cardiac function curve. Color the graph, noting that the points on the line refer to the conditions shown in Fig. 6.25. Note that the cardiac function curve has a steep portion in which cardiac output increases with filling pressure and a flat portion in which cardiac output is at its maximum value, independent of the filling pressure.*

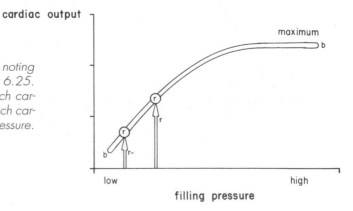

The cardiac function curve is moved upward by any factor that increases the pumping capability of the heart (Fig. 6.27). Some factors that render the heart hypereffective are increased heart rate, enhanced myocardial contractility (a measure of strength), and cardiac hypertrophy (increased muscle mass). On the other hand, the cardiac function curve is moved downward by any factor that decreases the pumping capability of the heart. Some factors that render the heart hypoeffective are decreased heart rate, diminished myocardial contractility, cardiac anoxia (very low oxygen levels in arterial blood), congenital heart disease, and valvular heart disease (Fig. 6.27).

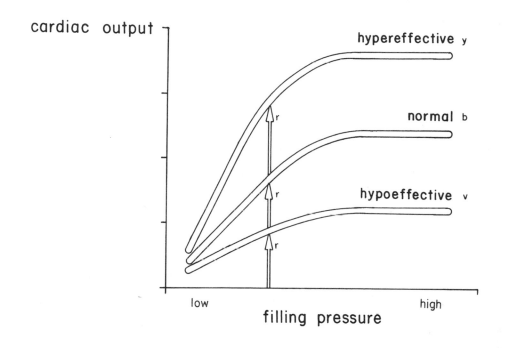

Figure 6.27 *Factors that modify the cardiac function curve. Color each of the curves, noting that the normal curve is the same as that shown in Fig. 6.26. Note also that the cardiac function curves for the hypereffective and hypoeffective hearts fall above and below the normal curve. Color the vertical line that indicates a fixed filling pressure and thus, the same fiber length. Note that the cardiac output associated with the same fiber length is high in the hypereffective heart, intermediate in the normal heart, and low in the hypoeffective heart.*

Regulation of blood pressure

Arterial blood pressure is maintained at a constant level by a number of mechanisms that have different time courses. As was described above, arterial blood pressure can be regulated by mechanisms that adjust: 1) cardiac output, 2) total peripheral resistance, and 3) blood volume (Fig. 6.18).

Short-term regulation of blood pressure is provided by baroreceptor reflexes that adjust cardiac function and total peripheral resistance. Intermediate mechanisms include the capillary fluid shift mechanism, which adjusts blood volume, and the renin-angiotensin system (Fig. 7.14), which adjusts total peripheral resistance and blood volume. Long-term regulation of blood pressure is provided by the kidney-body fluid system (Fig. 7.10), which increases blood volume when pressure is low and decreases blood volume when pressure is high.

Arterial blood pressure is also maintained by chemical factors that regulate the contraction of vascular smooth muscle. As noted above, these chemical agents include norepinephrine, epinephrine, angiotensin, and antidiuretic hormone (Fig. 6.21).

Baroreceptor reflexes

Baroreceptor reflexes are an example of a general reflex arc in which a response is mediated by the sequential operation of sensory receptors, afferent pathways, coordinating centers, efferent pathways and effector organs (Fig. 4.15).

Baroreceptors are sensory receptors that respond to the stretch of the arterial walls in which they reside. Arterial baroreceptors are located at the carotid sinus (the input to the brain) and the aortic arch (the output of the heart). They generate neural signals related to the blood pressure as well as its rate of change (Fig. 6.28) and transmit these signals to cardiovascular control centers in the brainstem. The afferent pathway from the carotid sinus baroreceptors is through the glossopharyngeal nerve (cranial nerve IX) (Fig. 6.29) and the afferent pathway from the aortic arch baroreceptors is through the vagus nerve (cranial nerve X).

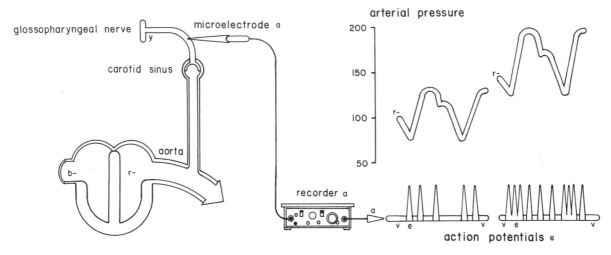

Figure 6.28 *Transduction characteristics of baroreceptors. Color the blood in the heart; note that the carotid sinus barorecep-tors are exposed to arterial blood pressure. Color the glossopharyngeal nerve, the microelectrode, and the recorder. Color the arterial blood pressure tracings and the corresponding membrane potentials. Note that the frequency of action potentials generated by the baroreceptors increases when blood pressure rises. Compare this figure with Fig. 4.18.*

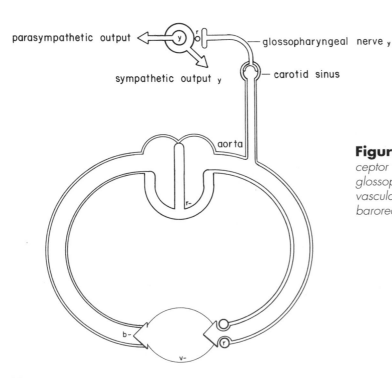

Figure 6.29 *Afferent pathway of the carotid sinus barore-ceptor reflex. Color the circulation as in Fig. 6.1. Color the glossopharyngeal nerve, its neurotransmitter, and the cardio-vascular control center. Note that nerve impulses from the baroreceptors inhibit the cardiovascular control center.*

At rest, the cardiovascular control center delivers a steady stream of parasympathetic (vagal) impulses to the heart and a steady stream of sympathetic impulses to both the heart and the systemic circuit (Fig. 6.30). Parasympathetic impulses decrease heart rate and mildly decrease myocardial contractility, which is an expression of muscle strength. Conversely, sympathetic impulses increase heart rate and increase myocardial contractility (Fig. 6.6). Sympathetic impulses also cause vasoconstriction and venoconstriction. Vasoconstriction increases arterial blood pressure by increasing total peripheral resistance (TPR). Venoconstriction increases venous return by mobilizing some of the blood contained in the veins (Fig. 6.18).

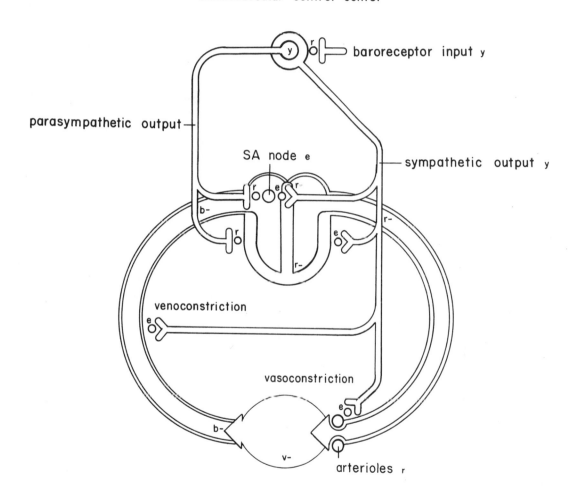

Figure 6.30 *Efferent pathways of the baroreceptor reflex. Color the glossopharyngeal nerve, its neurotransmitter, and the cardiovascular control center. Color the parasympathetic and sympathetic pathways and their neurotransmitters. Note that the parasympathetic fibers innervate the heart while the sympathetic fibers innervate both the heart and the circuit. Note also that parasympathetic impulses inhibit cardiac function, while sympathetic impulses stimulate cardiac function.*

Reflex response to hemorrhage

The immediate fall in arterial blood pressure (hypotension) due to a loss of blood volume causes the baroreceptors to send fewer inhibitory impulses to the cardiovascular control center (Fig. 6.29). This withdrawal of inhibitory input causes the control center to decrease its parasympathetic output to the heart and to increase its sympathetic output to both the heart and the circuit (Fig. 6.30).

The adjustments in neural output to the heart increase its rate and contractility, rendering it a hypereffective pump (Fig. 6.27). The adjustments in neural output to the systemic circuit cause vasoconstriction, which increases total peripheral resistance (Fig. 6.18), and venoconstriction, which increases venous return. Arterial pressure is therefore increased by the com-bined action of an increased venous return, an enhanced pumping capability of the heart, and a higher total peripheral resistance of the systemic circuit (Fig. 6.31). These adjustments increase both cardiac output and total peripheral resistance, and thereby help restore arterial blood pressure to its normal level (Fig. 6.32).

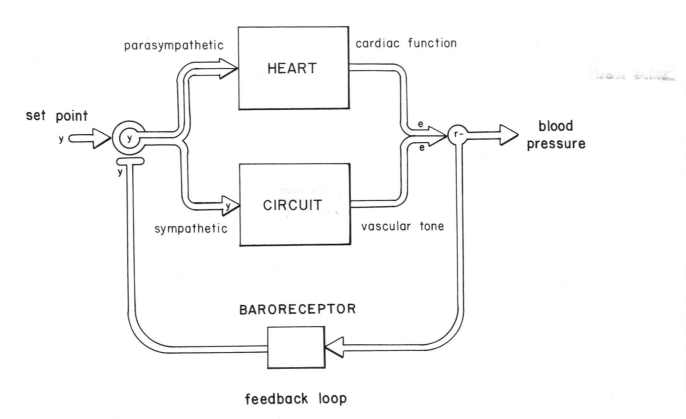

Figure 6.31 *Block diagram of a blood pressure control system. Color the block diagram, noting that the control of arterial blood pressure is achieved through adjustments in both cardiac function and vascular tone. Compare this figure with Fig. 1.7.*

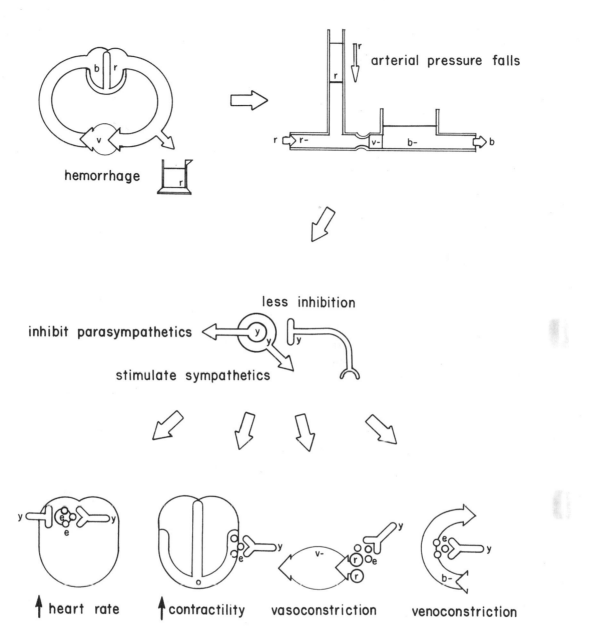

arterial pressure falls

hemorrhage

less inhibition

inhibit parasympathetics

stimulate sympathetics

↑heart rate   ↑contractility   vasoconstriction   venoconstriction

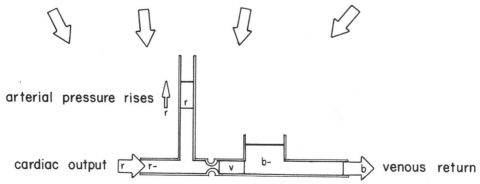

arterial pressure rises

cardiac output   venous return

Figure 6.32 *Cardiovascular response to hemorrhage. Color the circulation and its model, noting that a loss of blood volume causes blood pressure to fall and stimulate baroreceptor reflexes. Move downward as you color the remaining parts of the figure. Identify the actions that can be attributed to the operation of baroreceptor reflexes. Note that the compensatory rise in arterial blood pressure reflects the combined action of adjustments in cardiac function and vascular tone.*

chapter **seven**
renal system

The renal system cleanses the blood of metabolic waste products, regulates the constituents of body fluids, and helps control arterial blood pressure.

Structure of the kidney

Each kidney contains a renal artery, a renal vein, and a ureter (Fig. 7.1). The kidney filters the blood and excretes unwanted substances in the urine. The urine formed by the kidney passes through the ureters into the urinary bladder, where it is stored until it is eliminated from the body.

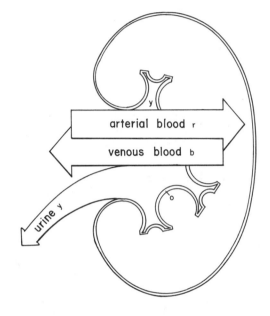

Figure 7.1   *The kidney. Color the diagram, noting the directions of the arrows. Arterial blood enters the kidney through the renal artery, venous blood leaves the kidney through the renal vein, and urine leaves the kidney through the ureter.*

Structure of the nephron

The nephron is the functional unit of the kidney. Nephrons consist of a system of blood vessels and kidney tubules. The blood vessels consist of two arterioles and two capillary beds that are connected in series.

Blood enters the first capillary bed, which is called the glomerulus, through the afferent arteriole and leaves the glomerulus through the efferent arteriole. From there, it flows through the second capillary bed, which is made up of the peritubular capillaries, before it returns to the venous circuit (Fig. 7.2).

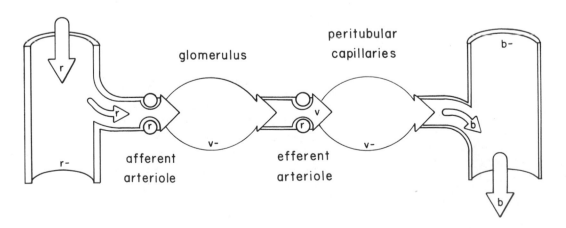

arterial blood

glomerulus

peritubular capillaries

afferent arteriole

efferent arteriole

venous blood

Figure 7.2 *Blood vessels of the nephron. Color the blood vessels from left to right, identifying the structures as you go. Note that blood entering the kidney through the renal artery passes through two arterioles and two capillary beds before it leaves the kidney through the renal vein. Compare this figure with Fig. 7.1.*

Fluid that filters through the glomerular membrane enters Bowman's capsule. From there, it flows through a long kidney tubule; it is in this tubule that it is transformed into urine. The kidney tubule is divided into four segments: 1) a proximal tubule, which receives glomerular filtrate from Bowman's capsule; 2) a loop of Henle, which dips into the medulla (the inner region of the kidney) before it returns to the cortex (the outer region of the kidney); 3) a distal tubule, which lies within the cortex, and 4) a collecting duct, which drains urine into the urinary bladder (Fig. 7.3).

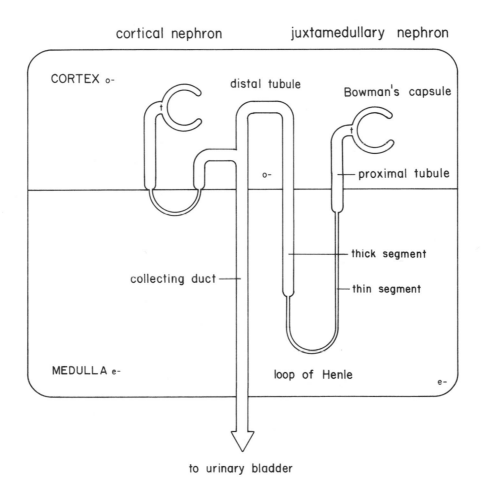

Figure 7.3 *Tubules of the nephron. Color and compare the tubules of each nephron. Color the cortex and medulla. Note that the tubules of the cortical nephron reside mainly in the cortex of the kidney, while the tubules of the juxtamedullary nephron dip into the medulla, where they are exposed to an osmotic gradient that can remove water from their fluid (Fig. 7.23). For this reason, juxtamedullary nephrons play an important role in regulating the concentration of urine.*

The kidney tubule is surrounded by peritubular capillaries that receive blood from the efferent arteriole. Most of the peritubular capillaries are located in the cortex close to the proximal tubules, distal tubules, and collecting ducts. The vasa recta is a thin capillary that surrounds the loop of Henle as it descends into the medulla and ascends back to the cortex.

Function of the nephron

The function of the nephron is to cleanse the blood of unwanted substances. Some examples of unwanted substances are: 1) the waste products of metabolism, including urea (Fig. 10.19), creatinine and uric acid; 2) excess electrolytes such as sodium, potassium, and chloride; and 3) excess hydrogen ions.

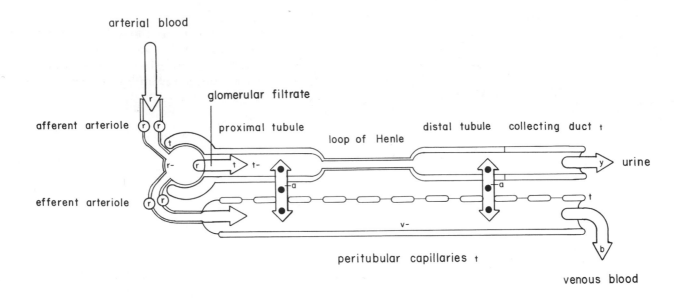

Figure 7.4 *Exchange of substances between the kidney tubules and the peritubular capillaries. Begin by coloring the tubules of the kidney and the peritubular capillaries. Color the arrow labeled arterial blood, the afferent and efferent arterioles, and the arrow labeled venous blood. Color the blood in the glomerulus and peritubular capillaries. Color the arrow labeled glomerular filtrate, the fluid in the kidney tubules, and the arrow labeled urine. Finish the picture by coloring the arrows that indicate the exchange of substances between the fluid in the kidney tubules and the blood in the peritubular capillaries.*

The nephron cleanses the blood by filtering it through a glomerular membrane; the result of this filtration is glomerular filtrate. The glomerular filtrate passes through kidney tubules where wanted substances are removed from the filtrate and returned to the blood while unwanted substances are excreted in the urine (Fig. 7.4). The excretion of unwanted substances in the urine is accomplished by two different mechanisms: 1) a failure of the kidney tubular cells to transport them back into the peritubular capillary blood; or 2) active secretion of the substances from the peritubular capillary blood into the kidney tubular cells (Fig. 7.5).

Figure 7.5 *Reabsorption and secretion. Color the parts of the nephron as in Fig. 7.4. Color the active transport mechanisms labeled reabsorption (a sodium co-transport mechanism) and secretion (a sodium counter-transport mechanism). Color the flash that indicates that the energy for these processes is derived from the breakdown of ATP. Note that reabsorption transports substances from the kidney tubules into the blood while secretion transports substances from the blood into the kidney tubules.*

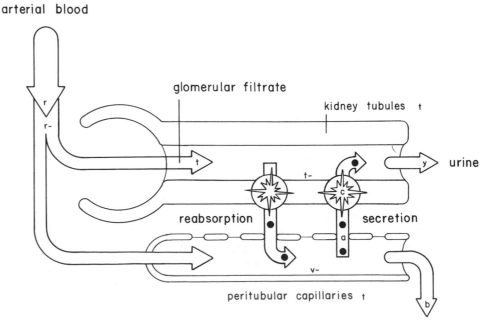

gray blue canary green flesh black navy orange pink red sienna tan violet white yellow azure [-] means use light pressure

The glomerular membrane

The glomerular membrane is made up of a layer of endothelium that is perforated with small holes called fenestrae, a basement membrane that consists of a loose meshwork of fibers called fibrillae, and a layer of epithelium that contains spaces between its cells called slit pores (Fig. 7.6). The dimensions of the pores and the nature of the basement membrane make the glomerular membrane highly permeable to small molecules but impermeable to red blood cells and plasma proteins. Glomerular filtrate can therefore be regarded as plasma minus plasma proteins.

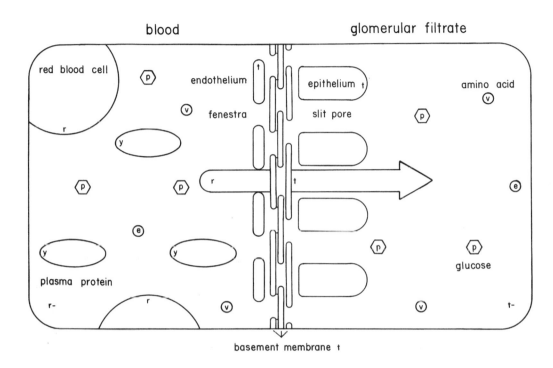

Figure 7.6 *Glomerular membrane. Color the membrane and identify the epithelial cells, basement membrane, slit pores, and fenestrae. Color and count the components of blood and the glomerular filtrate. Note that glucose (hexagons) and amino acids (circles) appear in equal concentrations on both sides of the glomerular membrane because they are small enough to fit through the pores of the membrane. Note also that red blood cells and plasma proteins (ellipses) do not pass through the membrane because they are too big to fit through the pores. Recall that nondiffusible plasma proteins exert a strong osmotic pull for water that prevents excessive filtration of water across the membranes of the capillaries (Fig. 6. 22). Finish the picture by coloring the arrow; noting its similarity to that shown in Fig. 7.4. Note also that glomerular filtrate can be regarded as blood plasma minus plasma proteins.*

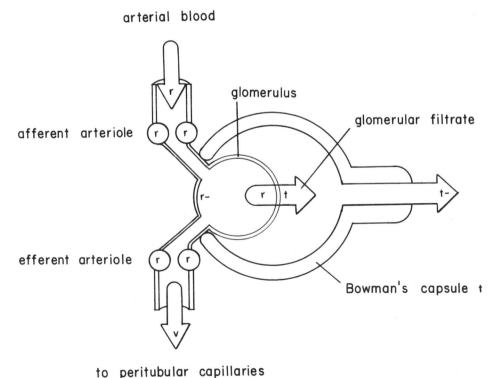

Figure 7.7 *Bowman's capsule. Color the arrow labeled arterial blood, the arterioles, the blood and the remaining arrow. Note that the glomerulus resides between the afferent and efferent arterioles. Identify the glomerular membrane and color the arrow that indicates the filtration of fluid across it. Finish the picture by coloring Bowman's capsule and the fluid it contains. Compare this figure with Fig. 7.2.*

Forces determining glomerular filtration rate

Glomerular filtration rate (GFR) depends on the permeability of the glomerular membrane for water (K) and the balance between the pressures in the capillary and Bowman's capsule (Fig. 7.7):

$$GFR = K\,[\,(Pc - Pi) - (\pi c - \pi i)\,]$$

where Pc and Pi are the hydrostatic pressures in the capillary and Bowman's capsule, and πc and πi are the osmotic pressures of blood and glomerular filtrate, respectively (Fig. 7.8).

hydrostatic pressures

osmotic pressures

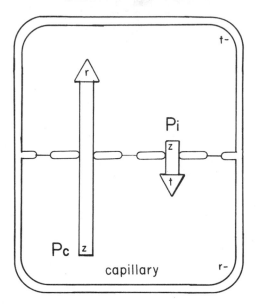

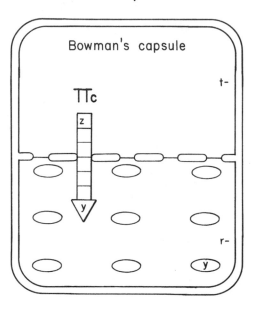

Figure 7.8 *Effects of pressures on glomerular filtration rate. Color the arrows that depict the rate at which water flows across the glomerular membrane by filtration (unmarked arrows) and osmosis (hatched arrow). Note the magnitude and direction of each arrow and identify its corresponding hydrostatic or osmotic pressure. Finish the picture by coloring the background areas on both sides of the membrane. Compare this figure with Fig. 6.22.*

The rate at which the kidney forms glomerular filtrate depends on the relative magnitudes of both the outward and inward forces. The substitution of normal values of Pc (60 mmHg, an outward force), Pi (18 mmHg, an inward force), πc (32 mmHg, an inward force) and πi (0 mmHg, an outward force) into the above equation yields a net pressure gradient of only 10 mmHg, i.e.,

(60 – 18) – (32 – 0) = 10. Because of the high permeability of the glomerular membrane, this modest pressure gradient of 10 mmHg enables the kidneys to produce 180 liters of glomerular filtrate per day; 179 of which are returned to the blood while the remaining one liter becomes urine (Fig. 7.9).

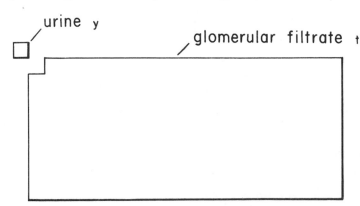

Figure 7.9 *Urine formed from glomerular filtrate. Color the diagram and compare the relative amounts of urine and glomerular filtrate that are formed by the kidney each day.*

Effect of arterial blood pressure on glomerular filtration rate

The glomerular filtration rate must be held constant if the kidney is to function properly. If the GFR were too low, the kidney would return too many unwanted molecules to the blood. On the other hand, if it were too high, the kidney would not return enough wanted molecules to the blood.

Local feedback mechanisms within the kidney enable the GFR to be held reasonably constant over a wide range of arterial blood pressures (from 75 to 150 mmHg) (Fig. 7.10). These tubuloglomerular feedback mechanisms rely on the chemistry of the filtrate in the distal tubule to regulate the degree of constriction of the afferent and efferent arterioles (Fig. 7.11). The two regulating mechanisms are: 1) the afferent arteriolar vasodilator mechanism; and 2) the efferent arteriolar vasoconstrictor mechanism.

Figure 7.10 *Effects of blood pressure on kidney function. Color the graphs that show the effects of arterial blood pressure on glomerular filtration rate and urine output. Note from the horizontal line that glomerular filtration rate remains essentially constant over a wide range of arterial blood pressure. This means that the kidney has mechanisms that can maintain a constant glomerular pressure in the face of marked changes in arterial pressure. In contrast, note that urine output is low during hypotension (low blood pressure) and high during hypertension (high blood pressure). These adjustments in urine output alter blood volume in such a way as to help maintain a normal level of blood pressure.*

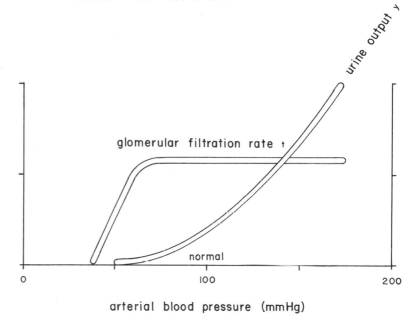

Figure 7.11 *Effect of arteriolar constriction on glomerular filtration rate. Color the panels from left to right. Begin each panel at the top by coloring the afferent and efferent arterioles, the blood, and each of the three arrows. Color the bottom panel, noting the glomerular capillary pressure in each condition. Note that GFR decreases (short arrow in middle panel) when capillary pressure falls and increases (long arrow in right panel) when capillary pressure rises. Thus, constriction of the afferent arteriole decreases GFR while constriction of the efferent arteriole increases GFR.*

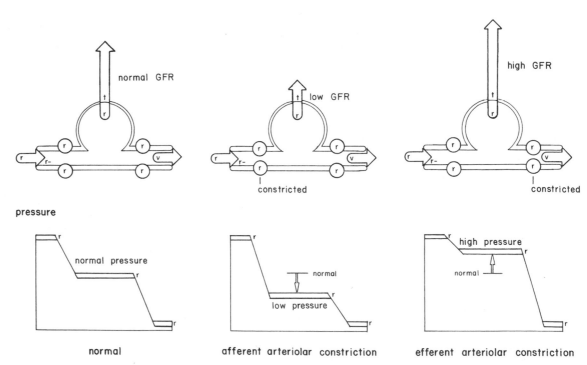

Tubuloglomerular feedback mechanisms

Specialized epithelial cells in the distal tubule form what is called the macula densa. These cells are in close contact with smooth muscle cells of the arterioles, which are called the juxtaglomerular cells. The macula densa and the juxtaglomerular cells are collectively known as the juxtaglomerular apparatus (Fig. 7.12).

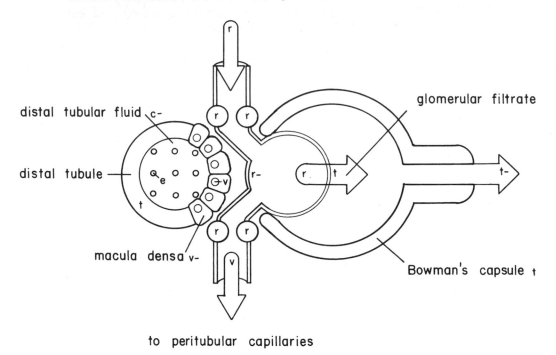

Figure 7.12 *The juxtaglomerular apparatus. Color Bowman's capsule, the blood, and the blood vessels as in Fig. 7.7. Color the distal tubule, the macula densa, and the distal tubular fluid. Note that the macula densa comes in contact with the cells of the afferent and efferent arterioles.*

A low GFR causes excessive reabsorption of sodium and chloride ions in the distal tubule so that the cells of the macula densa are exposed to a more dilute fluid (Fig. 7.13); this stimulates the cells of the macula densa to secrete a substance that dilates the afferent arterioles. This afferent arteriolar vasodilator mechanism increases glomerular capillary pressure and helps to raise GFR back to its normal level (Fig. 7.11).

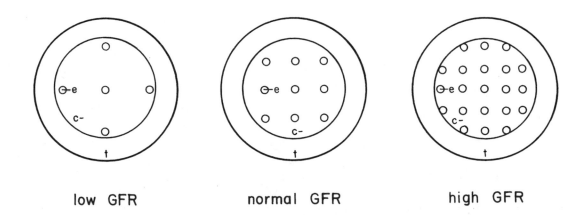

Figure 7.13 *Effect of GFR on distal tubular fluid. Color the molecules of sodium, the fluid, and the distal tubule in each condition. Note that the concentration of sodium in the distal tubular fluid varies with the glomerular filtration rate. For this reason, the sodium concentration in the distal tubule can serve as an indicator of GFR.*

In addition, a dilute fluid at the macula densa stimulates the release of renin into the blood. Renin is an enzyme that catalyzes the formation of angiotensin from angiotensinogen, which is already present in the blood. Angiotensin is a vasoactive agent that constricts the efferent arteriole (Fig. 7.14). This efferent arteriolar vasoconstrictor mechanism increases glomerular capillary pressure and helps raise GFR back to its normal level (Fig. 7.11).

Effect of arterial blood pressure on urine output

Hypertension raises glomerular capillary pressure which, in turn, increases urine output. The increased urine output reduces blood volume and helps restore normal levels of arterial blood pressure. A doubling of arterial pressure (to 200 mmHg) produces an 8-fold increase in urine output (Fig. 7.10).

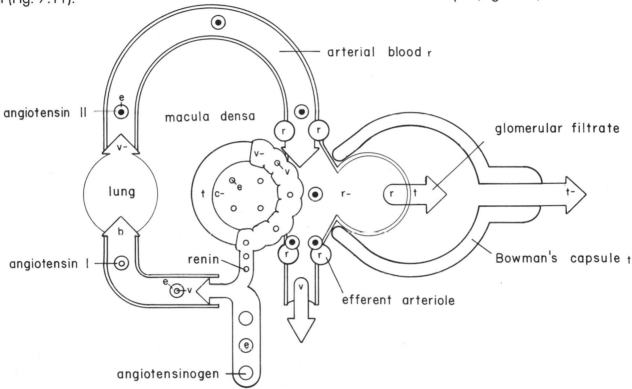

Figure 7.14 *Efferent arteriolar vasoconstrictor mechanism. Begin by coloring the distal tubular fluid, noting that it is dilute (Fig. 7.13). Color the macula densa, the renin it releases, and the angiotensinogen molecules that combine with the renin. Color the angiotensin I molecules and note that they become angiotensin II molecules as they pass through the lung. Color the angiotensin II molecules, noting that they ultimately come in contact with the efferent arteriole. Color the efferent arteriole. Finish the picture by coloring the remaining structures as in Fig. 7.12. Compare this figure with Fig. 1.10.*

Conversely, hypotension lowers glomerular capillary pressure which, in turn, decreases urine output. The decreased urine output increases blood volume and helps restore normal levels of arterial blood pressure. A halving of arterial blood pressure (to 50 mmHg) causes a complete cessation of urine output.

The strong influence of arterial blood pressure on urine output explains how the kidney-body fluid mechanism provides long-term regulation of blood volume and thus, arterial blood pressure (Fig. 6.18).

Reabsorption and secretion of substances in the kidney tubules

As the glomerular filtrate passes through the kidney tubules, the tubular epithelial cells reabsorb substances from the filtrate and secrete some of them into the filtrate (Fig. 7.4). Nutrients such as glucose and amino acids are completely reabsorbed in the proximal tubules, while metabolic waste products such as urea and creatinine are poorly reabsorbed. Inulin, a large polysaccharide that is used as an indicator substance for measuring body fluid volumes (Fig. 3.15), is neither reabsorbed nor secreted. Para-aminohippuric acid (PAH), which is another substance that is used in the study of kidney function, is actively secreted (Fig. 7.15).

Figure 7.15 *Reabsorption and secretion of selected substances. Begin each panel by coloring the kidney tubules and the peritubular capillaries. Color and count the molecules in the arterial blood, kidney tubules, venous blood and urine. Note that the molecules that enter the kidney in arterial blood leave the kidney in the venous blood and the urine. Finish each panel by coloring the arrows. Compare this figure with Fig. 7.4. Note that glucose is completely reabsorbed, urea is poorly reabsorbed, inulin is ignored, and para-aminohippuric acid is secreted.*

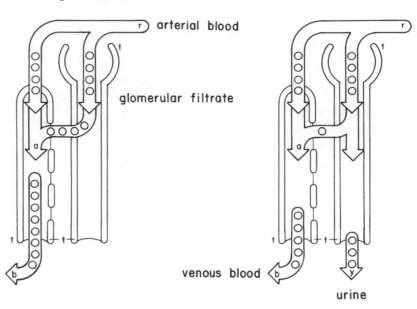

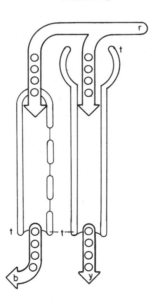

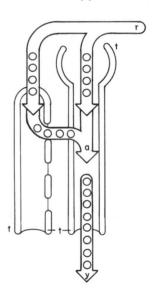

A sodium-potassium pump in the basolateral membrane of the proximal tubular cells uses energy derived from ATP to pump sodium ions out of the tubular cells and into the space between the tubular cells and the peritubular capillaries (Fig. 7.5). This removal of positively charged sodium ions creates an electrochemical gradient that pulls sodium ions from the lumen of the proximal tubule into the tubular cells. Glucose and amino acids are transported from the lumen into the proximal tubular cells by a sodium co-transport mecha-

nism (Fig. 3.12). Thus, as sodium moves down its electrochemical gradient to enter the cell, it pulls a glucose or amino acid molecule along with it. This mechanism enables the kidney to completely reabsorb glucose and amino acids in the proximal tubule (Fig. 7.15). Because the active transport mechanism for glucose limits the maximum rate at which the proximal tubular cells can reabsorb glucose (Fig. 3.13), high blood levels of glucose, as occurs in diabetes mellitus, can lead to the appearance of glucose in the urine (Fig. 7.16).

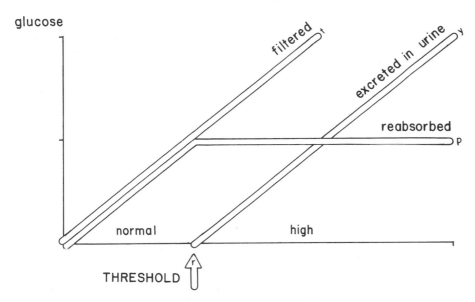

glucose

filtered t

excreted in urine y

reabsorbed P

normal

high

THRESHOLD r

blood glucose concentration

Figure 7.16 *Effect of blood glucose concentration on glucose reabsorption. Color each of the lines, noting that the glucose that filters into the glomerulus will either be reabsorbed or will appear in the urine. Since there is a maximum rate at which the kidney tubules can reabsorb glucose from glomerular filtrate, high blood levels of glucose can cause glucose to appear in the urine. The highest concentration of blood glucose that the kidney can reabsorb is called the threshold. Compare this figure with Fig. 3.13.*

Metabolic waste products such as urea and creatinine are poorly reabsorbed by the kidney tubules. About half the urea molecules and almost all the creatinine molecules that enter the proximal tubules end up in the urine. (Fig. 7.15). Inulin is a test substance that does not cross the membranes of the epithelial cells that form the kidney tubules. All of the inulin molecules that enter the proximal tubule from Bowman's capsule end up in the urine.

Active secretion of substances is accomplished by a sodium counter-transport mechanism in which transported substances move in a direction that is opposite to that of sodium (Fig. 3.12). Substances that are actively secreted by kidney tubules include hydrogen ions, potassium ions, and para-aminohippuric acid (PAH) (Fig. 7.15).

Reabsorption of water in the kidney tubules

Water is reabsorbed from the kidney tubules by osmosis. Osmotic pressure gradients are generated by the transport of solutes from the tubular fluid into the tubular cells. The proximal tubules reabsorb 65% of the water in glomerular filtrate, the loop of Henle reabsorbs 15%, and the distal tubule reabsorbs 10%. The remaining 10% of the glomerular filtrate passes on to the collecting duct where 9.3% of the water is usually reabsorbed, leaving 0.7% to become urine (Fig. 7.17). The actual amount of water reabsorbed in the collecting duct varies, depending on the amount of antidiuretic hormone (ADH) released by the posterior pituitary gland.

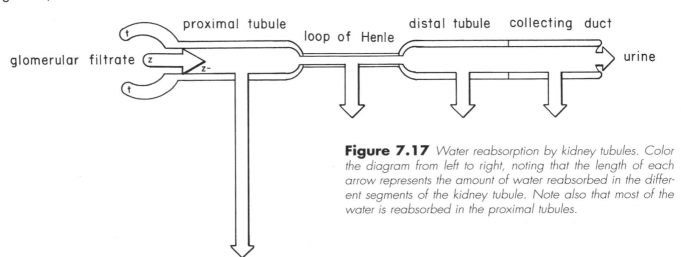

proximal tubule   loop of Henle   distal tubule   collecting duct

glomerular filtrate z   urine

t   z-   t

Figure 7.17 *Water reabsorption by kidney tubules. Color the diagram from left to right, noting that the length of each arrow represents the amount of water reabsorbed in the different segments of the kidney tubule. Note also that most of the water is reabsorbed in the proximal tubules.*

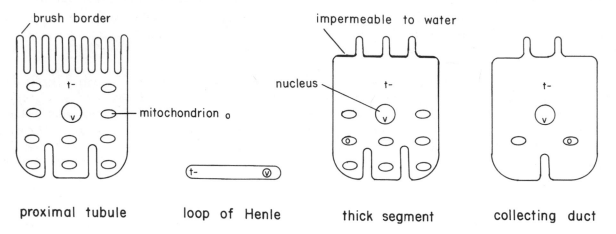

Figure 7.18 *Tubular epithelial cells of the kidney. Color each of the tubular epithelial cells and compare their mitochondrial content, geometry, and water permeability.*

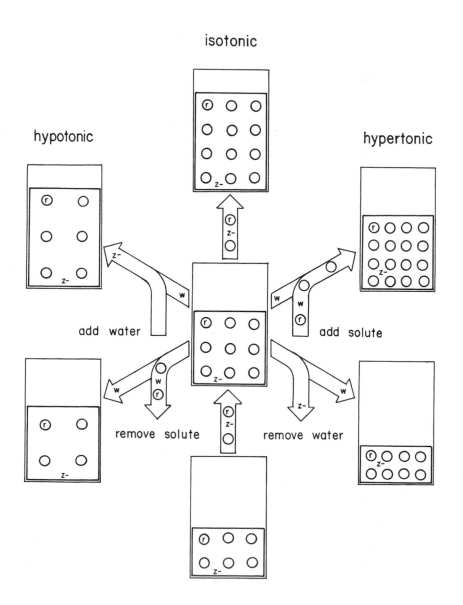

Figure 7.19 *Determinants of concentration. Color and count the molecules in each rectangular container. Color the water in each container, noting that the concentration of molecules can be visualized from the space between them. Color the arrows between the container in the center and those at the left. Note that the addition of water or the removal of solute makes the solution hypotonic (more dilute). Color the arrows between the container at the center and those at the right. Note that the addition of solute or the removal of water makes the solution hypertonic (more concentrated). Finish the picture by coloring the remaining vertical arrows, noting that the addition or subtraction of the same solution (isotonic) changes the volume of fluid but not its concentration.*

Tubular epithelial cells

The proximal tubular epithelial cells are well adapted for reabsorption of solutes and water. They are permeable to water, contain large numbers of mitochondria to provide energy for active transport mechanisms, and have a well-developed brush border that contains protein carrier molecules used in co-transport and counter-transport mechanisms (Fig. 7.18). The cells of the thin segment of the loop of Henle have no brush border. The cells of the thick segment of the loop of Henle and the initial portion of the distal tubule are well-adapted for the transport of sodium and chloride ions. They have a rudimentary brush border and are impermeable to water. The late distal tubule and the collecting duct are also impermeable to water in the absence of ADH (Fig. 7.18).

Concentrations of substances in the urine

The concentration of a substance in the urine depends on the number of molecules of that substance in the urine and the total volume of water in the urine (Fig. 7.19).

Since glucose is completely reabsorbed in the proximal tubule, its concentration in urine is normally zero (Fig. 7.20). Urea is a poorly reabsorbed metabolic waste product; about half of the urea molecules are reabsorbed in the kidney tubules, while over 99% of the water is reabsorbed. Stated another way, half of the urea molecules that entered the proximal tubule mix with less than 1% of the water that entered the proximal tubule. This results in a urea concentration in urine that is 65 times its concentration in plasma (Fig. 7.20). All of the inulin molecules that entered the proximal tubule mix with less than 1% of the water that entered the proximal tubule to yield an inulin concentration in urine that is 125 times its concentration in plasma (Fig. 7.20).

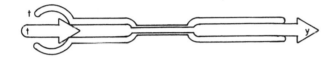

number of molecules

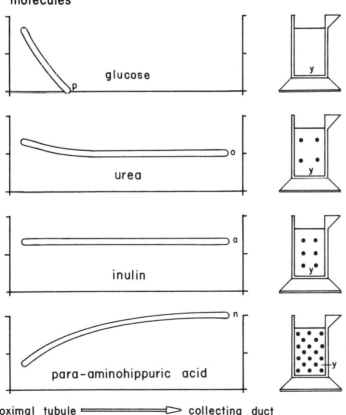

urine

Figure 7.20 *Concentrations of selected substances in urine. Color the schematic diagram of the kidney tubule at the top. For each substance, color the line that indicates the number of molecules in the tubular fluid as it flows from the proximal tubule to the collecting duct. Color the graduated cylinder at the right and note the concentration of each substance in the urine. Note that the number of molecules decreases for substances that are reabsorbed, such as glucose, and increases for substances that are secreted, such as para-aminohippuric acid. Note also that the concentration of substances in urine depends both on the number of molecules and the volume of water. Compare this figure with Fig. 7.15 and Fig. 7.17.*

Para-aminohippuric acid (PAH) is secreted by the proximal tubules into the tubular fluid. The number of PAH molecules that pass into the urine is determined by the sum of the PAH molecules that filter into the proximal tubule plus the PAH molecules that are added to the tubular fluid by active secretion. The resulting mixture of PAH molecules and water yields a PAH concentration in urine that is 585 times its concentration in plasma (Fig. 7.20).

Plasma clearance

Plasma clearance is a measure of the ability of the kidneys to cleanse the plasma of a given substance (Fig. 7.21). The plasma clearance of inulin is used to measure glomerular filtration rate, and the plasma clearance of PAH is used to measure renal blood flow.

The plasma clearance (in ml/min) for any particular substance can be calculated from the product of urine flow (in ml/min) and the ratio of the concentrations of the substance in urine [Cu] and plasma [Cp]:

$$\text{plasma clearance} = \text{urine flow} \, [Cu]/[Cp]$$

Since inulin passes freely through the glomerular membrane, the concentrations of inulin in plasma and glomerular filtrate are equal. Because inulin is neither reabsorbed nor secreted in the kidney tubules, all of the plasma that filters through the glomerulus is cleared of inulin (Fig. 7.15). The number of inulin molecules that appear in the urine can be used to determine the volume of plasma that filtered through the glomerulus. For these reasons, inulin clearance can be used to calculate glomerular filtration rate (Fig. 7.22).

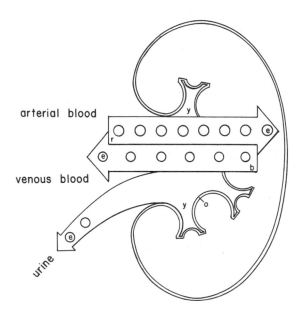

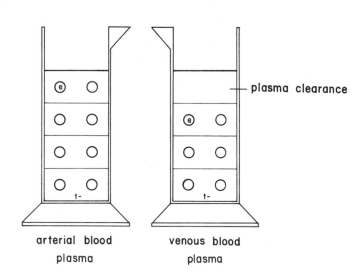

Figure 7.21 *Plasma clearance. Begin at the left by coloring the outline of the kidney. Color and count the molecules that enter the kidney in the arterial blood. Color and count the molecules that leave the kidney in the venous blood and in the urine. Color the arrows. Color and count the molecules in each of the graduated cylinders; note that these numbers are the same as those in the corresponding blood supply at left. Color the plasma in both cylinders and note the fraction of venous blood plasma that has been cleared of the substance by the kidney.*

Some of the PAH in arterial blood filters through the glomerular membrane, while the remaining PAH enters the peritubular capillaries, where almost all of it is secreted into the kidney tubules (Fig. 7.15). As a result, almost all of the blood (about 90%) that enters the kidney is cleared of PAH. For these reasons, PAH clearance can be used to calculate renal blood flow (Fig. 7.22).

Countercurrent multiplier mechanism

The concentration of particles in water is measured by its osmolality, which is defined as the number of moles of all particles per kilogram of water.

Glomerular filtrate has essentially the same osmolality as plasma (300 mOsm/L). The osmolality remains unchanged in the proximal tubule because solutes and water are reabsorbed in approximately equal proportions. The osmolality of tubular fluid decreases in the thick portion of the loop of Henle and the early distal tubule because sodium, chloride, and potassium ions are transported out of these tubules, which are impermeable to water (Fig. 7.18), without an accompanying osmotic flow of water. As a result, the fluid in the late distal tubule is dilute (100 mOsm/L).

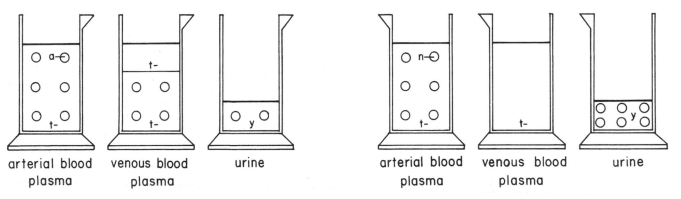

inulin clearance   **PAH clearance**

arterial blood plasma   venous blood plasma   urine

arterial blood plasma   venous blood plasma   urine

Figure 7.22 *Inulin and PAH clearance. Color and count the inulin and PAH molecules in each of the graduated cylinders. Color the fluid in each of the cylinders; compare the volume of blood plasma that has been cleared of inulin with the volume that has been cleared of PAH. Only that fraction of the plasma that filtered across the glomerular membrane has been cleared of inulin, while all of the plasma that entered the kidney has been cleared of PAH. For these reasons, inulin clearance is used to measure the rate at which plasma filters through the glomerulus. Similarly, PAH clearance is used to measure the rate at which blood flows through the kidney.*

Since the descending loop of Henle is permeable to water, the osmolality of the fluid inside the tubule is similar to that of the surrounding interstitial fluid. The pumping of sodium ions out of the thick portion of the loop of Henle and the early distal tubule, in conjunction with the infusion of new sodium ions from the proximal tubule, enables the kidney to function as a countercurrent multiplier mechanism (Fig. 7.23). An important feature of the countercurrent multiplier mechanism is that it establishes an osmotic gradient in the interstitial fluid that surrounds the collecting duct (Fig. 7.24).

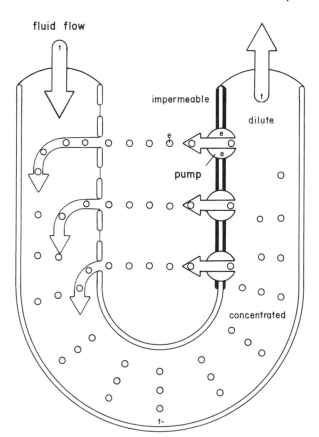

fluid flow

impermeable

dilute

pump

concentrated

Figure 7.23 *Countercurrent multiplier mechanism. Begin at the upper right by coloring the pump and the molecules it transports through the impermeable membrane. Color each of the molecules from this pump as you follow them in a counterclockwise direction. Color the arrow labeled fluid flow and note that it is the downward flow of fluid in the descending limb that returns the molecules to the pump where they can again be removed from the solution. Repeat this process for the two remaining pumps. Note that this countercurrent multiplier mechanism establishes a concentration gradient in which the fluid at the bottom of the ascending limb is highly concentrated while the fluid at the top is dilute. Finish the picture by coloring the fluid and the remaining arrow.*

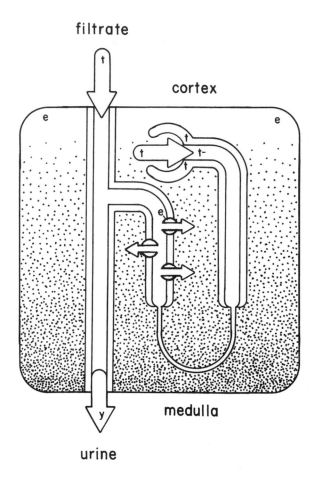

filtrate

cortex

medulla

urine

Figure 7.24 *Osmotic gradients in the kidney. Color the pumps, filtrate, kidney tubules, and interstitial fluid. Note that the operation of the countercurrent multiplier mechanism establishes a concentration gradient in the fluid that surrounds the kidney tubules.*

Regulation of the concentration of urine

The high osmolality of the medullary interstitial fluid that surrounds the collecting duct provides a driving force that can be used to remove water from the fluid in the collecting duct. However, the actual amount of water that is removed from the fluid in the collecting duct depends on the permeability of this tubule to water. The permeability of the collecting duct is regulated by the

level of antidiuretic hormone (ADH), a hormone released by the posterior pituitary gland (Fig. 11.8).

When the level of ADH is high, the permeability of the collecting duct is increased, more water is reabsorbed, and a small volume of concentrated urine is excreted. In the absence of ADH, the collecting duct is impermeable to water and a large volume of dilute urine is excreted (Fig. 7.25).

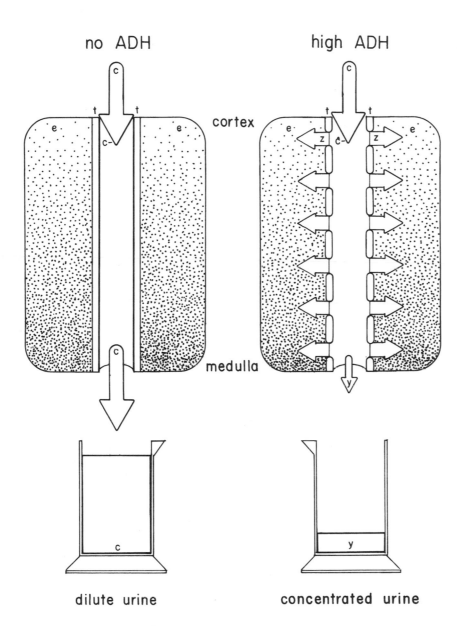

no ADH   high ADH

cortex

medulla

dilute urine   concentrated urine

Figure 7.25 *Regulation of urine concentration. Color the kidney tubules and the interstitial fluid in each panel. In the left panel, color the arrow at the top, the lumen of the tubule, the arrow at the bottom, and the urine in the graduated cylinder. Note that a large volume of dilute urine is formed when no water is removed from the filtrate as it passes through the tubule. In the right panel, color the arrow at the top, the lumen of the tubule, the water that is reabsorbed, the arrow at the bottom, and the urine in the graduated cylinder. Note that a small volume of concentrated urine is formed when water is removed from the filtrate as it passes through the tubule.*

Regulation of sodium concentration in extracellular fluid

A normal sodium concentration of 142 mEq/L in extracellular fluid is maintained through a balance between the thirst mechanism, which regulates water intake and the osmoreceptor-ADH system, which regulates water output by the kidney.

The thirst mechanism employs sensory receptors in the hypothalamus that respond to intracellular dehydration. These receptors can be stimulated by a high sodium concentration in extracellular fluid, a high potassium concentration in intracellular fluid, or a low blood volume.

The osmoreceptor-ADH system employs osmoreceptors in the hypothalamus that respond to the sodium concentration of the extracellular fluid. When the concentration of sodium is high, the neural output from the osmoreceptors stimulates the posterior pituitary gland to secrete ADH (Fig. 7.26). ADH increases the permeability of the distal tubule and collecting duct to water. More water is reabsorbed and the concentration of sodium in extracellular fluid is reduced to the normal level.

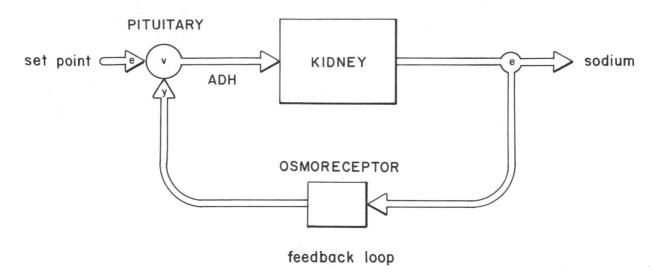

Figure 7.26 *Block diagram of a sodium control system. Color the block diagram of the osmoreceptor-ADH system and compare it with that shown in Fig. 1.7.*

Regulation of potassium concentration in extracellular fluid

The sodium-potassium pump in the proximal tubules and thick segment of the loop of Henle actively reabsorb over 90% of the potassium ions that enter the proximal tubules. Given the normal dietary intake of potassium, the maintenance of normal levels of potassium in extracellular fluid (4 meq/L) requires that potassium ions be secreted into the tubular fluid. The epithelial cells of the late distal tubules and cortical collecting ducts are well-adapted for secreting potassium ions (Fig. 7.18). The rate at which these cells secrete potas-

sium depends on the concentration of potassium ions in extracellular fluid and on the level of aldosterone, a hormone that is secreted by the adrenal cortex (Fig. 11.9).

High concentrations of potassium ions and low concentrations of sodium ions in extracellular fluid stimulate the secretion of aldosterone. Aldosterone secretion is also stimulated by the blood level of angiotensin II (Fig. 7.14). Aldosterone decreases the concentration of potassium in extracellular fluid by stimulating the sodium-potassium pump in the kidney tubules to secrete more potassium (Fig. 7.27).

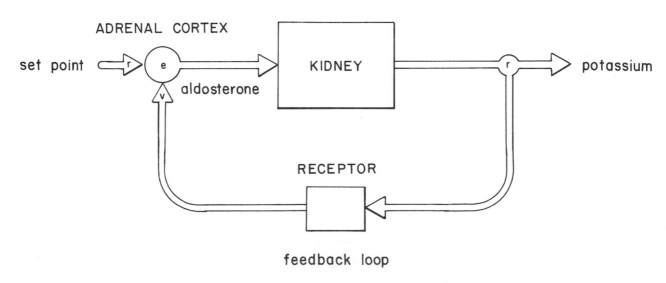

Figure 7.27 *Block diagram of a potassium control system. Color the block diagram of the potassium control system and compare it with that shown in Fig. 1.7.*

chapter **eight**
respiratory system

The respiratory system supplies oxygen to, and removes excess carbon dioxide from, the blood (Fig. 8.1).

Gas exchange in the lung

Gas exchange between air and blood in the lung occurs across the pulmonary membrane, which is the boundary between alveolar gas and pulmonary capillary blood, by the process of passive diffusion (Fig. 8.2). Oxygen (O_2) diffuses from the alveolus into the blood, while carbon dioxide (CO_2) diffuses simultaneously from the blood into the alveolus (Fig. 8.3).

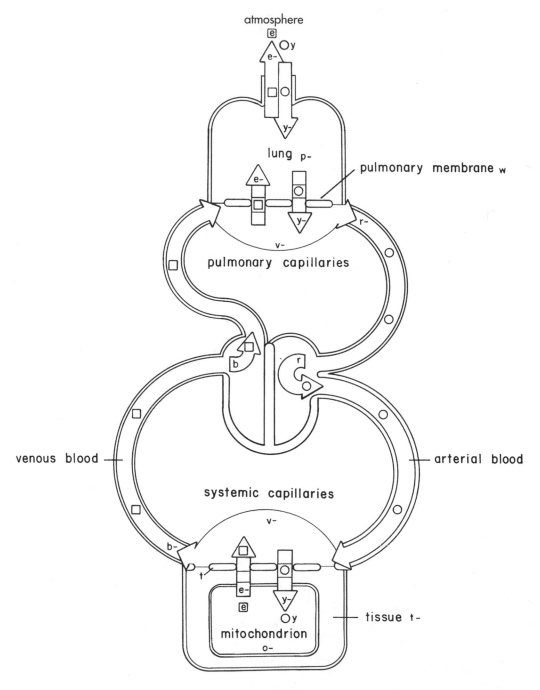

Figure 8.1 Transport of oxygen and carbon dioxide. Color the oxygen molecules (circles) and their arrows as they are transported from the atmosphere through the blood to the mitochondrion, the site where oxygen is exchanged for carbon dioxide. Color the carbon dioxide molecules (squares) and their arrows as they are transported in the opposite direction, from the mitochondrion to the atmosphere. Note that gas exchange between the lung and blood and between the blood and tissues occurs across capillary membranes by diffusion (hatched arrows). Finish the picture by coloring the background areas of the lung, cardiovascular system, tissue, and mitochondrion. Compare this figure with Fig. 6.1.

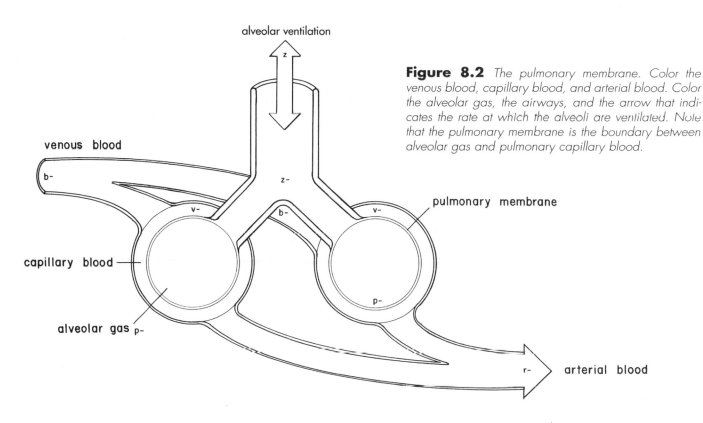

Figure 8.2 *The pulmonary membrane. Color the venous blood, capillary blood, and arterial blood. Color the alveolar gas, the airways, and the arrow that indicates the rate at which the alveoli are ventilated. Note that the pulmonary membrane is the boundary between alveolar gas and pulmonary capillary blood.*

Figure 8.3 *Diffusion of gases across the pulmonary membrane. Color the oxygen molecules and their diffusion arrow, noting that oxygen diffuses from the alveolar gas into the red blood cell. Color the carbon dioxide molecules and their diffusion arrow, noting that carbon dioxide diffuses from the capillary blood into the alveolar gas. Color the background area on both sides of the pulmonary membrane. Note that all of the oxygen is carried in the red blood cell while most of the carbon dioxide is carried in blood plasma. Compare this figure with Fig. 8.2.*

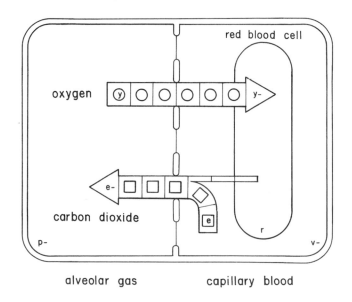

The rate at which a gas diffuses across the pulmonary membrane is determined by three factors: 1) the diffusion constant of the gas, which is a measure of how easily it passes through a membrane; 2) the area and the thickness of the membrane (Fig. 3.5); and 3) the partial pressures of the gas on either side of the membrane.

Partial pressure gradients, rather than concentration gradients, provide the driving force for diffusion in systems that have air-liquid interfaces. Gases in the lung therefore diffuse from a region of higher partial pressure to one of lower partial pressure. At equilibrium, the partial pressures on both sides of the membrane are equal and diffusion ceases.

Diffusion constants for oxygen and carbon dioxide

The diffusion constant for any particular gas in the lung depends on the solubility of the gas and its molecular weight; heavy molecules diffuse more slowly than do light ones. Carbon dioxide diffuses 20 times faster than oxygen, even though it is a heavier molecule, because of its much greater solubility in the pulmonary membrane.

Structure of the airways

The branches of the tracheobronchial tree bifurcate, meaning that they divide into two smaller branches, a total of 23 times. The tracheobronchial tree terminates in the 300 million alveoli whose membranes make up the largest part of the pulmonary membrane (Fig. 8.4).

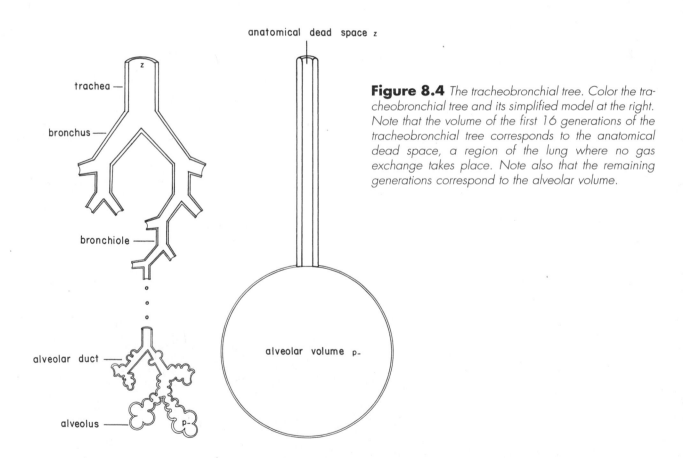

anatomical dead space z

trachea

bronchus

bronchiole

alveolar duct

alveolus

alveolar volume p-

Figure 8.4 *The tracheobronchial tree. Color the tracheobronchial tree and its simplified model at the right. Note that the volume of the first 16 generations of the tracheobronchial tree corresponds to the anatomical dead space, a region of the lung where no gas exchange takes place. Note also that the remaining generations correspond to the alveolar volume.*

In the first 16 bifurcations, or divisions, the walls of the tracheobronchial tree are too thick for gases to diffuse across them. The volume of this region of the lung, where no gas exchange takes place, is called the anatomical dead space (V_D). In the remaining divisions, the airway walls are thin enough for gas exchange to occur between the alveoli and the blood vessels that surround them; the volume of this region of the lung is called the alveolar volume (Fig. 8.4).

Geometry of the pulmonary membrane

The pulmonary membrane is ideally suited for diffusion because it is extremely thin (0.1 – 1.0 microns) and has a very large surface area (about 80 m²) (Fig. 3.5). Two examples of conditions that decrease the rate at which gases diffuse in the lung are emphysema, which decreases the area of the pulmonary membrane, and pulmonary edema, which increases its thickness.

Partial pressure gradients for oxygen and carbon dioxide

The partial pressure gradients for oxygen and carbon dioxide provide the driving force for the diffusion of these gases across the pulmonary membrane, the systemic capillaries, and the mitochondrial membranes (Fig. 8.1).

Inspired air is a mixture of nitrogen (N_2), oxygen (O_2), carbon dioxide (CO_2), and water vapor (H_2O). Dalton's law states that the total pressure of a mixture of gases is determined by the sum of the partial pressures of each of its constituents (Fig. 8.5). Barometric pressure (P_B), which is 760 mmHg at sea level, is therefore equal to the sum of the partial pressures of nitrogen (PN_2), oxygen (PO_2), carbon dioxide (PCO_2), and water vapor (PH_2O):

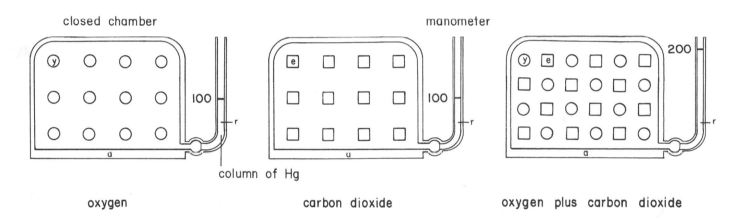

closed chamber — manometer — 200 — 100 — column of Hg — 100

oxygen — carbon dioxide — oxygen plus carbon dioxide

Figure 8.5 *Partial pressures. Color and count the round oxygen molecules in the left panel. Color its chamber and the level of mercury in the manometer, which indicates that the pressure exerted by this gas on the walls of the chamber happens to be 100 mmHg, i.e., PO_2 = 100 mmHg. Repeat the process for the square carbon dioxide molecules in the middle panel, noting that the same number of molecules exerts the same pressure on the walls of the chamber, i.e., PCO_2 = 100 mmHg. Finish the picture by coloring the right panel, noting that the gas mixture in this chamber represents the sum of the oxygen molecules from the left chamber plus the carbon dioxide molecules from the middle chamber. In accordance with Dalton's law, the pressure exerted by this mixture of gases (P_{TOTAL} = 200 mmHg) can be calculated from the sum of the partial pressures of each of its constituents (i.e., P_{TOTAL} = PO_2 + PCO_2).*

$$P_B = PN_2 + PO_2 + PCO_2 + PH_2O$$

Inspired air is completely saturated with water vapor in the mouth and pharynx. Since the partial pressure of water vapor (PH_2O) at body temperature is 47 mmHg, the partial pressure of oxygen in inspired air can be calculated by the product of its fractional concentration in dry air, which is 20.8%, and (P_B – 47), i.e., PO_2 = 20.8 % (760 – 47) = 150 mmHg. This represents the total force that is available to drive oxygen from inspired air into the mitochondria, where it is ultimately consumed (Fig. 8.1).

Similarly, the partial pressure of carbon dioxide in inspired air can be calculated from the product of its fractional concentration, which is 0.03%, and $(P_B - 47)$, i.e., $PCO_2 = 0.03 \% (760 - 47) = 0$ mmHg. Table 8.1 compares the partial pressures of oxygen and carbon dioxide in inspired air, alveolar gas, arterial blood, and mixed venous blood (Fig. 8.6).

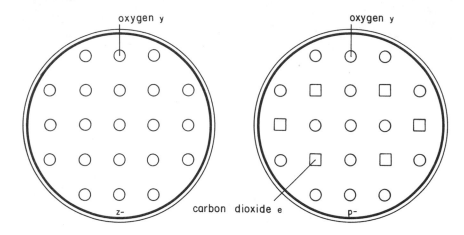

inspired air   alveolar gas

Figure 8.6 *Composition of inspired air and alveolar gas. Color and count the round oxygen molecules and square carbon dioxide molecules in inspired air and alveolar gas. Note that alveolar gas differs from inspired air in that it has fewer oxygen molecules and more carbon dioxide molecules. Compare the concentrations of oxygen and carbon dioxide in inspired air and alveolar gas with the corresponding partial pressures listed in Table 8.1. Finish the picture by coloring the background areas.*

Table 8.1 Partial pressures of oxygen and carbon dioxide				
	Inspired air	Alveolar gas	Arterial blood	Mixed venous blood
PO_2 (mmHg)	150	100	100	40
PCO_2 (mmHg)	0	40	40	46

In going from the atmosphere to the mitochondria, PO_2 decreases and PCO_2 increases. Since gases diffuse from a region of higher partial pressure to one of lower partial pressure, these partial pressure gradients con-tinuously drive O_2 from the atmosphere into the mito-chondria (Fig. 8.7) and drive CO_2 from the mitochon-dria into the atmosphere (Fig. 8.8).

Figure 8.7 *Partial pressure gradients for oxygen. Color the arrows that indi-cate the flow of oxygen from the atmos-phere into the matrix of the mitochondri-on. Color all of the structures in the top panel from left to right. Color the bar graph in the bottom panel, which indi-cates the partial pressure of oxygen in the structure directly above it. The difference between the heights of the steps indicates the partial pressure gradient between adjacent structures. Note that these par-tial pressure gradients enable oxygen to diffuse continuously from the atmosphere into the mitochondrion, where it is ulti-mately consumed. Note also that the par-tial pressures of oxygen in alveolar gas and arterial blood are the same. Compare this figure with Fig. 8.1 and*

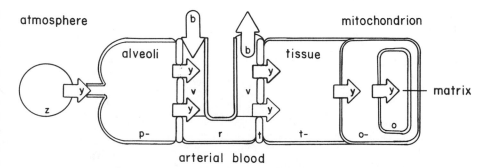

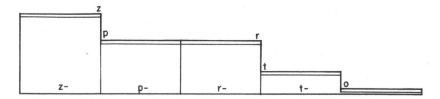

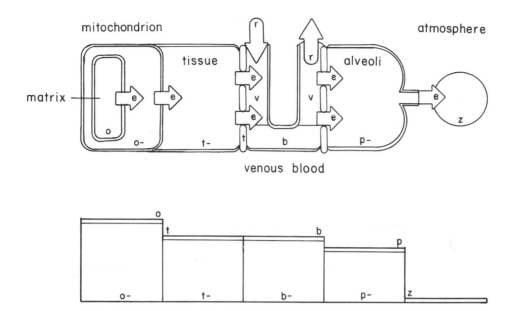

Figure 8.8 *Partial pressure gradients for carbon dioxide. Color the arrows that indicate the flow of carbon dioxide from the matrix of the mitochondrion into the atmosphere. Color all of the structures in the top panel from left to right. Color the bar graph in the bottom panel, which indicates the partial pressure of carbon dioxide in the structure directly above it. The difference between the heights of the steps indicates the partial pressure gradient between adjacent structures. Note that these partial pressure gradients enable carbon dioxide to diffuse continuously from the mitochondrion into the atmosphere where it is ultimately expired. Note also that the partial pressures of carbon dioxide in the tissue and mixed venous blood are the same. Compare this figure with Fig. 8.7 and Table 8.1.*

Table 8.1 shows that the partial pressures of both oxygen and carbon dioxide in alveolar gas and arterial blood are equal. This occurs because the time that the blood spends in the pulmonary capillary is long enough to allow the blood gases to come into equilibrium with the alveolar gases (Fig. 8.9). For this reason, it is the partial pressures of oxygen and carbon dioxide in alveolar gas that determine the partial pressures of oxygen and carbon dioxide in arterial blood. These partial pressures, in turn, determine the concentrations of oxygen and carbon dioxide in arterial blood.

Oxygen carriage by blood

Essentially all of the O_2 in blood is carried by hemoglobin molecules that are contained in the red blood cells. Because of its low solubility in plasma, only a negligible amount of O_2 is carried by the blood in a dissolved state.

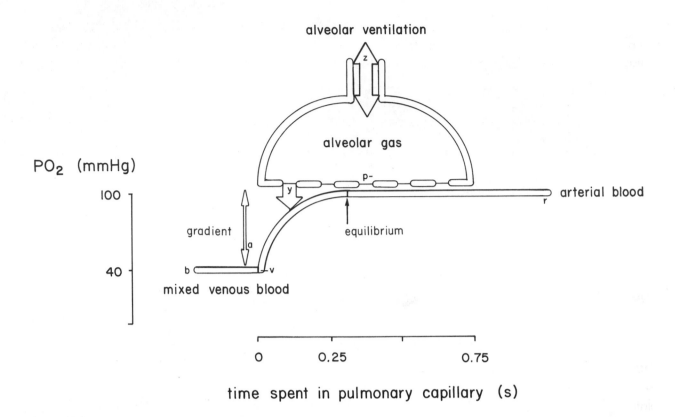

PO₂ (mmHg)

time spent in pulmonary capillary (s)

Figure 8.9 *Dynamics of gas exchange in the lung. Color the alveolar gas and the arrow labeled alveolar ventilation. Color the horizontal line at the left, which indicates the partial pressure of oxygen in mixed venous blood. Identify and color the arrow labeled gradient and note that the partial pressure gradient for oxygen corresponds to the amount by which the PO₂ in alveolar gas exceeds that in mixed venous blood. Color the arrow that indicates the diffusion of oxygen down its partial pressure gradient, i.e., from the alveolus into the blood. Finish the picture by coloring the remainder of the line, noting that the PO₂ in the blood equilibrates with the PO₂ in alveolar gas well before the blood leaves the lung. For this reason, the partial pressure of oxygen in arterial blood is the same as that in alveolar gas.*

The hemoglobin molecule consists of two alpha chains and two beta chains that each contain a heme, which is an iron porphyrin group, that binds loosely to an oxygen molecule. Each complete hemoglobin molecule (Hb_4) can bind reversibly with up to four O_2 molecules (Fig. 8.10).

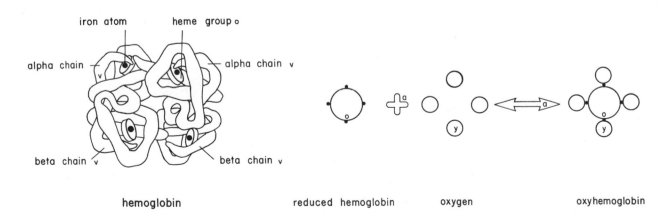

Figure 8.10 *Hemoglobin. Identify and color the chains of the hemoglobin molecule and the sites where oxygen molecules are carried. Color the reaction at the right, noting that each hemoglobin molecule can combine reversibly with four molecules of oxygen.*

$$Hb_4 + 4\,O_2 \rightleftharpoons Hb_4O_8$$

The oxygen saturation of blood (SO$_2$) specifies the percentage of the total number of hemoglobin sites that are

occupied by O$_2$ molecules. At 100% saturation, for example, all of the sites are filled with O$_2$, whereas at 50% saturation only half of the sites are filled with O$_2$ (Fig. 8.11).

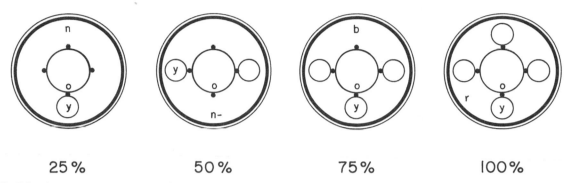

| 25% | 50% | 75% | 100% |

Figure 8.11 *The oxygen saturation of blood. Color the hemoglobin and oxygen molecules in each condition, noting that the oxygen saturation represents the percentage of the total number of sites on hemoglobin that are filled with oxygen. Color the background area in each condition, noting that the color of the blood reflects its oxygen saturation.*

The oxyhemoglobin dissociation curve

The oxyhemoglobin dissociation curve describes the relationship between the oxygen saturation of hemoglobin, or SO$_2$, and the partial pressure of oxygen (PO$_2$), or oxygen tension, that is imposed on the blood. The oxyhemoglobin dissociation curve is characterized by a steep, S-shaped portion, and a flat, nearly horizontal portion (Fig. 8.12).

The steep portion of the curve corresponds to the range of oxygen tensions over which SO$_2$ is dependent on PO$_2$, while the flat portion corresponds to the range of

oxygen tensions over which SO$_2$ is independent of PO$_2$. At the normal arterial PO$_2$ of 100 mmHg, which corresponds to a point on the flat portion of the curve, nearly 100% of the hemoglobin sites are occupied by oxygen molecules. At the normal mixed venous PO$_2$ of 40 mmHg, which corresponds to a point on the steep portion of the curve, only around 75% of the hemoglobin sites are occupied by oxygen molecules. This difference between the oxygen saturations of arterial and venous blood indicates that, at rest, the tissues extract from arterial blood only one-quarter of the oxygen that it carries.

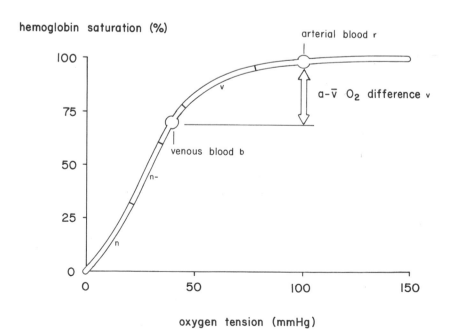

Figure 8.12 *The oxyhemoglobin dissociation curve. Color the oxyhemoglobin dissociation curve, comparing the colors of its segments with the blood depicted in Fig. 8.11. Identify the points that correspond to the partial pressures of oxygen in arterial and mixed venous blood and compare them with those listed in Table 8.1. Note that the oxygen saturation of arterial blood is nearly 100%, indicating that essentially all of the hemoglobin sites are filled by oxygen molecules. Note that the oxygen saturation of mixed venous blood is around 75% and color the arrow that indicates the corresponding a-v̄ O$_2$ difference.*

The a-$\bar{v}$ O$_2$ difference

Given that the nominal hemoglobin concentration in blood is 15 g Hb per 100 ml of blood, and that each gram of hemoglobin can carry 1.34 ml O$_2$, the oxygen content of arterial blood (at 100% saturation) is 20 ml O$_2$ per 100 ml of blood. Similarly, the oxygen content of mixed venous blood, which is 75% saturated, is 15 ml O$_2$ per 100 ml of blood.

The difference between the oxygen content of arterial blood and mixed venous blood, which is 5 ml O$_2$ per 100 ml of blood at rest, is called the a-$\bar{v}$ O$_2$ difference and it represents the oxygen that is consumed by the tissues. Under conditions of increased metabolism, the tissues extract more oxygen from arterial blood, the a-$\bar{v}$ O$_2$ difference widens, and the PO$_2$ of venous blood falls accordingly (Fig. 8.13).

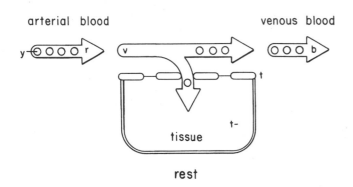

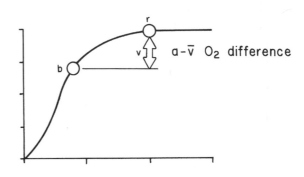

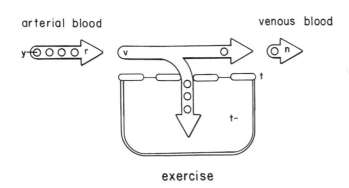

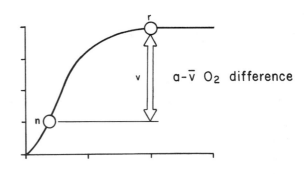

Figure 8.13 *Effect of oxygen uptake on a-$\bar{v}$ O$_2$ difference. For each condition, color the tissue and the membrane. Color and count the oxygen molecules. Note that the difference between the number of oxygen molecules in arterial and venous blood represents the number that is taken up by the tissues. Color the arrows that indicate arterial blood, capillary blood, and venous blood. Color the corresponding arterial and venous blood points on the oxyhemoglobin dissociation curve and the arrow that indicates the a-$\bar{v}$ O$_2$ difference. Since the saturation of arterial blood is 100% in both conditions, note that a widened a-$\bar{v}$ O$_2$ difference during exercise causes a corresponding reduction in the oxygen saturation of venous blood.*

Carbon dioxide carriage by blood

Carbon dioxide is carried by the blood in three different forms: 1) as a bicarbonate ion (HCO$_3^-$) in plasma; 2) as carbamino compounds, which are formed when CO$_2$ molecules combine with NH$_2$ groups in proteins, such as hemoglobin; and 3) as a dissolved molecule (Fig. 8.14).

The bicarbonate ion is formed in a reaction between CO2 and H2O that is catalyzed by the enzyme carbonic anhydrase (CA), which is present in the red blood cell but is absent in blood plasma:

$$CO_2 + H_2O \overset{[CA]}{\rightleftharpoons} H_2CO_3 \rightleftharpoons H^+ + HCO_3^-$$

Of the CO2 that is picked up by the blood in the systemic capillaries (Fig. 8.1), 60% is carried in the form of bicarbonate ions, 30% is carried in the form of carbamino compounds, and the remaining 10% is dissolved in blood.

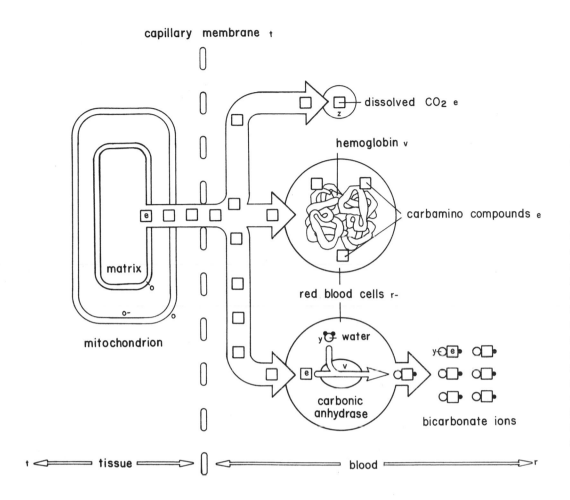

Figure 8.14 *Carriage of carbon dioxide by the blood. Color the capillary membrane, the arrows at the bottom, the mitochondrion, and the CO_2 molecules that it produces. Color the CO_2 molecule that is in a dissolved state. Color the red blood cell just below, its hemoglobin molecule, and the CO_2 molecules that are carried in carbamino compounds. Finish the picture by coloring the red blood cell at the bottom, the carbonic anhydrase, the water molecule, and the bicarbonate ions (HCO_3^-) that are formed by the reaction between carbon dioxide (CO_2) and water (H_2O). Note the relative numbers of CO_2 molecules that are carried in the different states.*

The lung and chest wall

The outer surface of the lung and the inner surface of the thoracic cage are covered with slippery pleural membranes that slide easily over each other. This arrangement allows the lung to passively follow the movement of the chest wall, which is made up of the rib cage plus the diaphragm (Fig. 8.15). Thus, the lung inflates when the vertical and/or lateral dimensions of the chest wall increase, and deflates when these dimensions decrease (Fig. 8.16).

Figure 8.15 *The lung and chest wall. Color the lung and chest wall, noting that the pleural cavity lies between them. Contraction of the respiratory muscles alters the pressure in the pleural cavity which, in turn, provides the driving force to expand or collapse the lung.*

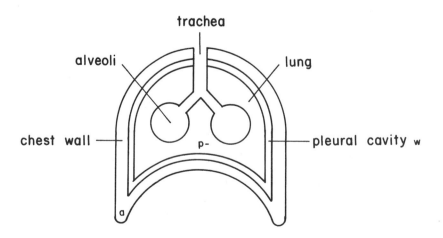

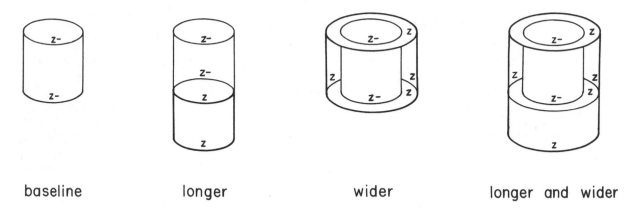

Figure 8.16 *Effect of chest wall dimensions on lung volume. Color the cylinders in each condition, noting that the volume of a cylinder is made larger by increases in its length and/or width.*

The force that moves the chest wall is provided by the contraction of the respiratory muscles, which alters the pressure in the pleural cavity that surrounds the lung. The respiratory muscles are skeletal muscles that are divided into a group of inspiratory muscles and a group of expiratory muscles (Fig. 8.17). The volume of the lung increases when the inspiratory muscles shorten and decreases when the expiratory muscles shorten.

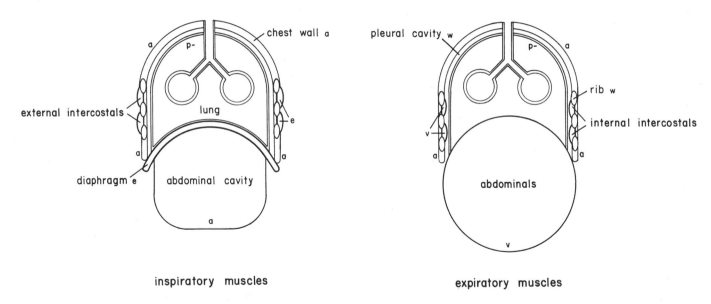

Figure 8.17 *The respiratory muscles. Color the inspiratory muscles, noting that the diaphragm and the rib cage collectively form the chest wall (Fig. 8.15). Color the expiratory muscles, noting their relationship to the inspiratory muscles. Finish the picture by coloring the lung and the remainder of chest wall in each panel.*

Inspiratory muscles

The diaphragm is the most important inspiratory muscle. It is a large, dome-shaped sheet of muscle that separates the thoracic cavity from the abdominal cavity. By pushing the abdominal contents down and out, the contraction of the diaphragm increases the vertical dimension of the chest wall (Fig. 8.18).

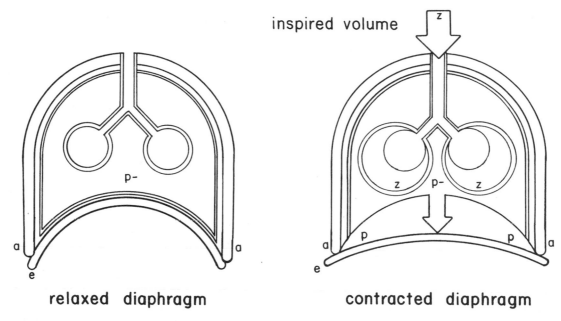

inspired volume

relaxed diaphragm   contracted diaphragm

Figure 8.18 *Action of the diaphragm. Color the rib cage, lung, and diaphragm in the left panel, noting the domed configuration of the relaxed diaphragm. Color the same structures in the right panel, noting the flattened configuration of the contracted diaphragm. Note also that the length of the contracted diaphragm is shorter than the length of the relaxed diaphragm. Diaphragmatic contraction increases the vertical dimension of the chest wall and thereby increases lung volume (Fig. 8.16). Color the arrow that indicates the volume of air that is inspired during diaphragmatic contraction and color the corresponding increase in alveolar volume. Color the rest of the picture, noting that the volume of inspired air is equal to the volume that is displaced by the descent of the diaphragm, i.e., the difference between the positions of the relaxed and contracted diaphragms.*

The fibers of the external intercostal muscles connect adjacent ribs. Contraction of the external intercostal muscles pulls the ribs upward and outward, thereby increasing the anteroposterior (AP) and lateral diameters of the chest wall (Figure 8.19).

The accessory muscles of inspiration include a group of neck muscles that expand the upper part of the rib cage. These muscles are not used at rest, but they may contract vigorously during periods of increased ventilation.

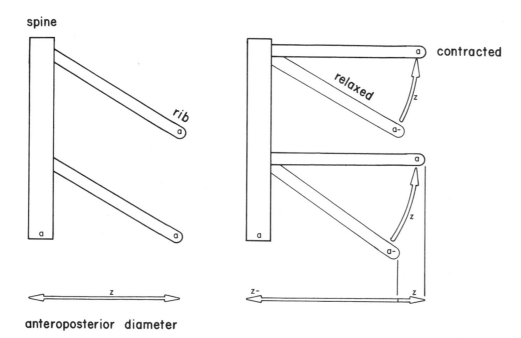

anteroposterior diameter

Figure 8.19 *Action of the external intercostal muscles. Color the ribs and spine for the condition at the left, which corresponds to relaxed external intercostal muscles. Color the arrow that indicates the corresponding anteroposterior (AP) diameter of the rib cage. Color the ribs and spine for the condition at the right, which corresponds to contracted external intercostal muscles. Color the arrow that indicates the AP diameter of the rib cage. Note that the elevation of the ribs increases the AP and lateral diameters of the chest wall and thereby increases the volume of the lung (Fig. 8.16).*

115

Expiratory muscles

Expiratory muscles are not usually active during quiet breathing. The lung and chest wall are stretched during inspiration, which is the period in which air flows into the lung and the lung inflates. The elastic properties of the lung and chest wall enable them to recoil passively to their resting positions during expiration, which is the period in which air flows out of the lung and the lung deflates.

The muscles of the anterior abdominal wall are the most important expiratory muscles. Contraction of the abdominal muscles increases intra-abdominal pressure and forces the diaphragm upward, thereby decreasing the vertical dimension of the chest wall (Fig. 8.16). Contraction of the internal intercostal muscles moves the ribs downward and inward. This action, which is the opposite of that produced by the external intercostal muscles, decreases the AP and the lateral diameters of the chest wall.

Mechanical properties of the lung

The mechanical properties of the lung are divided into an elastic component and a resistive component. The elastic component is due to the elastic fibers in the lung and chest wall and the surface tension forces that occur at the air-liquid interface in the lung. The resistive component is due to the geometry of the airways in the lung.

Elastic properties of matter

Elasticity is the property of matter that enables it to return to its original shape after being deformed by an external force.

The elastic behavior of a spring can be expressed graphically by plotting its length (in cm) against the force (in g) that is applied to stretch the spring. The length-force data obtained using a range of forces, or weights, determine a line in a length-force plane. The slope of the line thus formed represents the compliance of the spring (in cm/g), a measure of the ease with which the spring can be stretched, and the y-intercept represents its unstretched length (Fig. 8.20). Thus, the compliance of the spring can be visualized from the steepness of the slope of its length-force line, and the resting length of the spring can be visualized from its y-intercept.

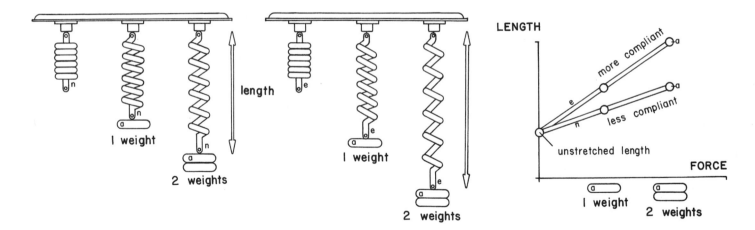

Figure 8.20 *Elastic properties of springs. Color the spring at the left, noting its length under each of the three weighted conditions. Color the weights and the line at the right, noting that each weighted condition corresponds to a point on the line. Repeat the procedure for the spring at the right. Note that both springs have the same unstretched length and the same y-intercept on their length-force line. Note also that the spring on the right is more compliant (less stiff) than the one on its left and therefore has a length-force line with a steeper slope.*

Elastic properties of the lung

In a similar manner, the elastic behavior of the lung can be expressed graphically by plotting the volume of the lung (in ml) against the pressure (in cmH$_2$O) that is applied at the airway opening to inflate the lung (Fig. 8.21). The volume-pressure data obtained using a range of inflation pressures determine a line in a volume-pressure plane. The slope at any point on the line thus formed represents the compliance of the lung (in ml/cmH$_2$O), a measure of the ease with which the lung can be inflated, and the y-intercept indicates the volume of the lung when the applied pressure is zero. Thus, the compliance of the lung can be visualized from the steepness of the slope of its volume-pressure curve.

The slope of the volume-pressure curve for the lung is steep at low inflation pressures and tapers off at high inflation pressures, indicating that the compliance of the lung decreases with increasing lung volume. In other words, the lungs become stiffer when they are inflated to a large volume (Fig. 8.21).

Half of the elastic behavior of the lung is due to elastic and collagenous fibers within the lung itself; the other half is due to surface tension forces that occur at the air-liquid interfaces in the alveoli. The cells lining the alveoli secrete a substance called surfactant that reduces surface tension forces and makes the lung more compliant. Surfactant reduces the work of breathing because it makes it easier for the inspiratory muscles to expand the lung.

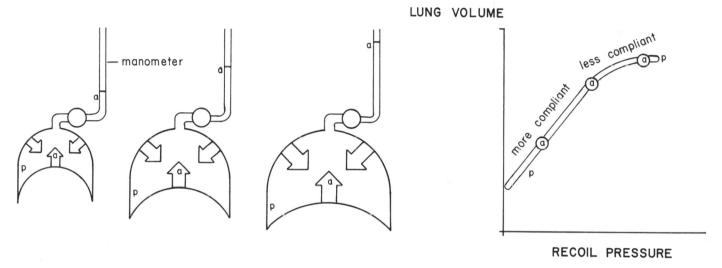

Figure 8.21 *Elastic properties of the lung. Color the figures for each of the three conditions on the left. Note that the lung recoil pressure in each condition is measured by the height of the column of water in the manometer, and color the corresponding points on the line at the right. By analogy to the analysis shown in Fig. 8.20, the y-intercept specifies the lung volume that would occur in the absence of external pressures, and the slope of the line indicates the compliance of the lung. Note that the volume-pressure curve for the lung is linear at low inflation pressures and curvilinear at high inflation pressures. These results show that the compliance of the lung decreases when it is inflated to a large volume.*

Resistive properties of the lung

The resistive properties of the lung are due to the narrow airways through which air flows during inspiration and expiration. The resistance to airflow in the lung is similar to the resistance to blood flow in the circulation (Fig. 6.20) in that it depends critically on the diameter of the airways.

The airways of the tracheobronchial tree contain smooth muscle cells that contract when they are exposed to acetylcholine, which is the neurotransmitter used by the parasympathetic nervous system. Contraction of bronchial smooth muscle narrows the airways and increases airway resistance; this process is called bronchoconstriction (Fig. 8.22). In contrast, bronchial smooth muscle cells relax when they are exposed to epinephrine or norepinephrine. This widens the airways in a process called bronchodilation, and decreases the airway resistance (Fig. 8.22)

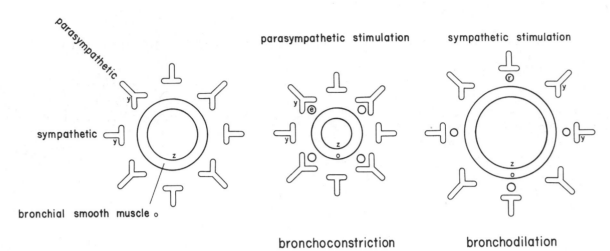

Figure 8.22 *Effect of bronchial muscle tone on airway diameter. For each condition, color the smooth muscle and its lumen, the parasympathetic and sympathetic nerve fibers, and their neurotransmitters. Note that parasympathetic stimulation causes bronchial smooth muscle to contract, which constricts the airway and increases airway resistance. Note also that sympathetic stimulation causes bronchial smooth muscle to relax, which dilates the airway and decreases airway resistance. Compare this figure with Fig. 6.21, noting the difference between the effects of sympathetic stimulation on vascular smooth muscle and bronchial smooth muscle.*

Pulmonary ventilation

The ventilation of the lung is an important determinant of the oxygen and carbon dioxide tension in alveolar gas and, thus, arterial blood (Fig. 8.9). Two different measures of ventilation are minute ventilation and alveolar ventilation.

Minute ventilation refers to the rate at which air moves into and out of the trachea. Minute ventilation ($\dot{V}_E$, in L/min) is determined by the product of tidal volume (V_T, the volume of air inspired per breath in L) and respiratory frequency (f, the number of breaths per minute).

Thus,

$$\dot{V}_E = V_T \cdot f$$

Alveolar ventilation refers to the rate at which air moves into and out of the alveoli. Part of the inspired volume ventilates the dead space, where no gas exchange takes place, while the remaining part ventilates the alveoli, where gas exchange takes place (Fig. 8.4). Alveolar ventilation ($\dot{V}_A$, in L/min) is determined by the product of the volume of air entering the alveoli per breath and the respiratory frequency (Fig. 8.23).

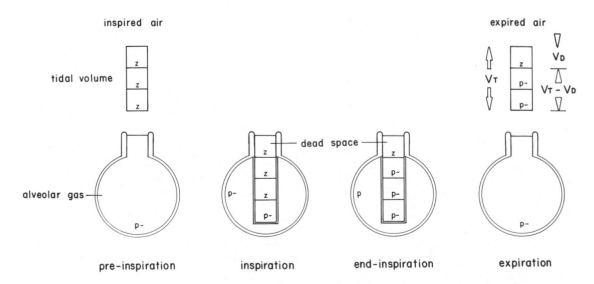

Figure 8.23 *Pulmonary ventilation. Color the panels from left to right, noting the similarity between this schematic lung and that shown in Fig. 8.4. Note that inspired air equilibrates with alveolar gas by end-inspiration. Compare the composition of gases in the inspired and expired air, noting that only that fraction of the tidal volume that exceeds the dead space volume actually ventilates the alveoli.*

Since only that portion of the tidal volume (V_T) that exceeds the dead space (V_D) actually enters and ventilates the alveoli, it follows that

$$\dot{V}_A = (V_T - V_D) \cdot f$$

The remaining portion of the tidal volume (V_D) is wasted ventilating dead space. Note that $\dot{V}_A$ becomes zero when V_T equals V_D; this shows that alveolar ventilation ceases when the tidal volume fails to exceed the dead space.

Effect of breathing pattern on alveolar ventilation

Since minute ventilation is determined by the product of V_T and f, it follows that a given minute ventilation can be achieved by a spectrum of V_T–f combinations, ranging from a rapid-shallow to a slow-deep breathing pattern (Fig. 8.24). Because the respiratory frequency determines the number of times that the dead space will be ventilated per minute (Fig. 8.23), a slow-deep breathing pattern provides more alveolar ventilation than does a rapid-shallow breathing pattern. Thus, the small tidal volumes used in rapid-shallow breathing are inefficient because an excessive amount of energy is wasted ventilating dead space where no gas exchange takes place (Fig. 8.25).

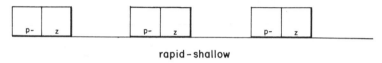

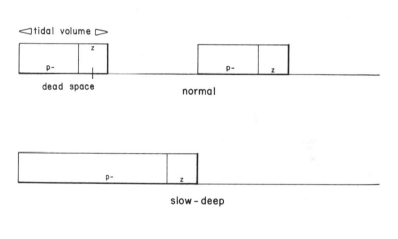

Figure 8.24 *Breathing patterns. Color the rectangles that represent samples of expired air that were produced during rapid-shallow, normal, and slow-deep breathing patterns. Note that each breathing pattern produces the same total volume of expired air over the 10-second period.*

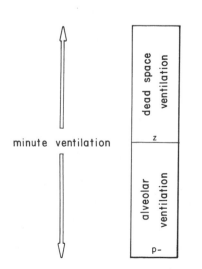

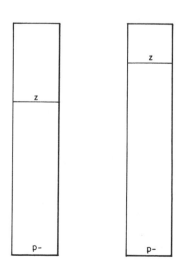

Figure 8.25 *Effect of breathing pattern on alveolar ventilation. Color the bar graphs from left to right, noting that they represent the ventilation associated with each of the breathing patterns shown in Fig. 8.24. Note that the rapid-shallow, normal, and slow-deep breathing patterns provide the same minute ventilation, but different dead space and alveolar ventilations.*

Effect of alveolar ventilation on arterial blood gases

The relationship between alveolar ventilation and arterial blood gases is governed by two alveolar gas laws.

The first alveolar gas law states that the level of CO_2 in alveolar gas represents the balance between the rate of CO_2 production by metabolizing tissues and the rate of CO_2 removal by alveolar ventilation. Increasing the rate of CO_2 production or decreasing its rate of removal will increase PCO_2, but changing them both proportionally does not alter PCO_2.

The second alveolar gas law states that the level of PO_2 in alveolar gas depends on the level of PCO_2 in alveolar gas. In other words, any change in alveolar PCO_2 must be accompanied by an opposite change in alveo-lar PO_2. As a result, only certain combinations of PCO_2 and PO_2 levels can coexist in alveolar gas.

Hypoventilation is defined as a condition in which the rate of CO_2 production by the tissues exceeds the rate of CO_2 removal by the lung. Hypoventilation therefore produces a high level of PCO_2 (hypercapnia) and a low level of PO_2 (hypoxia) in alveolar gas (Fig. 8.26). Since blood gases equilibrate with alveolar gases in the lung (Fig. 8.9), hypoventilation also produces a high level of PCO_2 (hypercarbia) and a low level of PO_2 (hypoxemia) in arterial blood.

Hyperventilation is defined as a condition in which the rate of CO_2 removal by the lung exceeds the rate of CO_2 production by the tissues. Hyperventilation produces a low level of PCO_2 and a high level of PO_2 in alveolar gas and arterial blood (Fig. 8.26).

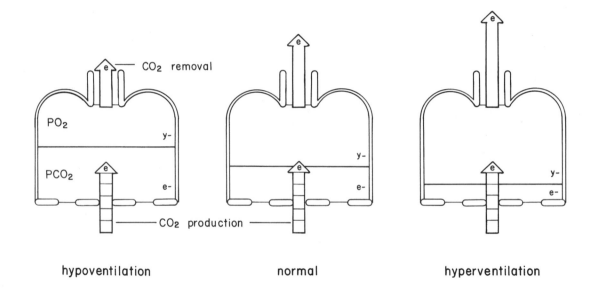

Figure 8.26 *Effect of alveolar ventilation on arterial blood gases. Color the panels from left to right, noting that the length of the arrow at the bottom indicates the rate at which CO_2 enters the lung from metabolizing tissues. Note also that the length of the arrow at the top indicates the rate at which CO_2 is removed from the lung by alveolar ventilation. Note that hypoventilation causes the alveolar gas to have a high level of CO_2 (hypercapnia) and a low level of O_2 (hypoxia). Note also that hyperventilation causes the alveolar gas to have a low level of CO_2 and a high level of O_2.*

Regulation of arterial blood gases

A consequence of the alveolar gas laws described above is that the maintenance of normal levels of oxygen and carbon dioxide in arterial blood requires that alveolar ventilation be matched precisely to the rate of CO_2 production by the tissues. The sections below describe the operation of respiratory reflexes that adjust ventilation in order to maintain the normal levels of carbon dioxide, oxygen, and acidity in the blood.

Respiratory reflexes

The respiratory centers in the medulla and pons of the brainstem initiate and sustain a rhythmic breathing pattern. A variety of respiratory reflexes modulate this pattern in response to chemical, mechanical, and other stimuli.

Respiratory reflexes represent the sequential operation of: 1) sensory receptors that transmit neural signals along afferent pathways to the CNS; 2) coordinating centers in the CNS that transmit neural signals along efferent pathways to the respiratory muscles; 3) respiratory muscles, which convert their neural drive into respiratory muscle tension, which is the force that alters pleural pressure to move the lung; 4) the elastic and resistive properties of the lung, which determine the relationship between pleural pressure and lung volume (Fig. 8.27).

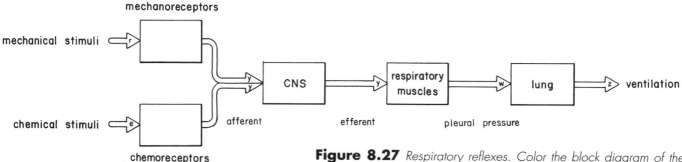

Figure 8.27 *Respiratory reflexes. Color the block diagram of the respiratory reflexes. Compare this figure with Fig. 4.1.*

Chemoreceptors

The arterial blood levels of PCO_2, PO_2, and pH are continuously monitored by chemoreceptors that sense the chemical composition of the fluid that surrounds them.

The most potent chemoreceptors are the central chemoreceptors, which are located in the brainstem on the surface of the medulla. The central chemoreceptors respond to the level of PCO_2 in arterial blood. Peripheral chemoreceptors, which are located in the carotid bodies and the aortic bodies, also sense the PCO_2, PO_2, and pH of their arterial blood supply (Fig. 8.28). The afferent pathway from the carotid body travels in the glossopharyngeal nerve (cranial nerve IX), while the afferent pathway from the aortic body travels in the vagus nerve (cranial nerve X).

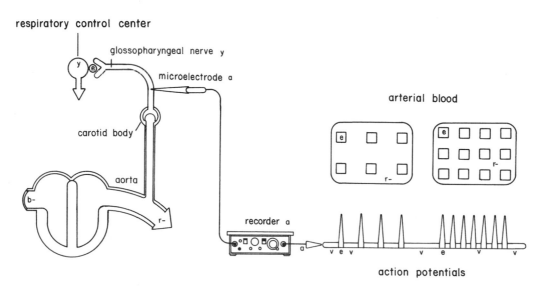

Figure 8.28 *Transduction characteristics of chemoreceptors. Color the blood in the heart, noting that the carotid body chemoreceptors are exposed to arterial blood. Color the glossopharyngeal nerve, its excitatory neurotransmitter, and the respiratory control center in the brainstem. Color the microelectrode and the recorder. Color the arterial blood samples and their CO_2 molecules, and then the corresponding recordings of the action potentials that are generated by the chemoreceptors. Note that the frequency of action potentials increases when blood levels of CO_2 rise. Compare this figure with Fig. 6.28.*

Chemoreceptor reflexes

Any deviation from the normal values of PCO_2, PO_2, or pH in the arterial blood stimulates chemoreceptor reflexes that alter ventilation in such a way as to restore their normal levels. The neural output from chemoreceptors stimulates the respiratory centers in the brainstem which, in turn, adjust ventilation by regulating the intensity and the timing of the respiratory muscle contractions (Fig. 8.29). The operation of chemoreceptor reflexes can be observed by measuring the changes in minute ventilation that occur when the blood levels of carbon dioxide and oxygen are varied.

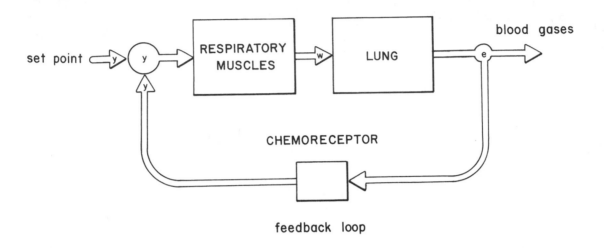

Figure 8.29 *Block diagram of a blood gas control system. Color the block diagram and compare it with that shown in Fig. 1.7.*

Ventilatory responses to carbon dioxide and oxygen

The ventilatory response to changes in arterial CO_2 tension can be measured when a subject breathes a gas mixture that increases the level of PCO_2 but does not change the level of PO_2 in the alveoli. Under conditions in which the blood levels of CO_2 gradually rise, central and peripheral chemoreceptor reflexes are stimulated which, in turn, increase ventilation. As ventilation increases, more CO_2 is blown off, and arterial PCO_2 is restored to its normal level (Fig. 8.26).

The relationship between ventilation and arterial PCO_2 that emerges from such studies shows that ventilation increases when arterial PCO_2 rises above its normal value of 40 mmHg and decreases when arterial PCO_2 falls below its normal value (Fig. 8.30). Thus, blood levels of PCO_2 strongly influence ventilation. The ventilatory response to CO_2 is reduced by drugs that depress the respiratory centers in the central nervous system, by respiratory muscle weakness, or by pathological conditions that increase the stiffness of the lung or narrow its airways.

The ventilatory response to oxygen can also be measured when a subject breathes a gas mixture that changes the PO_2 level, but not the PCO_2 level, of alveolar gas. Under conditions in which arterial blood levels of PO_2 gradually fall, peripheral chemoreceptor reflexes are stimulated which, in turn, increase ventilation. In contrast to the potency of altered carbon dioxide levels as a ventilatory stimulus, ventilation does not change appreciably when arterial PO_2 falls to moderately low levels. Thus, mild hypoxemia (low O_2 in arterial blood) only weakly stimulates ventilation, but severe hypoxemia strongly stimulates ventilation (Fig. 8.30).

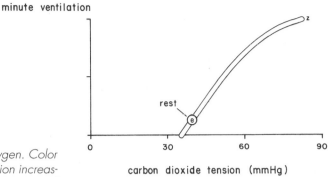

minute ventilation

rest
e

carbon dioxide tension (mmHg)

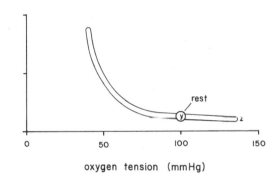

rest
y

oxygen tension (mmHg)

Figure 8.30 *Ventilatory responses to carbon dioxide and oxygen. Color the top graph, noting from the steep grade of the line that ventilation increases markedly in response to small increases in the carbon dioxide tension of arterial blood. Then color the bottom graph, noting that ventilation does not change appreciably during mild hypoxemia, but increases markedly during severe hypoxemia.*

Respiratory mechanoreceptors

Other respiratory reflexes originate in mechanoreceptors, such as lung irritant receptors, pulmonary stretch receptors, and respiratory muscle spindles and tendon

organs (Fig. 8.31). Mechanoreceptor reflexes provide a rapid form of respiratory regulation because they can alter ventilation before any changes in blood gases can stimulate chemoreceptor reflexes.

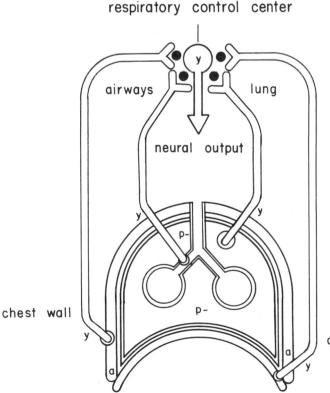

respiratory control center

airways lung

neural output

chest wall

diaphragm

Figure 8.31 *Respiratory mechanoreceptors. Color the afferent nerve pathways from the respiratory mechanoreceptors, noting that they transmit neural signals from the airways, lung, chest wall, and diaphragm to the respiratory control center in the brainstem. Finish the picture by coloring the respiratory control center, the lung, and the chest wall. Compare this figure with Fig. 8.27.*

123

Blood pH

The pH of arterial blood is held constant by the buffering action of the HCO_3^-/CO_2 system and by blood proteins; primarily hemoglobin.

The Henderson-Hasselbach equation states that the pH of blood can be calculated by adding a constant term (6.1) to a variable term given by the logarithm of the ratio of the HCO_3^- concentration to the CO_2 concentration:

$$pH = 6.1 + \log ([HCO_3^-]/[CO_2])$$

Since $\log (20) = 1.3$, the pH of blood will be 7.4 whenever $[HCO_3^-]/[CO_2]$ is 20, i.e., $6.1 + \log 20 = 6.1 + 1.3 = 7.4$. One implication of the Henderson-Hasselbach equation is that the pH of blood can be maintained at its normal value of 7.4 by the balanced operation of the renal system, which regulates the HCO_3^- concentration, and the respiratory system, which regulates the CO_2 concentration.

carbon dioxide e   bicarbonate n

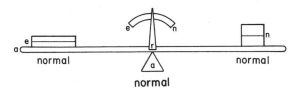

normal   normal

normal

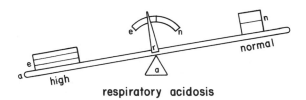

high   normal

respiratory acidosis

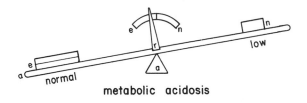

normal   low

metabolic acidosis

Figure 8.32 *Acid-base disturbances. For each condition, color the balance, the pointer, and the pH scale. Then color and count the carbon dioxide and bicarbonate rectangles on each side the balance. Note that an abnormal pH occurs whenever the levels of CO_2 and HCO_3^- do not exactly counterbalance one another.*

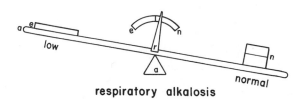

low   normal

respiratory alkalosis

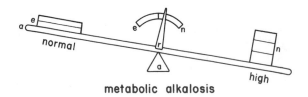

normal   high

metabolic alkalosis

Acid-base disturbances

Another implication of the Henderson-Hasselbach equation is that the pH of blood will deviate from its normal value of 7.4 whenever the $[HCO_3^-]:[CO_2]$ ratio deviates from its normal value of 20:1. Alkalosis (pH > 7.4) occurs when $[HCO_3^-]:[CO_2]$ is greater than 20:1 and acidosis (pH < 7.4) occurs when $[HCO_3^-]:[CO_2]$ is less than 20:1. It follows from these considerations that an abnormal pH could be due to an abnormal level of HCO_3^- (a metabolic component) and/or an abnormal level of CO_2 (a respiratory component) (Fig. 8.32).

In summary, acidosis can be due to a high level of CO_2 (respiratory acidosis) and/or a low level of HCO_3^- (metabolic acidosis), and alkalosis can be due to a low level of CO_2 (respiratory alkalosis) and/or a high level of HCO_3^- (metabolic alkalosis).

Compensated acid-base disturbances

In reality, however, an abnormal pH that is due to a disturbance in one component is usually partially or fully compensated by an opposite adjustment in the other component, thereby enabling the pH of the blood to be maintained within normal limits (Fig. 8.33). For example, respiratory acidosis due to chronically elevated CO_2 levels, as can occur in long-standing lung disease, is usually accompanied by a compensatory metabolic alkalosis due to the elevation of HCO_3^- levels by the kidney.

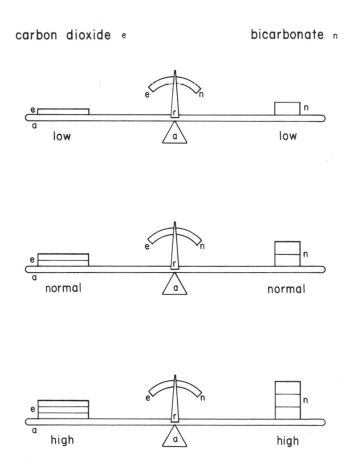

Figure 8.33 *Compensated acid-base disturbances. For each condition, color the balance, the pointer, and the scale. Then color and count the carbon dioxide and bicarbonate rectangles on each side of the balance. Note that a normal pH results whenever the levels of CO_2 and HCO_3^- exactly counterbalance one another. Compare this figure with Fig. 8.32.*

chapter **nine**
gastrointestinal system

The gastrointestinal system digests food and absorbs the products of digestion into the body.

Topology of the gastrointestinal tract

The gastrointestinal (G.I.) tract consists of a very long tube (about 11 feet) of varying shape that begins at the mouth and ends at the anus. It is hollow throughout and its lumen opens to the outside at both ends. Food that is in the lumen of the G. I. tract, therefore, is topologically outside of the body (Fig. 9.1).

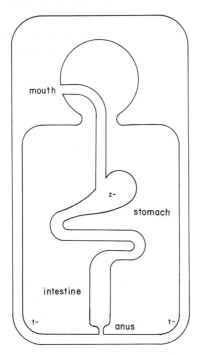

Figure 9.1 *Topology of the gastrointestinal tract. Begin by coloring in the stomach and continue to color the entire area without crossing any lines. Note that the interior, or lumen, of the G.I. tract is continuous with the external environment; that is, substances in the lumen are outside of the body.*

The G.I. tract functions as a boundary that allows only certain substances to pass through its walls and enter the body. Digestion is the process by which food is converted to forms that can pass through the gastrointestinal wall; absorption is the actual passage of these substances through the wall.

Structure of the gastrointestinal tract

The parts of the G.I. tract outlined below are the mouth, esophagus, stomach, small intestine, and large intestine; these form a continuous tube. The accessory organs of digestion are the pancreas, liver, and gall bladder; these secrete digestive fluids into the G.I. tract (Fig. 9.2).

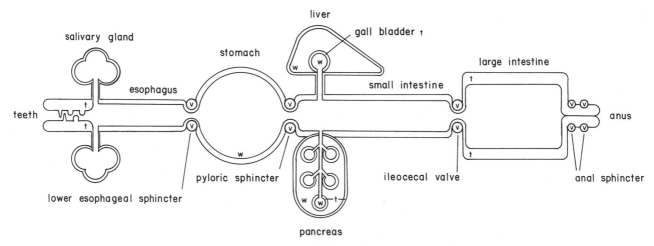

Figure 9.2 *Structure of the gastrointestinal system. Follow the path of the ingested food by coloring this schematic illustration of the G.I. tract and its accessory organs from left to right. Note that the salivary glands, pancreas, and liver (via the gall bladder) release substances into the lumen. Identify the sphincters, which prevent backflow and control the rate at which the food moves toward the anus.*

In the mouth, food is chewed and mixed with saliva. Saliva is a fluid secreted by the sublingual, submandibular, parotid, and buccal salivary glands in the mouth; this will be described later.

The esophagus is a muscular tube that connects the mouth and the stomach. At its point of connection with the stomach there is a ring of smooth muscle called the lower esophageal sphincter; constriction of this sphincter prevents reflux, or backflow, of food from the stomach into the esophagus. When constriction of this sphincter is weak, as is the case in normal infants, reflux of food occurs easily.

The stomach is a stretchable organ that can hold approximately 1 liter of food. Gastric glands in the stomach lining secrete digestive fluids, which include digestive enzymes and hydrochloric acid (HCl). Muscular contraction of the stomach mixes food with gastric secretions and propels the mixture through a ring of smooth muscle, called the pyloric sphincter, into the small intestine.

The small intestine is the major site of digestion and absorption. It consists of consecutive sections called the duodenum, jejunum and ileum. The ileocecal valve separates the small intestine from the large intestine.

The large intestine consists of consecutive sections called the ascending, transverse, descending, and sigmoid colon. Unabsorbed material from the small intestine moves slowly through the large intestine before the material is further dehydrated to form feces. Feces pass through the rectum and exit the body through the anus; defecation is controlled by two anal sphincters.

Accessory organs of digestion

The accessory organs of digestion are the pancreas, liver, and gall bladder (Fig. 9.2). The pancreas secretes a number of enzymes that digest food. It also secretes sodium bicarbonate ($NaHCO_3$), which neutralizes the hydrochloric acid released in the stomach. The liver produces bile, a detergent that enables fat to mix with water. The bile is concentrated and stored in a sac called the gall bladder.

Both the pancreas and gall bladder release their secretions into ducts that empty into the duodenum. Since the lumen of the G.I. tract is topologically outside the body (Fig. 9.1), secretions by these accessory organs are considered to be exocrine, i.e., "outside" secretions.

Regulation of gastrointestinal function

The G.I. tract moves food along at a pace that is coordinated with the state of digestion of the food, and it secretes fluids that contain lubricants, enzymes, and detergents. The gastrointestinal system controls its activities through hormonal and neural mechanisms. In addition to local controls, G.I. activities are regulated by the autonomic nervous system (Fig. 9.3). In general, the parasympathetic nervous system, via the vagus nerve, increases the propulsion of food along the G.I. tract, increases the secretion of digestive fluids, and increases blood flow in the G.I. tract. The sympathetic nervous system inhibits these activities.

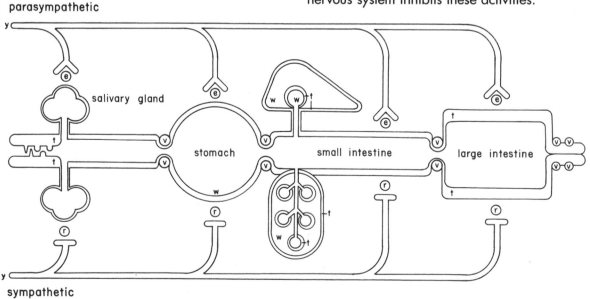

Figure 9.3 *Autonomic control of the gastrointestinal system. Color the G.I. tract and its accessory organs as in Fig. 9.2. Color the innervation by the parasympathetic and sympathetic branches of the autonomic nervous system.*

Stimulation of these processes by the parasympathetic nervous system begins early in the digestive process. It often precedes ingestion, as the sight or smell of food initiates the cephalic ("brain") control of processes that prepare the body for the entry of food. These processes include salivation, propulsion of food along the G.I. tract, hydrochloric acid secretion, and insulin release.

Structure of the gastrointestinal wall

The layers of the gastrointestinal wall (going from the lumen to the inside of the body) are: 1) the mucosa; 2) the submucosa; 3) a circular layer of smooth muscle; 4) a longitudinal layer of smooth muscle; and 5) the serosa (Fig. 9.4).

The mucosa, or epithelial lining, consists of a variety of mucus-secreting, enzyme-secreting, absorptive, and endocrine (hormone-secreting) cells. The submucosa is a layer of connective tissue that supports blood vessels, lymphatic vessels, and nerves. The circular smooth muscle forms a ring around the lumen; its contraction constricts the lumen. The longitudinal smooth muscle is arranged along the length of the G.I. tract so that its contraction shortens a segment of the tract. The serosa is comprised of connective tissue; it forms the covering of the G.I. tract that separates it from the rest of the abdominal organs.

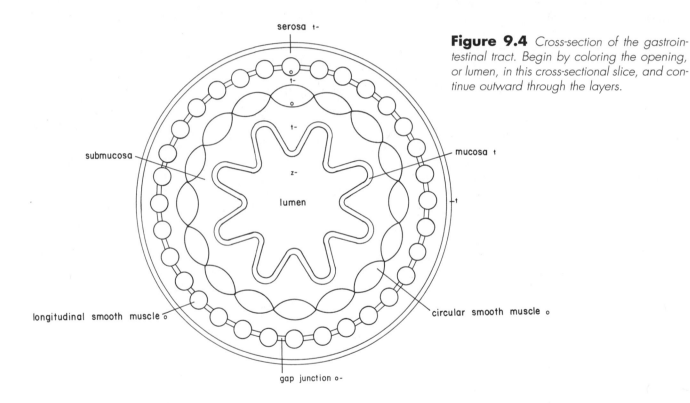

Figure 9.4 *Cross-section of the gastrointestinal tract. Begin by coloring the opening, or lumen, in this cross-sectional slice, and continue outward through the layers.*

Gastrointestinal smooth muscle

The fibers of the circular and longitudinal smooth muscle layers are arranged in bundles. The individual fibers in each bundle are connected to each other by gap junctions that allow ions to flow between them (Fig. 5.19). This arrangement enables action potentials to spread from one smooth muscle fiber to the next so that the muscle fibers can contract as a single unit.

The electrical activity of the smooth muscle of the G.I. tract is characterized by slow waves and spikes (Fig. 9.5). The slow waves represent spontaneous changes in resting membrane potential, and the spikes represent action potentials that arise whenever the membrane potential exceeds a threshold level (typically −40 mV). The smooth muscle of the G.I. tract is depolarized by muscle stretch, parasympathetic stimulation, and acetylcholine, and is hyperpolarized by sympathetic stimulation and norepinephrine.

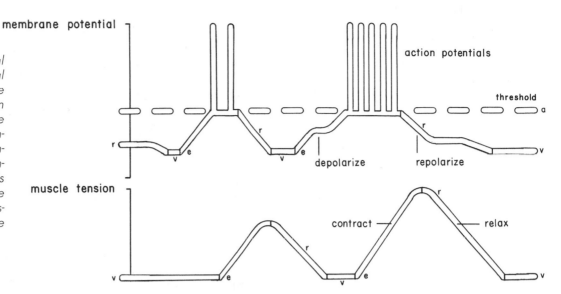

Figure 9.5 *Electrical activity of gastrointestinal smooth muscle. Color the recordings of the changes in membrane potential and the corresponding muscle tension. Note that action potentials arise when the membrane potential exceeds threshold. Note also that the action potentials cause muscle contraction. Compare this figure with Fig. 5.9.*

The enteric nervous system

The local nervous system of the G.I. tract is located within its wall and is called the enteric nervous system (Fig. 9.6). It consists of a myenteric plexus (Auerbach's plexus), which lies between the longitudinal and circular smooth muscle layers, and a submucosal plexus (Meissner's plexus) that lies in the submucosa. The myenteric plexus controls peristalsis (described below) whereas the submucosal plexus controls the secretions of the mucosal cells that line the G.I. tract. The enteric nervous system is generally stimulated by parasympathetic impulses and inhibited by sympathetic impulses.

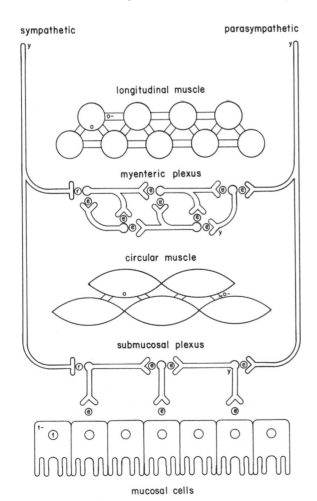

Figure 9.6 *The enteric nervous system. Color the longitudinal and circular smooth muscle cells and their gap junctions. Color the mucosal cells. Color the myenteric plexus, the submucosal plexus, and their innervation by the sympathetic and parasympathetic nervous systems. Note that these plexuses are excited by parasympathetic stimulation and inhibited by sympathetic stimulation. Compare this figure with Figs. 9.3 and 9.4.*

Peristalsis

Peristalsis is the coordinated series of muscular contractions that moves food along the G.I. tract; food normally moves caudally (from mouth to anus). When a bolus of food stretches a segment of the G.I. tract, the smooth muscle behind the bolus contracts while the smooth muscle in front of the bolus relaxes (Fig. 9.7). This coordinated contraction of the circular and longitudinal muscle layers produces a wave of constriction that propels food forward at a rate that is appropriate for digestion and absorption. Peristaltic activity is increased by parasympathetic stimulation and decreased by sympathetic stimulation.

Control of gastric emptying

Progression of food from the stomach to the small intestine is determined not only by the rate and strength of peristaltic contractions of the stomach, but also by the degree of constriction of the pyloric sphincter, a thick ring of smooth muscle located at the junction of the two organs (Fig. 9.2). Distention of the stomach by incoming food causes the sphincter to relax so that the gastric contractions can propel food, which is called chyme once it is mixed with gastric secretions, into the duodenum (Fig. 9.8). The sphincter is usually partly open so that small amounts of chyme (about 5 ml) squirt into the duodenum with each wave of gastric peristalsis.

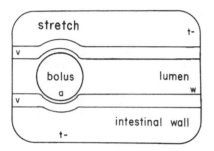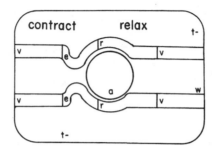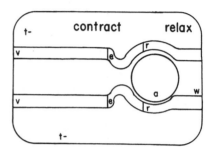

Figure 9.7 *Peristalsis. Color the bolus of food in each panel, noting that it progresses from left to right. In the left panel, color the intestinal wall and notice its stretched portion; in the middle and right panels, color the intestinal wall, noting the contracted muscle behind the bolus and the relaxed muscle ahead of it.*

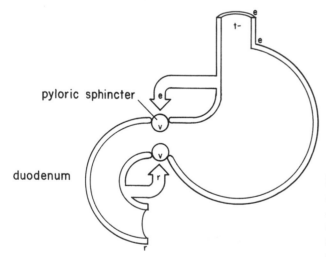

Figure 9.8 *Regulation of gastric emptying. Color the pyloric sphincter, the stomach, and the outline of the stomach and duodenum, including the two arrows. Note that the green arrow from the stomach relaxes the sphincter when the stomach is distended and that the red arrow from the duodenum constricts the sphincter when the duodenum is distended or when the chyme is acidic.*

Distention of the duodenum or acidity of the duodenal contents stimulates the enteric nervous system to decrease the intensity of gastric peristalsis and increase the constriction of the pyloric sphincter, thereby decreasing gastric emptying. Thus, the degree of constriction of the pyloric sphincter reflects the balance between dilating effects from the stomach and constricting effects from the duodenum (Fig. 9.8).

Secretions of the gastrointestinal system

The G.I. system secretes a large amount of fluid which provides lubrication, emulsification, and chemical breakdown of ingested food (Figs. 9.9, 9.10).

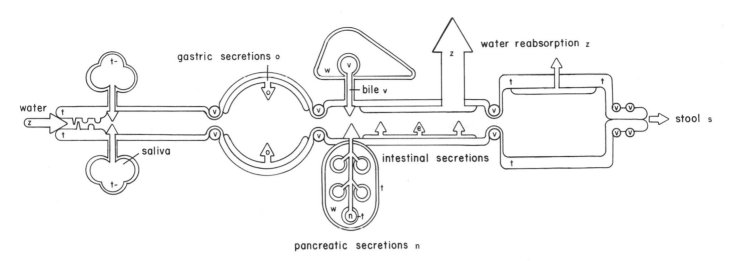

Figure 9.9 *Secretions of the gastrointestinal system. Color the intestinal wall and sphincters. Color the secretions of the salivary glands, stomach, pancreas, gall bladder, and intestinal mucosa into the lumen and the water leaving the lumen through the small and large intestines. Color the arrows depicting the amount of water entering the mouth and the stool leaving the anus.*

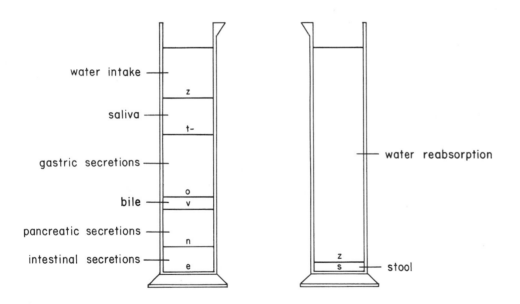

Figure 9.10 *Fluid balance in the gastrointestinal system. Color the portions of fluid entering the G.I. tract from ingested fluids and G.I. secretions, shown in the graduated cylinder at left. Color the fluid in the cylinder at right that represents the fluid absorbed by the G.I. tract and the fluid lost in feces. Note that normally the amount of water that is lost in feces is a very small fraction of that which enters the G.I. tract.*

Salivary secretions

The salivary glands secrete saliva, a fluid made up of two types of secretions. Some salivary glands (e.g. parotid) secrete a watery fluid that contains salivary amylase (an enzyme that digests starch); others (e.g. buccal glands) secrete a thick, slippery fluid called mucus, which is high in the protein mucin. The cells that line the esophagus also secrete mucus. The parasympathetic nervous system, stimulated by many taste and tactile sensations on the tongue, increases the secretion of saliva.

Gastric secretions

The gastric, or oxyntic, glands contain the parietal cells, which secrete hydrochloric acid (HCl), the chief cells, which secrete pepsinogen (an inactive form of pepsin, an enzyme that digests protein), and mucous neck cells, which secrete mucus (Fig. 9.11).

133

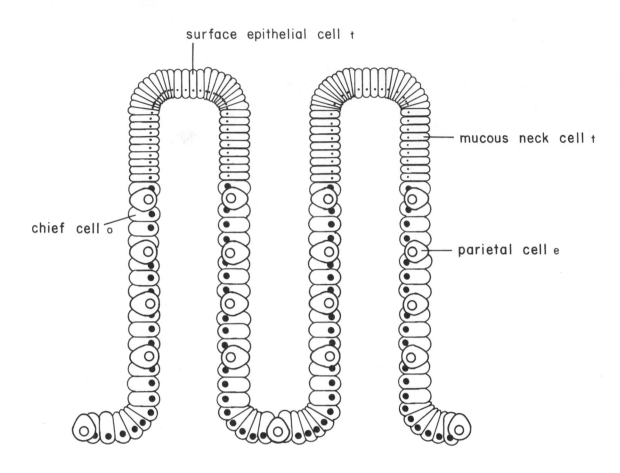

surface epithelial cell t

mucous neck cell t

chief cell o

parietal cell e

Figure 9.11 *Gastric oxyntic gland. Color the chief, parietal and mucous neck cells of the gastric oxyntic gland. Note that both mucous neck cells and surface epithelial cells secrete protective mucus.*

Hydrochloric acid sterilizes the upper portion of the G.I. tract (as far as the mid-ileum) and begins protein digestion by converting pepsinogen into pepsin, which is an active proteolytic, or protein-digesting, enzyme that works best in an acid environment. Since pepsin would digest the chief cell itself, it is adaptive that it is activated only after it is released from the cell; many other protein-digesting enzymes are also secreted in inactive forms.

Mucus secretion by mucous neck cells and epithelial cells on the surface of the stomach protects the gastric lining from being digested by pepsin and HCl. An imbalance between HCl and mucus secretion can cause ulceration, which is a deterioration of the mucosal lining of the stomach or duodenum.

Regulation of gastric secretions

The vagus nerve of the parasympathetic nervous system stimulates the gastric glands to secrete hydrochloric acid, pepsinogen, and mucus. In addition, hydrochloric acid release is stimulated by the hormone gastrin; the presence of protein in the stomach stimulates endocrine cells in the gastric mucosa to secrete gastrin into the blood. Gastrin release is inhibited when the contents of the stomach are highly acidic (pH < 2).

Pancreatic exocrine secretions

The acinar cells are the exocrine cells of the pancreas; they secrete digestive enzymes into the pancreatic duct (Fig. 9.12). These include active forms of enzymes that digest carbohydrates (pancreatic amylase) and fats (pancreatic lipase) and inactive forms of enzymes that digest proteins (trypsinogen, chymotrypsinogen, and procarboxypeptidase).

The inactive forms of the proteolytic enzymes are activated as follows. Trypsinogen becomes trypsin in the presence of enterokinase, an enzyme produced by intestinal cells; trypsin then acts to convert chymotrypsinogen to chymotrypsin, and procarboxypeptidase to carboxypeptidase.

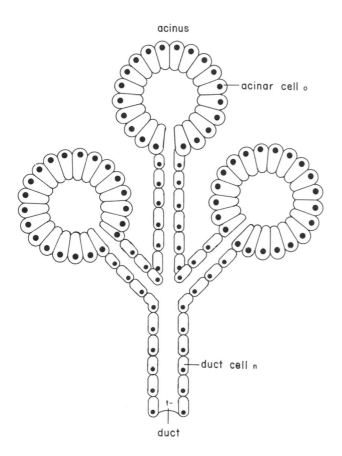

acinus

acinar cell ₒ

duct cell ₙ

duct

Figure 9.12 *Acinar and duct cells of the pancreas. Color this cross-section of a pancreatic acinus and the ducts that collect the secretions from the opening in each acinus. Note that the small ducts from individual acini converge to form a larger duct. Note also that the acinar cells secrete digestive enzymes while the duct cells secrete sodium bicarbonate.*

The cells that line the pancreatic duct (Fig. 9.12) secrete large amounts of sodium bicarbonate (NaHCO$_3$), which neutralizes the acidity of the chyme that enters the duodenum from the stomach.

Regulation of pancreatic exocrine secretions

The secretion of digestive enzymes by the acinar cells of the pancreas is stimulated by the hormone cholecystokinin (CCK), which is secreted into the blood by endocrine cells in the duodenum in response to the presence of food (Fig. 9.13).

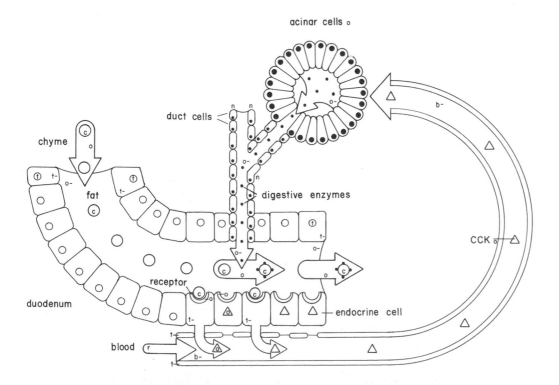

acinar cells ₒ

duct cells

chyme

fat

digestive enzymes

receptor

duodenum

endocrine cell

blood

CCK

Figure 9.13 *Regulation of pancreatic enzyme secretion. Color the entering fat, its receptors, and the cells of the duodenum. Color the hormone, CCK, that is released in response to receptor stimulation as you follow its path through the blood to the pancreatic acinar cells. Color these cells and the secretion they produce when they are stimulated by CCK. Complete the picture, noting that the ingested fat is digested by the pancreatic enzymes that are secreted. Compare this figure with Fig. 1.10.*

The secretion of bicarbonate by the duct cells of the pancreas is regulated by the hormone secretin, which is released into the blood by endocrine cells in the duodenum in response to the acidity of the chyme. This release of HCO_3^- neutralizes H^+, restores the pH to about 7, and provides an environment that is favorable to digestive enzyme activity (Fig. 9.14).

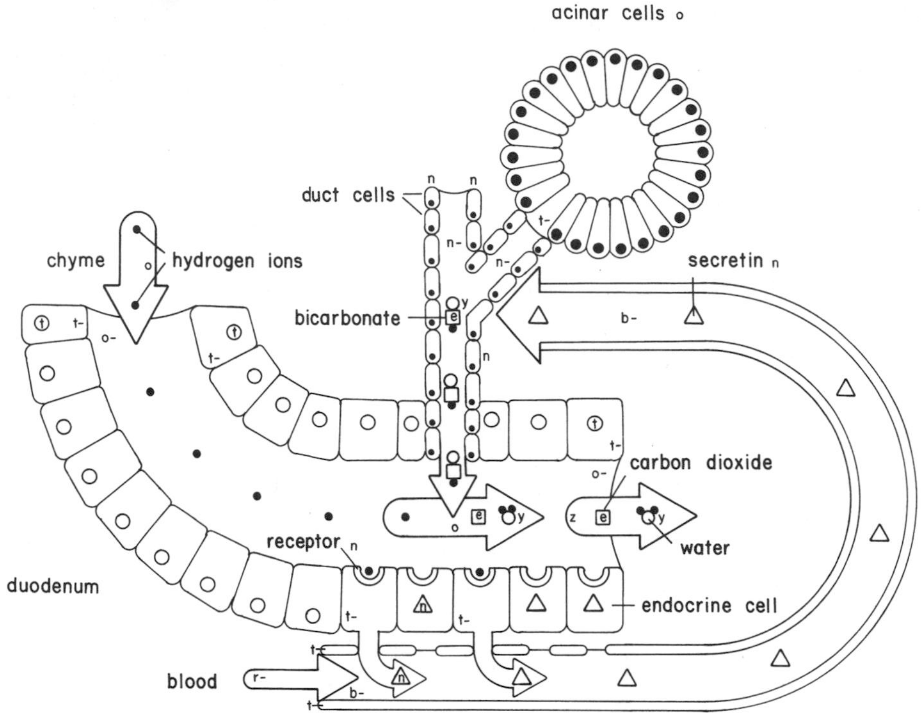

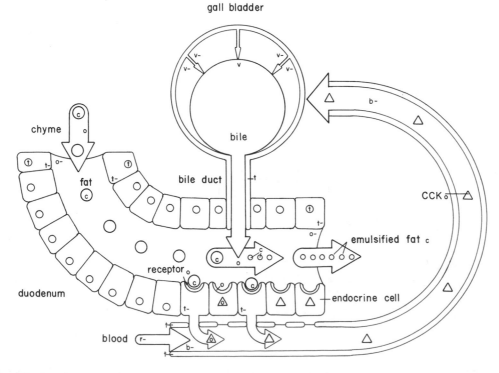

Figure 9.14 *Regulation of bicarbonate secretion. Color the entering acidic chyme, the acid receptors, and the cells of the duodenum. Color the hormone, secretin, that is released in response to receptor stimulation as you follow its path through the blood to the pancreatic duct cells. Color these cells and the secretion they produce when they are stimulated by secretin. Complete the picture, noting that the acid is neutralized by the bicarbonate. Compare this figure with Figs. 8.14 and 9.13.*

Bile secretion by the liver

The liver synthesizes bile, which is a mixture of bile salts, bile acids, cholesterol, phospholipids, fatty acids, and water. The gall bladder receives bile continuously from the liver, and stores and concentrates it. In response to the presence of fat, endocrine cells in the duodenum release cholecystokinin into the blood; CCK causes the gall bladder to contract and send bile through the bile duct into the duodenum (Fig. 9.15).

Figure 9.15 *Regulation of bile secretion. Color the entering fat droplets, their receptors, and the cells of the duodenum. Color the hormone, CCK, that is released in response to receptor stimulation, as you follow its path through the blood to the gall bladder. Color the gall bladder and the bile that is released when it is stimulated by CCK. Complete the picture, noting that the fat droplets are emulsified by the bile that is secreted. Compare this figure with Figs. 9.13 and 9.14.*

Intestinal secretions

Intestinal cells secrete a lubricating fluid and produce a number of digestive enzymes that carry out the final steps in the process of digestion. These enzymes remain attached to the cells that comprise the mucosal lining of the G.I. tract and digest nutrients near the cell surface.

Hydrolysis and condensation

The digestive enzymes break down the compounds in foods by hydrolysis, a reaction in which water is added at the bond to be broken, and OH becomes part of the product on one side of the bond, while H becomes part of the product on the other side (Fig. 9.16). Condensation, or dehydration synthesis, is the opposite reaction to hydrolysis; in condensation the two compounds are linked when OH is removed from one compound and H is removed from the other; in this process water is produced (Fig. 9.16).

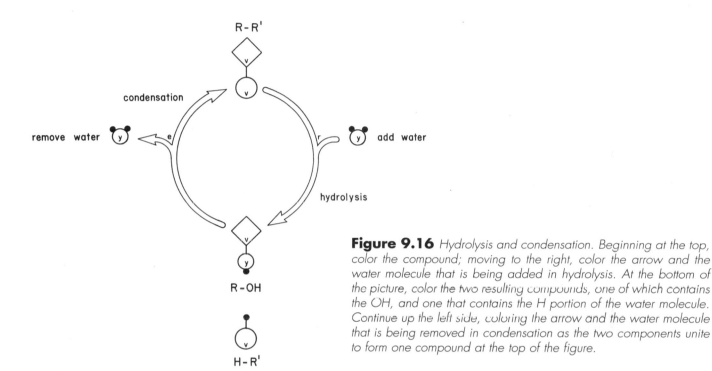

Figure 9.16 *Hydrolysis and condensation. Beginning at the top, color the compound; moving to the right, color the arrow and the water molecule that is being added in hydrolysis. At the bottom of the picture, color the two resulting compounds, one of which contains the OH, and one that contains the H portion of the water molecule. Continue up the left side, coloring the arrow and the water molecule that is being removed in condensation as the two components unite to form one compound at the top of the figure.*

Absorption

Most of the absorption in the G.I. tract occurs across the wall of the small intestine. Anatomical features of the small intestine that greatly increase the surface area for absorption include: 1) intestinal folds, 2) the villi, which are finger-like projections of the mucosa into the lumen, and 3) the microvilli, which are projections of the mucosal cell membrane into the lumen to form a brush border (Fig. 9.17). Of these anatomical features, the microvilli make the greatest contribution to increasing the area available for absorption (Fig. 9.18).

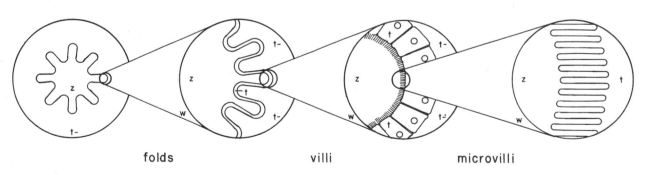

folds   villi   microvilli

Figure 9.17 *Folds, villi, and microvilli. Color the views of a cross-section of the G.I. tract that portray increasing magnification from left to right. Each feature increases the area of the mucosa that comes in contact with the contents of the lumen.*

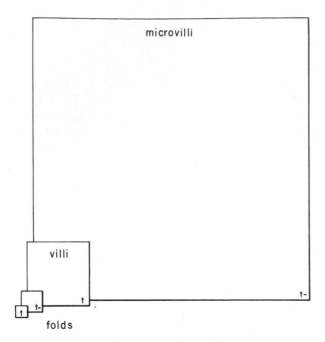

Figure 9.18 *Effects of folds, villi, and microvilli on surface area. Color the areas that correspond to the features shown in Fig. 9.17; compare the size of the smallest (straight tube, no adaptations) to the largest (all three features) surface area. Note that the microvilli make the largest relative contribution to increasing the surface area of the G.I. tract.*

Transport mechanisms for absorption

Digested materials in the lumen enter mucosal cells and exit them on the other side to enter the submucosa (Figs. 9.4, 9.19) by a variety of transport mechanisms. Water and lipids are absorbed by passive diffusion; many water-soluble vitamins are transported by facilitated diffusion; glucose is absorbed by sodium co-transport and amino acids are absorbed by active transport. The transport mechanism responsible for bringing substances into the mucosal cell from the lumen may differ from the mechanism that transports them out of the cell into the submucosa (Fig. 9.4).

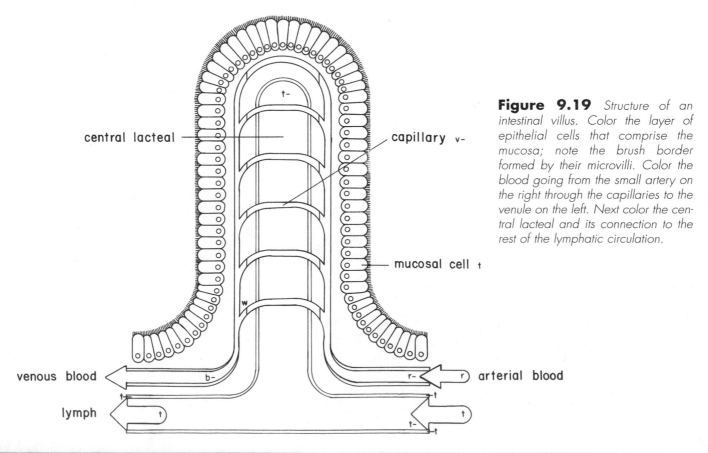

Figure 9.19 *Structure of an intestinal villus. Color the layer of epithelial cells that comprise the mucosa; note the brush border formed by their microvilli. Color the blood going from the small artery on the right through the capillaries to the venule on the left. Next color the central lacteal and its connection to the rest of the lymphatic circulation.*

Absorption of water

Water is absorbed through the mucosal cells by osmosis. The osmotic gradient is established by the absorption of other substances, especially sodium. Since large amounts of sodium are absorbed daily, it is responsible for much of the water absorption in the G.I. tract.

Most (about 80%) of water absorption occurs in the small intestine; this includes water from the meal plus water from G.I. secretions. Further water absorption occurs in the first half of the large intestine (Fig. 9.9). Feces normally contains less than 2% of the water entering the G.I. tract each day (Fig. 9.10).

Transport of water-soluble substances

Once water-soluble substances like glucose or amino acids pass through the mucosal cell, they enter capillaries that unite to form venules (Fig. 9.19) and ultimately join to form the hepatic portal vein, which brings blood to the liver (Fig. 9.20). This arrangement of blood vessels is known as a portal system, since arterial blood first enters one tissue (the intestine) and the venous blood from that tissue enters another tissue (the liver) before returning to the heart.

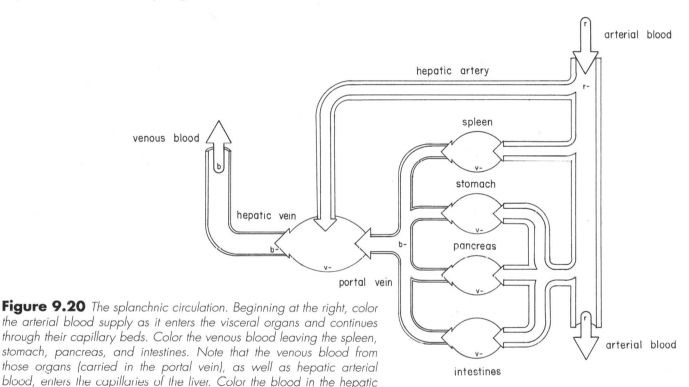

Figure 9.20 *The splanchnic circulation. Beginning at the right, color the arterial blood supply as it enters the visceral organs and continues through their capillary beds. Color the venous blood leaving the spleen, stomach, pancreas, and intestines. Note that the venous blood from those organs (carried in the portal vein), as well as hepatic arterial blood, enters the capillaries of the liver. Color the blood in the hepatic vein that returns blood from the liver to the heart.*

Thus, the absorbed nutrients first pass through the liver before they are distributed to other tissues by the general circulation (Fig. 9.20). The strategic location of the liver allows it to screen the newly absorbed, water-soluble compounds, thereby controlling blood levels of glucose, amino acids, water-soluble vitamins, and other substances.

Transport of fat-soluble substances

Since fat does not dissolve in water, fat-soluble substances must be packaged to allow them to be suspended in plasma. This packaging occurs in the mucosal cells, which form lipoprotein (lipid and protein) particles called chylomicrons, which will be described later.

These fat-containing particles do not enter the capillaries that bring blood to the villi but are instead taken up by lacteals, which are open-ended ducts of the lymphatic circulation (Fig. 9.19). The chylomicrons enter the blood when the fluid in the lymphatic vessels enters the general circulation at the left subclavian vein (Fig. 6.24). Since the movement of lymph is slow, it takes a few hours for dietary fat to appear in the blood after consumption of a meal. In contrast to water-soluble substances, absorbed fat does not first pass through the liver before entering the general circulation.

Nutrients

Nutrients are digestible substances in food that: 1) provide energy; 2) form the structures of the body; or 3) regulate metabolic processes. The six categories of nutrients are carbohydrates, fats, proteins, vitamins, minerals, and water; the first three are energy-providing nutrients and will be discussed here.

Chemistry of carbohydrates

Carbohydrates are organic compounds that have a ratio of one carbon atom (C) for each water molecule (H_2O). Carbohydrates include monosaccharides and disaccharides (collectively called sugars), and polysaccharides (starches, glycogen and dietary fiber); fruits, vegetables, and grains are the main sources of carbohydrate in the diet.

Sugars

The fundamental unit of carbohydrate is the monosaccharide; chemical formulas of the monosaccharides have the C:H:O proportion of 1:2:1. Glucose, fructose, and galactose are monosaccharides with six carbons; they all have the formula $C_6H_{12}O_6$.

Disaccharides consist of two monosaccharides that are connected to each other by the process of condensation (Fig. 9.16). The disaccharides include maltose, sucrose, and lactose. Maltose is comprised of two glucose molecules and is found in fermented grain products like beer; sucrose is comprised of glucose plus fructose and is found in fruit and in table sugar; and lactose is comprised of glucose plus galactose and is found in milk and dairy products.

Digestion of disaccharides

Disaccharides are digested by hydrolysis into their original monosaccharide components (Fig. 9.21). The disaccharidases, which are maltase, sucrase, and lactase, are enzymes made by mucosal cells in the small intestine. Maltase digests maltose, isomaltase digests isomaltose, [a disaccharide (glucose + glucose) formed in starch digestion], sucrase digests sucrose, and lactase digests lactose.

Inadequate production of the enzyme lactase is responsible for the common condition of lactose intolerance; undigested lactose from dairy products is fermented by intestinal bacteria, which causes the production of gas, discomfort, and diarrhea.

Polysaccharides

Polysaccharides consist of straight or branched chains of monosaccharides that are linked together by condensation. Starch, a class of polysaccharides found in plants, is composed of chains of glucose and is the major source of energy in most diets. Glycogen is a branched polysaccharide that is important in metabolism but not in the diet; it will be discussed in chapter 10.

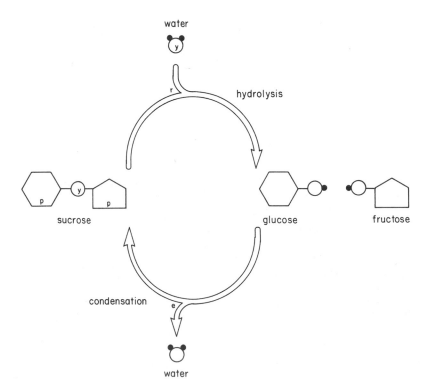

Figure 9.21 *Digestion of disaccharides. Color the sucrose molecule at left and continue clockwise with the arrow indicating hydrolysis. Color the water to be added and the two monosaccharides, glucose and fructose, that are formed. Note that the OH portion of the water molecule is added to one monosaccharide and the H portion of water is added to the other. Color the arrow for condensation and the water molecule that is removed. Note that condensation and hydrolysis are opposite reactions.*

Digestion of polysaccharides

Salivary amylase begins the hydrolysis of starch into shorter chains in the mouth and stomach (Fig. 9.22); the enzyme is soon deactivated by acid in the stomach. The chains of glucose are further hydrolyzed in the intestine by pancreatic amylase, which enters the duodenum at the pancreatic duct. The action of pancreatic amylase produces maltose and isomaltose; the latter is derived from starches whose glucose chains are branched. Maltose and isomaltose are hydrolyzed to glucose by intestinal maltase and isomaltase, respectively, as described above (Figs. 9.21, 9.23).

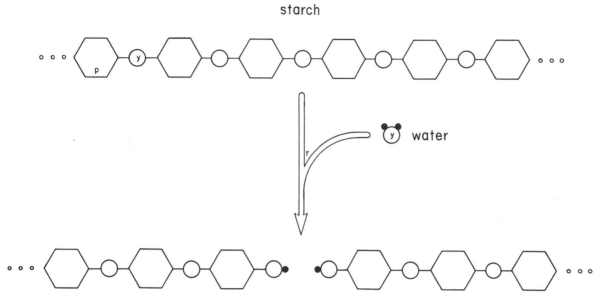

Figure 9.22 *Digestion of starch. Color the chain of glucose molecules that makes up the polysaccharide starch. Color the arrow indicating hydrolysis and the water molecule to be added. Complete the picture with the two shorter chains of glucose molecules that result from hydrolysis. Note that, as in Fig. 9.21, the water molecule is divided between the products.*

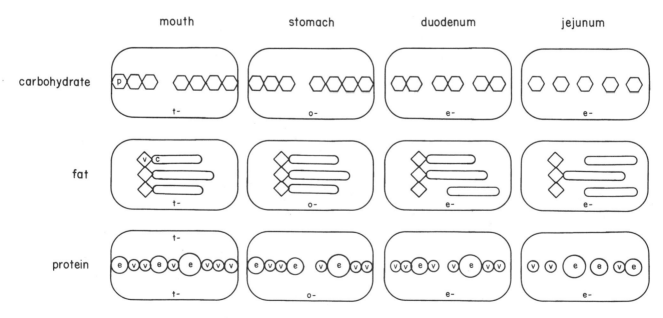

Figure 9.23 *Summary of nutrient digestion. For each class of nutrient, follow its row from left to right and color its forms at the stages of digestion observed in the mouth, stomach, duodenum, and jejunum. Finish the picture by coloring the backgrounds of the panels. Note that digestion of starch begins in the mouth, whereas digestion of protein begins in the stomach and that of fat in the duodenum. In the jejunum, digestion of all nutrients is virtually complete.*

Dietary fiber

Plants also contain an undigestible carbohydrate known as dietary fiber; the term dietary fiber also refers to lignin, a woody substance that is not carbohydrate but which contributes to plant structure. The linkage between glucose units in dietary fiber (e.g. cellulose) cannot be hydrolyzed by human gastrointestinal enzymes and so dietary fiber proceeds, undigested, through the G.I. tract, stimulating peristalsis as it stretches the intestinal wall (Fig. 9.7). The undigested material is partly fermented by bacteria in the ileum and colon, and it therefore promotes bacterial proliferation. These bacteria synthesize useful substances (for example, certain vitamins), and comprise about half of the fecal mass.

Absorption of carbohydrate

The monosaccharides that result from carbohydrate digestion, namely glucose, fructose, and galactose, enter the mucosal cells of the intestine by facilitated diffusion (fructose) and sodium co-transport (glucose and galactose) (Fig. 9.24). These monosaccharides pass through the mucosal cell and enter the capillaries (Fig.

9.19); the venous blood then transports them via the hepatic portal vein to the liver (Fig. 9.20).

The liver greatly alters the carbohydrate composition of the blood it receives. It converts galactose to glucose, converts fructose to glucose or fat, and stores a portion of glucose as glycogen. Therefore, the blood leaving the liver for the general circulation contains a lower level of glucose and virtually no galactose or fructose.

Chemistry of fats

The basic unit of dietary fat is the fatty acid, which consists of a straight chain of carbon (units of CH_2 linked together) with a carboxyl group (COOH) at one end. The length of the carbon chain, as well as the number and placement of carbon-to-carbon double bonds, differs among fatty acids. Saturated fatty acids have no carbon-to-carbon double bonds; monounsaturated fatty acids have one double bond and polyunsaturated fatty acids have two or more double bonds (Fig. 9.25). For example, butyric acid in butter is a short chain (4 carbons), saturated fatty acid, and linoleic acid in corn oil is a long chain (18 carbons) polyunsaturated fatty acid.

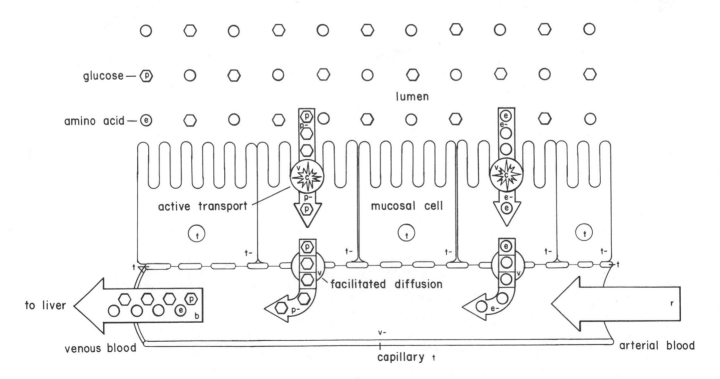

Figure 9.24 *Absorption of glucose and amino acids. Color the molecules of glucose, the mucosal cells, and the capillary blood. Next color the transport arrows and the energy flashes. Follow the molecules of glucose and amino acids through their respective transport systems as they enter the mucosal cells and then exit into the blood. Note that energy is required for the sodium co-transport mechanism that brings glucose into the mucosal cell and for the primary active transport mechanism that brings in amino acids. Color the large arrows that indicate blood flow and note the differences between the arterial and venous blood concentrations of glucose and amino acids.*

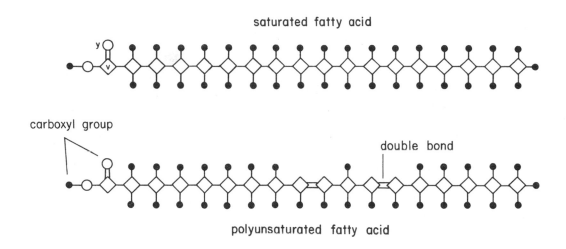

saturated fatty acid

carboxyl group

double bond

polyunsaturated fatty acid

Figure 9.25 *Structure of fatty acids. Color the carbon (diamonds) and oxygen (open circles) atoms that comprise the two fatty acids. Note the carboxyl group (COOH) at the left end of each. Note also that the polyunsaturated fatty acid (linoleic acid) has double bonds between its carbons at two locations (position 6 and position 9 from the right); at these carbon-to-carbon double bonds, a hydrogen atom has been removed from each of the participating carbon atoms. In contrast, the saturated fatty acid (stearic acid) has no missing hydrogen atoms; it is "saturated" with hydrogen.*

In foods and in adipose (fat storage) tissue, fatty acids are mainly found as triglycerides, which are also called triacylglycerols. Triglycerides are composed of three fatty acids attached by condensation to a glycerol mol-ecule, which is a three-carbon alcohol derived from glu-cose. The bond between each fatty acid and the glyc-erol molecule is called an ester linkage (Fig. 9.26).

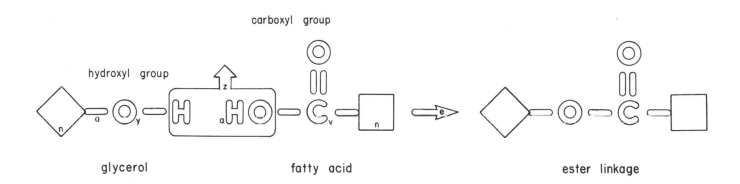

carboxyl group

hydroxyl group

glycerol

fatty acid

ester linkage

Figure 9.26 *Ester linkage. Color the portion of the glycerol molecule shown, noting its hydroxyl group (OH). Color the portion of the fatty acid shown, noting its carboxyl group (COOH). Color the region depicting the water that is removed. Finish the picture by coloring the arrow that indicates the process of esterification and the ester linkage that is formed between the glycerol and fatty acid. Since each glycerol molecule has three hydroxyl groups, it can make ester linkages with three fatty acids, thereby forming a triglyceride.*

Digestion of fat

The fat we ingest melts into large globules in the stomach. The interior of these globules is inaccessible to water-soluble substances, such as enzymes. Digestion of fat, therefore, requires that it be put into a form in which it can come into contact with digestive enzymes, mainly pancreatic lipase. When bile is released by the gall bladder, it divides the fat in the duodenum into smaller particles which then have a greater surface area exposed to the enzymes in the watery medium of the intestinal lumen (Fig. 9.15). This process is called emulsification.

Bile salts, bile acids, phospholipids, and cholesterol in bile have both lipophilic (lipid-soluble) and hydrophilic (water-soluble) regions (Fig. 9.27) and can therefore function as emulsifiers by orienting themselves so that the lipophilic portion is positioned in the fat globule and the hydrophilic portion is positioned in the watery fluid of the intestinal lumen. This bridging of fat and water disrupts the surface tension of the fat globules, which causes them to break into smaller droplets and allows them to remain suspended in the intestinal fluid.

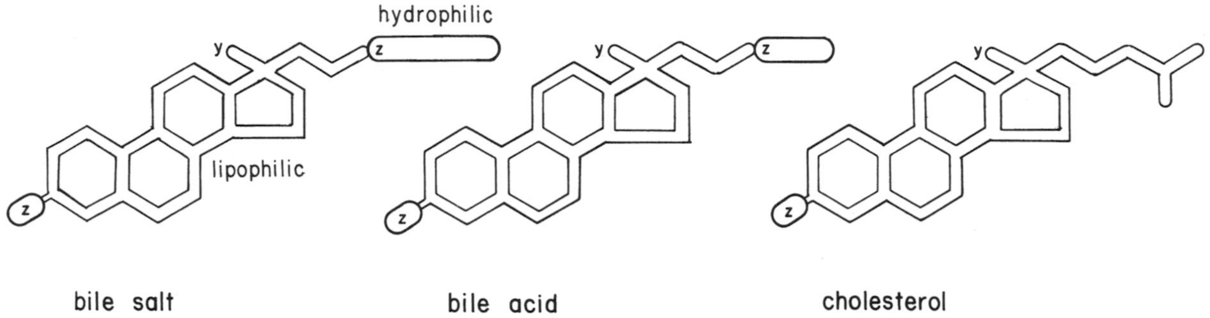

bile salt   bile acid   cholesterol

Figure 9.27 *Constituents of bile. Color the lipophilic and hydrophilic portions of the three compounds. Notice that bile acids and bile salts are derivatives of cholesterol. Compare the sizes of their hydrophilic portions and predict which would be best able to partition itself between fat and water layers; that is, which would be the best emulsifier. Bile contains these compounds as well as phospholipids, fatty acids, water, and various waste products, such as bile pigments.*

Pancreatic lipase hydrolyzes triglyceride into two fatty acids plus a monoglyceride, which is a glycerol with one fatty acid attached (Fig. 9.28). These digestion products are themselves not very soluble in water; they spontaneously aggregate with the bile to form micelles, which are small particles that can travel through the watery contents of the lumen to the membranes of the mucosal cells (Fig. 9.29).

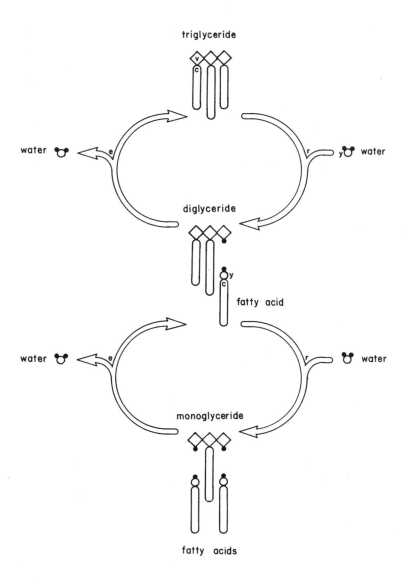

triglyceride

water

water

diglyceride

fatty acid

water

water

monoglyceride

fatty acids

Figure 9.28 *Digestion of triglycerides. Beginning at the top of the figure, color the 3-carbon glycerol portion and fatty acid portions of all molecules. Going downward on the right side, color the arrows that indicate lipolysis (hydrolysis) and the water molecules that are added. Going upward on the left side, color the arrows indicating esterification and the water molecules that are removed. Note that first a diglyceride (two fatty acids) and then a monoglyceride (one fatty acid) are formed in lipolysis of a triglyceride.*

Figure 9.29 *A micelle. Color the lipid center of the particle; color the hydrophilic portions of cholesterol, bile acids, bile salts, and phospholipids that protrude into the water layer. These hydrophilic groups permit the micelle to travel through the watery lumen of the G.I. tract to the mucosal cell membranes. Note that the lipophilic portions of these compounds are embedded in the lipid droplet. The hydrophilic portions on the outside of the particle prevent separate micelles from coalescing into a single, larger droplet.*

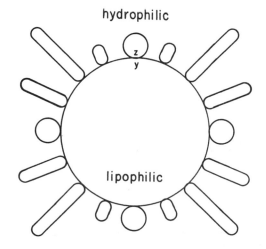

hydrophilic

lipophilic

Absorption of fat

Fatty acids, monoglycerides, phospholipids, and cholesterol diffuse into the mucosal cell. Within the cell, triglycerides are reformed from fatty acids and monoglycerides and packaged into a type of lipoprotein particle called a chylomicron (Fig. 9.30). Lipoprotein particles contain triglyceride at their center and are surrounded by a layer of cholesterol and phospholipid and covered on the surface by specific proteins.

The chylomicron leaves the mucosal cell by exocytosis and then enters the lymphatic circulation via an open-ended duct called a lacteal (Fig. 9.19), and eventually enters the general circulation (Fig. 6.24). Dietary fat is removed from the chylomicron by adipose tissue and is stored as triglyceride (chapter 10).

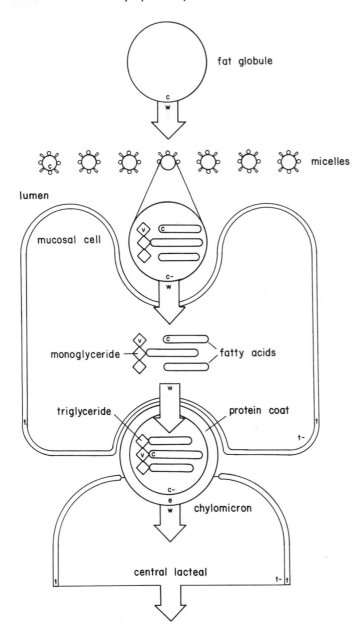

Figure 9.30 *Absorption of fat. Beginning at the top, color the fat globule and the micelles that are magnified to show the monoglyceride plus two fatty acids produced by digestion. Follow the monoglyceride and fatty acids into the mucosal cell and color them and the new triglyceride formed from them. Color the protein coat and other interior lipid components of the chylomicron into which the triglyceride is repackaged. Beginning at the top, follow the arrows, which indicate first the formation of the micelle, then the entry of the digested fat into the mucosal cell, its incorporation into the chylomicron, exocytosis of the chylomicron, and finally the flow of the lymph containing the chylomicron. Complete the picture by coloring the mucosal cell, the membranes, and the central lacteal.*

Chemistry of protein

The basic unit of protein is the amino acid (Fig. 9.31), which is defined as a compound which contains an amino group (NH_2) and a carboxyl group (COOH) on either side of a central (alpha) carbon; one of the remaining bonds from the alpha carbon is to H and the other bond is to a group that is specific to the identity of the particular amino acid. For example, the amino acid phenylalanine has a benzene ring, and alanine bears a methyl group.

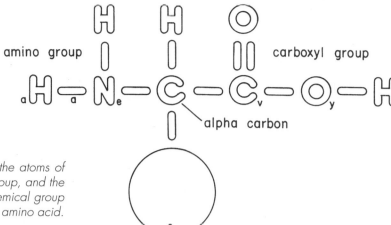

Figure 9.31 *Structure of an amino acid. Color the atoms of the amino acid; note the alpha carbon, the amino group, and the carboxyl group. Color the circle representing the chemical group and note that it differs according to the identity of the amino acid.*

There are 20 amino acids that are important in the diet because they are needed for human protein synthesis. Amino acids are linked through condensation; the linkages are called peptide bonds (Fig. 9.32).

In the diet, an enormous variety of proteins are found, since these are the structures and enzymes of the plant and animal tissues that are consumed. It is crucial that these intact proteins do not enter the body and act as enzymes and hormones that would alter our body functions. The breakdown of proteins into their constituent amino acids provides our body with the material needed for the construction of its own specific proteins.

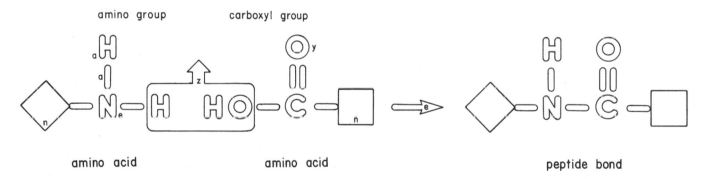

Figure 9.32 *Peptide bond. Color the atoms that make up the portions of the individual amino acids on the left side of the arrow; note the amino group of one and the carboxyl group of the other. Color the region that represents the water that is removed as these groups are joined. Next color the arrow that indicates the formation of the peptide bond and the dipeptide that results.*

Digestion of protein

Protein digestion breaks down dietary proteins to their constituent amino acids by hydrolyzing their peptide bonds (Fig. 9.33). Protein digestion begins in the stomach when Hydrochloric acid changes the shape of proteins, transforming pepsinogen into pepsin, which then hydrolyzes protein into shorter chains of amino acids. In the intestine, the active enzymes trypsin, chymotrypsin, and carboxypeptidase digest these chains into tripeptides (three amino acids), dipeptides (two amino acids), and single amino acids. Tripeptidases and dipeptidases produced by intestinal mucosal cells can hydrolyze tripeptides and dipeptides into single amino acids (Figs. 9.23, 9.33).

Absorption of protein

Amino acids are absorbed through the process of active transport by at least six carrier proteins, with different amino acids competing for transport by the same proteins (Fig. 9.24). Amino acids leave the mucosal cell and enter the capillaries (Fig. 9.19), which lead to the portal vein, carrying blood to the liver (Fig 9.20).

The liver removes about 80% of the amino acids absorbed from a meal and converts them to other nitrogen-containing compounds (e.g., creatine), incorporates them into blood proteins (e.g. albumin), and uses some as a source of energy. Therefore, the blood leaving the liver for the general circulation has a lower concentration of amino acids than the blood coming from the G.I. tract.

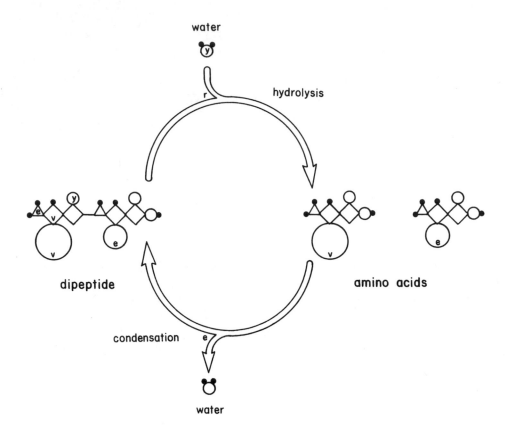

Figure 9.33 *Digestion of dipeptides. Color the amino acids that comprise the dipeptide and identify the peptide bond. Color the arrow indicating hydrolysis and the water molecule to be added. Complete the picture by coloring the individual amino acids that result. Note that, as in Fig. 9.32, it is an amino group on one side of the dipeptide and a carboxyl group on the other side that are involved in the reaction. Nitrogen is indicated by an open triangle.*

chapter **ten**
metabolism

Metabolism refers to the entire system of enzyme-cat-alyzed reactions in which matter and energy are exchanged between the cell and its environment. Its two aspects are anabolism, the building of compounds, which requires the addition of energy, and catabolism, the breakdown of compounds, which is accompanied by the release of energy (Fig.10.1).

Energy sources

The major sources of energy in the body are carbohy-drates, fats and proteins. These fuels contain chemical energy in the form of carbon-to-hydrogen bonds. Metabolic pathways release the energy in these fuels in a discrete, step-wise fashion, and capture it in the form of the high-energy bonds of ATP (adenosine triphos-phate). The various energy-requiring functions in the body (e.g., active transport, muscle contraction, and the synthesis of cellular structures) all use the energy stored in ATP; therefore, ATP can be regarded as the body's energy currency.

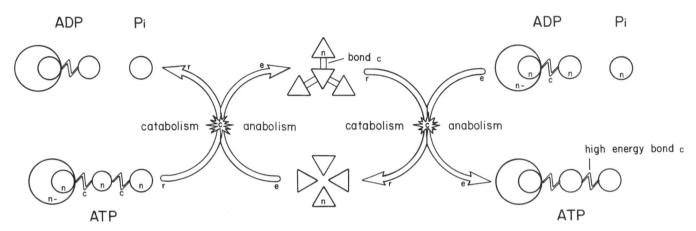

Figure 10.1 *Anabolism and catabolism. Begin at the lower left: color the molecule of ATP, the upward arrow and the flash that indicates the breaking of the high-energy bond of ATP. Color the resulting molecules of ADP and inorganic phosphate (Pi). Note the canary lines that symbolize the high energy bonds. In the middle panel, color the intact molecule, its bonds, and the breakdown products below it; color the arrow at its left indicating anabolism, the arrow at its right indicating catabolism, and the flash indi-cating the release of its bond energy. In the right panel, color the ADP, Pi, and ATP molecules and the arrow indicating the forma-tion of a high-energy bond in ATP. Note that the energy needed to build a compound can be derived from the breakdown of ATP and that the energy needed to synthesize ATP can be derived from the breakdown of a compound.*

Metabolism of carbohydrates

The form of carbohydrate that is found in the general circulation and is used by all cells is glucose, a 6-car-bon sugar (Fig. 10.2). Although the monosaccharides galactose and fructose are absorbed, they are convert-ed to other compounds (mainly glucose) by the liver before they enter the general circulation (Fig. 9.20). Glucose is unique among the metabolic fuels in that it is the only fuel that is normally used by the brain. For this reason, adequate levels of blood glucose must be main-tained.

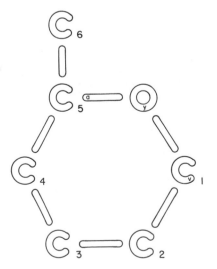

Figure 10.2 *Glucose molecule. Color the carbon and oxygen atoms and the bonds between them. Note that the carbons are numbered, and that the six-sided glucose molecule has oxygen in its ring while carbon number 6 lies outside the ring.*

Glucose is taken up by most cells through the process of facilitated diffusion; in muscle and adipose tissue this process is stimulated by the hormone insulin. When glucose enters a cell, a phosphate group from ATP is added to the glucose molecule; this process is called phosphorylation (Fig. 10.3). The compound that is formed, glucose 6-phosphate, cannot leave the cell; it is in this form that glucose enters metabolic pathways, where it is either used for energy or stored for use later.

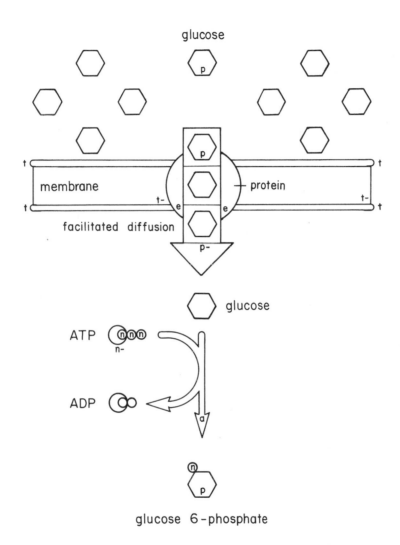

Figure 10.3 *Phosphorylation of glucose. Color the glucose molecules (hexagons) outside of the cell, the cell membrane, the transport protein, and the diffusion arrow. Color the glucose molecules that are transported through the cell membrane by facilitated diffusion. Color the glucose molecule in the cell, the molecules of ATP and ADP, the arrows denoting the phosphorylation reaction, and the product of the reaction, glucose 6-phosphate. Note that a phosphate group from ATP is added to a glucose molecule to form glucose 6-phosphate.*

Glycogen synthesis

Glucose is stored in cells as glycogen; liver and skeletal muscle contain the largest amounts of glycogen. Glycogen is a polysaccharide that is made up of branched chains of glucose molecules (Fig. 10.4); it is synthesized in the following way. Units of glucose 6-phosphate are converted to UDP-glucose (uridine diphosphate-glucose) by a transferal of the phosphate group to carbon number 1 and then its replacement by UDP (uridine diphosphate) (Fig. 10.5). The subsequent breakage of the bond between UDP and glucose provides the energy that is needed to add the glucose molecule to one of the many branches of an existing glycogen molecule.

Since this process is catalyzed by the enzyme glycogen synthase, glycogen synthesis is controlled by regulating the activity of this enzyme. For example, glycogen synthase activity is stimulated by the high insulin levels that follow the consumption of a meal (Fig. 11. 17).

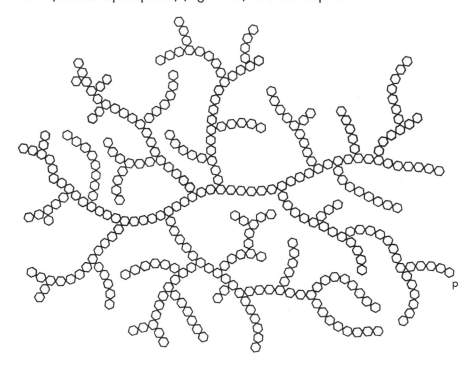

Figure 10.4 *Structure of glycogen. Color the glucose molecules that make up this molecule of glycogen; note the many branches.*

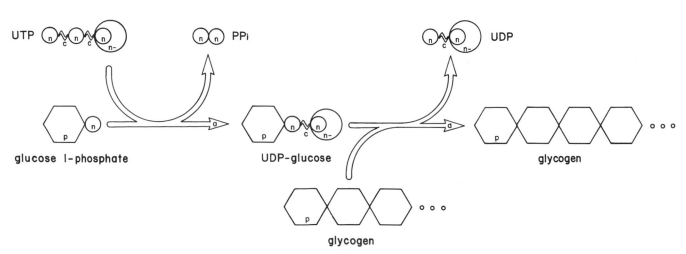

Figure 10.5 *Glycogen synthesis. Begin at left and color the molecules of glucose 1-phosphate, UTP, pyrophosphate (PPi), and UDP-glucose, and the arrow that indicates the reaction in which UDP is added, thereby displacing the existing phosphate group on glucose 1-phosphate. Next color the portion of the glycogen molecule below it, the arrows indicating addition of the glucose molecule, and the UDP which is released. Finally, color the portion of the glycogen molecule that has grown by one unit of glucose.*

Glycogenolysis

When the need for glucose increases, as happens during exercise or long after a meal, units of glucose are removed from the ends of the many branches of glycogen. This catabolic process is called glycogenolysis, which means the breakdown of glycogen. The enzyme glycogen phosphorylase removes glucose molecules by the process of phosphorolysis. Phosphorolysis is similar to hydrolysis (Fig. 9.16) except that it breaks bonds by adding a phosphate group instead of water across a bond (Fig. 10.6). Glycogen phosphorylase activity is stimulated by hormones that are released into the blood during exercise (Fig. 11.19) or when blood levels of glucose are low (Fig. 11.18).

Glycogenolysis produces units of glucose 1-phosphate (Fig. 10.6), which are quickly converted to glucose 6-phosphate; this causes the glycogen molecule to decrease in size. The molecules of glucose 6-phosphate can enter the pathway of glycolysis (see below), where some of their energy can be captured to form molecules of ATP.

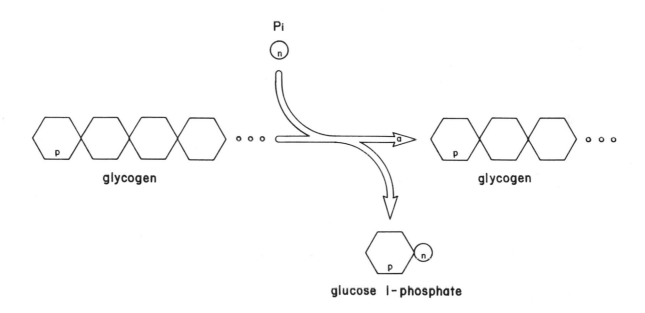

Figure 10.6 *Glycogenolysis. Color the glycogen molecule at the left, the phosphate group that is being added, the arrows indicating phosphorolysis, and the molecule of glucose 1-phosphate that is released. Finally, color the glycogen molecule that has been shortened by one unit of glucose.*

Glycogenolysis in liver and muscle

In the liver, the enzyme glucose 6-phosphatase can remove the phosphate group from glucose 6-phosphate. This enables the glucose molecule to leave the liver cell and enter the general circulation, causing blood levels of glucose to rise. Glycogen in the liver, therefore, can serve as a source of glucose for other tissues (Fig. 10.7).

In contrast, glucose that is produced by glycogenolysis in skeletal muscle does not leave the cell because the enzyme glucose 6-phosphatase is not present in muscle; consequently, glucose 6-phosphate must be metabolized within the muscle cell. For this reason, glycogen in muscle cannot serve as a source of glucose for other tissues.

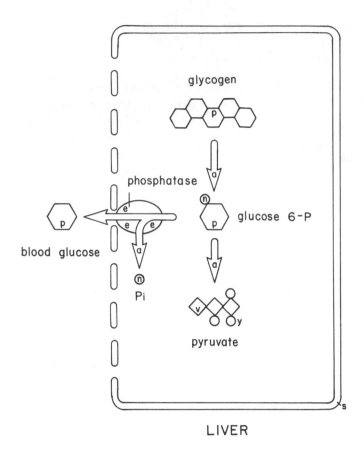

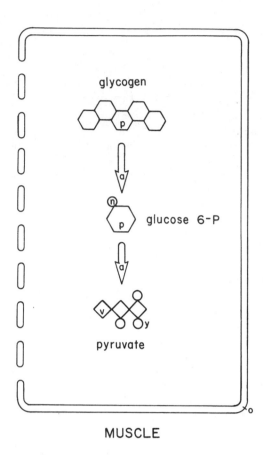

LIVER   MUSCLE

Figure 10.7 *Glycogenolysis in liver and muscle. In both panels, color the glycogen molecules at the top, the downward arrows indicating glycogenolysis, and the units of glucose 6-phosphate that are produced by glycogenolysis. Color the other downward arrows that indicate glycolysis and the 3-carbon molecules of pyruvate that are produced. In the panel at the left, also color the enzyme glucose 6-phosphatase, the arrow indicating the removal of the phosphate by the enzyme, and the arrow indicating that the glucose molecule can leave the cell after its phosphate has been removed. Color the phosphate group that is removed, the glucose molecule in the blood, and the cell membranes. Compare the two panels and consider the fates of glucose derived from glycogen in liver and muscle. Note that carbon is indicated by a diamond and oxygen by an open circle.*

Glycolysis

Glycolysis is a catabolic pathway that operates in the cytoplasm of all cells. Glycolysis is the only energy-yielding pathway that does not require oxygen; that is, it is anaerobic. Although glucose is the main compound that is metabolized by glycolysis, fructose from the diet and glycerol that is released during the breakdown of triglycerides (see below) are also both metabolized by this pathway in the liver.

In the first step of glycolysis, glucose is converted to glucose 6-phosphate (Fig. 10.3); note that the glucose 6-phosphate that is produced by glycogenolysis (Fig. 10.6) also enters glycolysis. The 6-carbon glucose molecule is split into two 3-carbon units and each of the units is converted to a molecule of the 3-carbon compound pyruvic acid. Pyruvic acid is often referred to as

pyruvate, which is the form in which the hydrogen ion is dissociated from the acid. The conversion of these 3-carbon units to pyruvic acid is an oxidative process; one in which electrons are removed. Since the proton from a hydrogen atom follows the electron that is removed, oxidation ultimately involves the removal of hydrogen atoms.

Hydrogen carriers

The hydrogen atoms that are removed during glycolysis are picked up by the coenzyme NAD (nicotinamide adenine dinucleotide, or NAD^+, which bears a positive charge). Coenzymes are organic compounds that perform various functions that are necessary for an enzyme to catalyze a reaction, such as temporarily binding to chemical groups that are being passed from one compound to another.

The coenzymes that carry hydrogen atoms are synthesized from vitamins, which are organic compounds that are required in the diet in small amounts. NAD⁺ is made from the vitamin niacin and FAD (flavin adenine dinucleotide) is made from the vitamin riboflavin. Coenzyme A, which transports a 2-carbon acetyl group to the Krebs cycle (see below), is made from the vitamin pantothenic acid. A deficiency of vitamins can lead to an inadequate production of coenzymes and a corresponding reduction in the activity of metabolic pathways that employ them.

NAD^+ picks up two hydrogen atoms at a time, during the steps of glycolysis (Fig. 10.8). This process is called reduction; $NADH + H^+$ is the reduced form of NAD^+. The hydrogen atoms that are carried by $NADH + H^+$ are then transferred to other compounds.

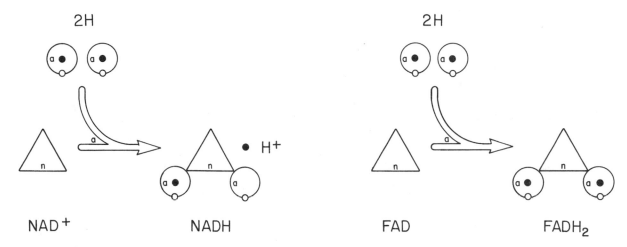

Figure 10.8 *Hydrogen carriers. In both panels, color the coenzymes NAD⁺ and FAD, the two hydrogen atoms that are being added in each reaction, and the arrows that indicate this addition. At left, color the NADH + H⁺ that is produced, noting the extra proton (H⁺) that remains when the two hydrogen atoms are added to NAD⁺. At right, color the FADH₂ that results from the addition of two hydrogen atoms to FAD.*

Anaerobic metabolism

Under anaerobic conditions, the hydrogen atoms that are carried by NADH + H⁺ are donated to pyruvic acid, which then becomes lactic acid, also referred to as lactate (Fig. 10.9). This mechanism enables NADH + H⁺ to become NAD⁺ again, which can then pick up more of the hydrogen atoms that are produced by glycolysis. This recycling of NADH + H⁺ to NAD⁺ through the production of lactic acid is an important step that enables glycolysis to continue under anaerobic conditions.

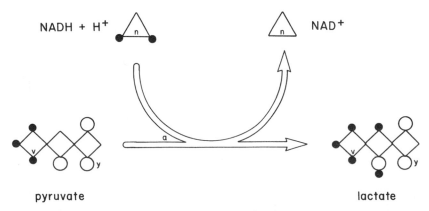

Figure 10.9 *Anaerobic recycling of NADH + H⁺ into NAD⁺. Color the molecule of pyruvate that was produced by glycolysis, NADH + H⁺, NAD⁺ and the molecule of lactate. Color the arrows showing that NADH + H⁺ donates two hydrogen atoms (filled circles) to pyruvate. Note that lactate differs from pyruvate only by the addition of these hydrogen atoms and that NAD⁺ has been regenerated by the reaction.*

The lactic acid that is produced during anaerobic metabolism diffuses out of the cell and into the blood where it can be taken up by cardiac muscle and used as fuel, or taken up by the liver and converted to glucose (see below).

Under aerobic conditions, lactic acid is not formed because NADH + H$^+$ donates its hydrogen atoms to the electron transport chain in the mitochondria, where energy is extracted from the hydrogen atoms and stored in the high-energy bonds of ATP (see below).

Gluconeogenesis

Glucose can be produced from non-carbohydrate substances by the energy-consuming pathway of gluconeogenesis, which means the "new creation of glucose." This pathway for the production of glucose is utilized when the breakdown of glycogen does not supply enough glucose to meet the needs of the brain or exercising muscle. The raw materials for gluconeogenesis are: 1) pyruvic acid, which can be derived from lactic acid or amino acids, 2) portions of amino acids, or 3) glycerol.

When an amino acid loses its amino group (Fig. 9.31), the portion that remains is called its carbon skeleton. Carbon skeletons can be used as an energy source, either by their direct consumption in metabolic pathways or by their conversion to glucose in the pathway of gluconeogenesis (Fig. 10.20). Glucose may also be produced from the glycerol that is released from adipose tissue when stored triglycerides are broken down into glycerol and fatty acids, in the process of lipolysis (Fig. 10.15).

For the most part, gluconeogenesis is the reverse of glycolysis. However, three of the steps of glycolysis are not reversible. In gluconeogenesis the reverse reactions for these steps are catalyzed by enzymes other than those that are involved in glycolysis. The fact that glycolysis does not operate in both directions means that glycolysis and gluconeogenesis are controlled separately and, although glycolysis is found in all tissues, gluconeogenesis only occurs in the liver (the exception is that during starvation it is also active in the kidney). The liver can release the glucose that it synthesizes by gluconeogenesis into the blood for use by other tissues (Fig. 10.7).

Cori cycle

During strenuous exercise, a considerable amount of lactic acid is produced by anaerobic metabolism in muscle cells; this lactic acid diffuses out of the muscle cells and into the general circulation. The liver can convert lactate to glucose through gluconeogenesis and release the glucose back into the blood; this process consumes energy. This mechanism, which is called the Cori cycle, provides muscle with a supply of glucose that enables it to continue to function anaerobically (Fig. 10.10).

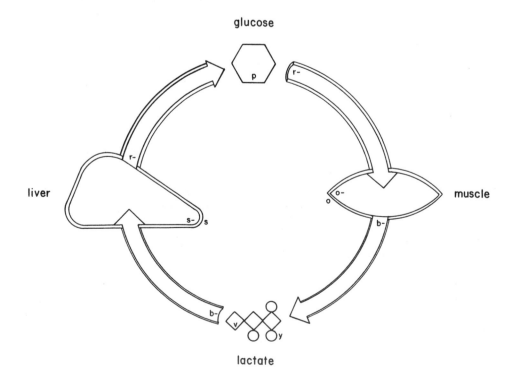

glucose

liver

muscle

lactate

Figure 10.10 *Cori cycle. Begin by coloring the glucose molecule at the top of the figure and continue clockwise, coloring the arterial blood that transports glucose to muscle and the subsequent release of lactate into venous blood. Color the molecule of lactate and the arrows indicating its transport to the liver, and then its conversion to glucose by gluconeogenesis. Complete the picture by coloring the liver and muscle. Note that the Cori cycle regenerates the glucose that was used anaerobically by muscle and therefore provides fuel that enables muscle to continue to function under anaerobic conditions. This process costs energy.*

Krebs cycle

All fuels can ultimately be converted to a form that can enter the Krebs cycle, which is the major energy-yielding pathway. The 3-carbon compound pyruvic acid that is produced by glycolysis can, in the mitochondria, lose one of its carbons as carbon dioxide to become a 2-carbon acetyl group that binds with coenzyme A. This is a one-way reaction that converts pyruvic acid to acetyl CoA, which can enter the Krebs cycle.

The Krebs cycle (Fig. 10.11) is an aerobic pathway that takes place in the mitochondria. In this pathway, the acetyl group undergoes a series of oxidations; its hydrogen atoms are picked up by the coenzymes NAD⁺ and FAD, which then become NADH + H⁺ and FADH$_2$, respectively (Fig. 10.8). The hydrogen atoms that are carried by NADH + H⁺ and FADH$_2$ (Fig 10.12) are transported to the electron transport chain (see below) where some of their energy is captured and stored in the high-energy bonds of ATP.

In the first reaction of the Krebs cycle, the 2-carbon acetyl group attaches to oxaloacetic acid (a 4-carbon compound derived from glucose), and forms citric acid, a 6-carbon molecule. The acetyl group is completely oxidized in subsequent reactions of the cycle to two molecules of carbon dioxide that diffuse out of the mitochondria and into the blood (Fig. 8.1). With each turn of the Krebs cycle, two molecules of carbon dioxide are produced, four pairs of hydrogen atoms are removed, and oxaloacetic acid is regenerated (Fig. 10.11).

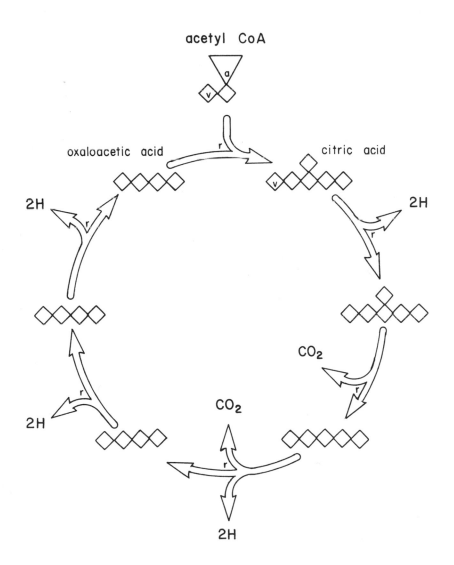

Figure 10.11 *Krebs cycle. Begin at the top by coloring the molecule of acetyl CoA that is entering the cycle; work clockwise as you color and count the carbon molecules (diamonds). Note that the 2-carbon acetyl group combines with the 4-carbon oxaloacetic acid to become the 6-carbon compound citric acid. Complete the picture by coloring the arrows at each step. Note the pairs of hydrogen atoms (2H) and the molecules of CO_2 that are removed in the process. Note also that citric acid loses two carbons as CO_2, that 8 hydrogen atoms are removed, and that oxaloacetic acid is regenerated at the completion of the cycle.*

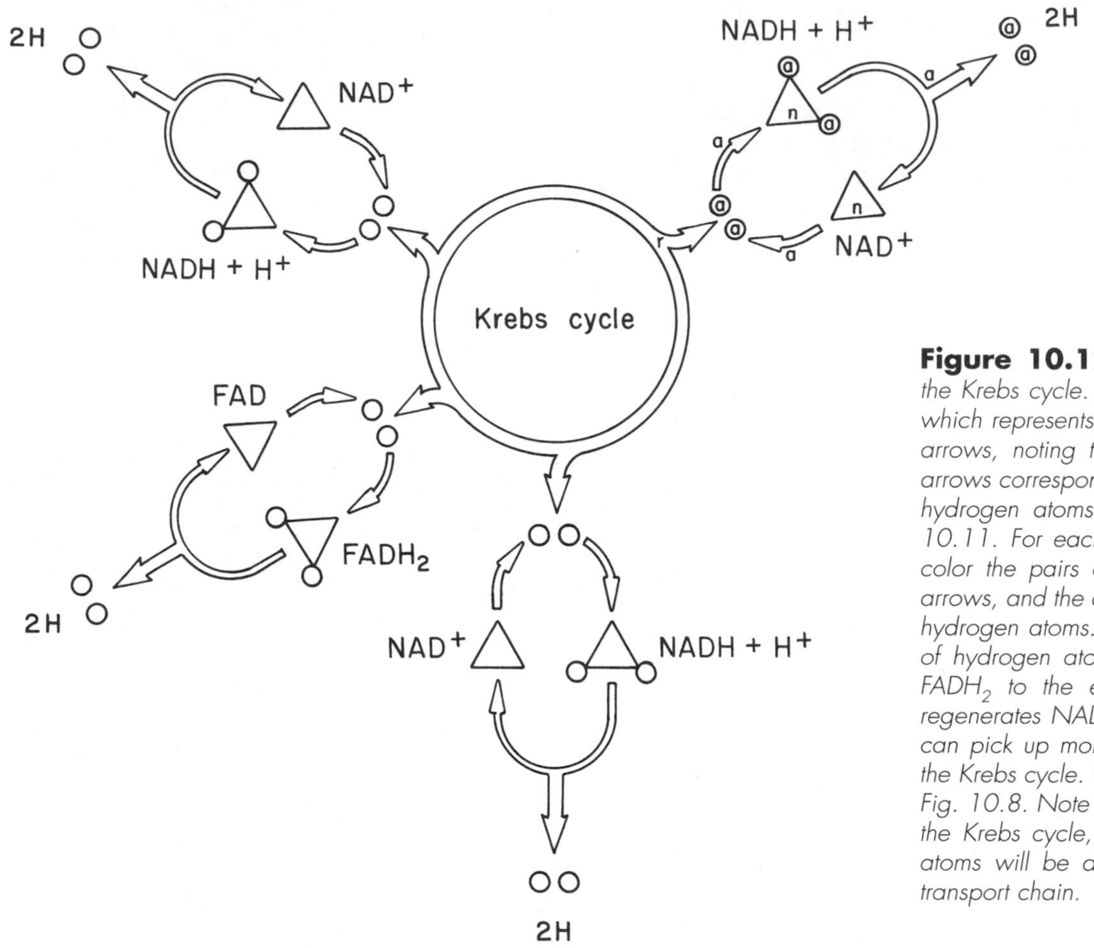

Figure 10.12 *Hydrogen carriers in the Krebs cycle. Color the central circle, which represents the Krebs cycle, and its arrows, noting that the positions of the arrows correspond to the positions where hydrogen atoms were removed in Fig. 10.11. For each position on the cycle, color the pairs of hydrogen atoms, the arrows, and the coenzymes that carry the hydrogen atoms. Note that the donation of hydrogen atoms by NADH + H+ or FADH$_2$ to the electron transport chain regenerates NAD+ and FAD so that they can pick up more hydrogen atoms from the Krebs cycle. Compare this figure with Fig. 10.8. Note also that for each turn of the Krebs cycle, four pairs of hydrogen atoms will be delivered to the electron transport chain.*

Electron transport chain

The hydrogen atoms that are removed in glycolysis and in the Krebs cycle are carried by NADH + H+ and FADH$_2$ to the inner mitochondrial membrane, where they are separated into their constituent electrons and protons (see below). A series of protein complexes, called cytochromes, that together are known as the electron transport chain, is situated within the inner mitochondrial membrane (Fig. 10.13). These compounds, which alternately function as electron donors and recipients, are ordered in such a way that the compound with the strongest tendency to lose electrons is at the beginning of the sequence and the compound with the strongest tendency to accept electrons is at the end. The compound that donates electrons at the beginning of the chain is NADH + H+ and the compound that accepts them at the end is oxygen. For this reason, the electron transport chain is an aerobic pathway and will not function in the absence of oxygen.

As electrons are passed down the electron transport

chain, they lose much of their energy. Part of this energy is captured and used to form the high-energy bonds of ATP in a process called oxidative phosphorylation; the remaining energy is released as heat. The proposed mechanism through which the electron transport chain synthesizes ATP is as follows.

Since the inner mitochondrial membrane is impermeable to protons, only the electrons from the hydrogen atoms enter the electron transport chain in the inner mitochondrial membrane, while the protons remain in the matrix (Fig. 10.13). The electrons are passed from one cytochrome to the next and some energy is released at each step. At three sites in the electron transport chain, the energy that is released is used to actively transport two protons across the inner mitochondrial membrane into the space between the inner and outer membranes. This produces a concentration gradient (due to the unequal distribution of protons) and an electrical gradient (due to unequal distributions of the positive charges) across the inner membrane.

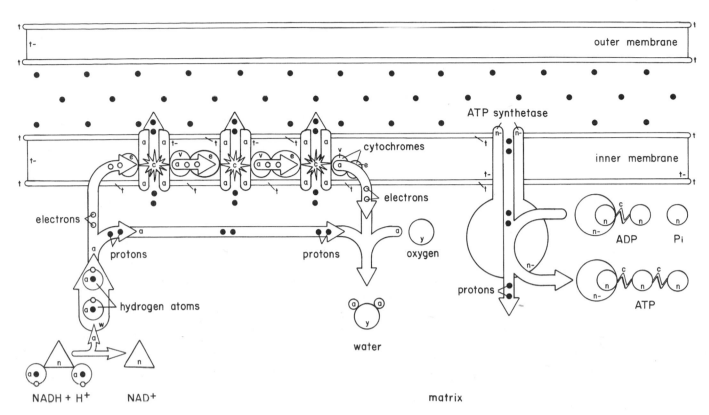

Fig. 10.13 *Electron transport chain. Color the membranes of the mitochondrion and note the location of the matrix, where the Krebs cycle takes place. Begin at the lower left by coloring the hydrogen atoms that are brought to the electron transport chain as part of NADH + H+. Color the coenzyme molecules, the pair of hydrogen atoms that are removed, and the arrows indicating their separation into their constituent protons and electrons. Note that the protons initially remain on the matrix side of the membrane. Color the arrows that show the passage of the electrons along the electron transport chain, coloring the cytochromes, the flashes, and the proton channels as you go. Note that a total of 6 protons are actively transported across the inner membrane for each pair of electrons. Also note the concentration gradient for protons that is established by this active transport mechanism. Finish this part of the picture by coloring the arrows that indicate the reuniting of protons and electrons to form the hydrogen atoms that combine with oxygen to form water. Color the oxygen and water molecules and note that these reactions cannot proceed in the absence of oxygen. At the right, color the enzyme ATP synthetase and note the channel that the protons pass through in going down their electrochemical gradients. Note that the energy that is released by the passage of a pair of protons back to the matrix is sufficient to synthesize one molecule of ATP from one molecule of ADP and one molecule of Pi. Color the molecules of ADP, Pi, and ATP, noting the high-energy bonds. Note also that a pair of hydrogen atoms that is carried by NADH + H+ yields 3 molecules of ATP. Each pair of hydrogen atoms that is carried as FADH$_2$ yields only 2 molecules of ATP because the electrons from these hydrogen atoms enter the electron transport chain at a point where their energy can only transport 4 protons across the inner membrane.*

Oxidative phosphorylation

The protons that have been actively transported across the membrane are then able to flow down their electrochemical gradients and re-enter the matrix through a channel within the enzyme ATP synthetase. The energy that is released when two protons pass through the enzyme is used to synthesize one molecule of ATP from one molecule of ADP (adenosine diphosphate) and one molecule of phosphate (Fig. 10.13).

Role of oxygen in electron transport chain

After passing through the electron transport chain, the electrons, now at lower energy, recombine with protons in the matrix to form hydrogen atoms, which then com-bine with oxygen to form water. Therefore, the function of oxygen in aerobic metabolism is to accept hydrogen atoms at the end of the electron transport chain.

The activity of the Krebs cycle is tightly coupled to that of the electron transport chain; if the electron transport chain is not processing hydrogen atoms, then the Krebs cycle will not operate. Since hydrogen atoms removed in the Krebs cycle are picked up by the coenzymes NAD+ and FAD, it is necessary for these coenzymes to unload hydrogen atoms so that they can return to the Krebs cycle and accept more hydrogen atoms. The electron transport chain is the site of this unloading, and its operation depends upon the presence of oxygen.

Therefore, in the absence of oxygen, the electron transport chain does not operate, NAD⁺ and FAD are not regenerated, and the Krebs cycle does not run.

Energy yield of aerobic versus anaerobic metabolism

Aerobic metabolism extracts much more energy from fuels than does anaerobic metabolism. Anaerobic metabolism of glucose in the pathway of glycolysis converts glucose to two molecules of lactic acid and captures enough energy to produce two molecules of ATP. In contrast, aerobic metabolism of glucose in the pathways of glycolysis and the Krebs cycle yields six molecules of carbon dioxide and captures enough energy to produce 36 molecules of ATP in skeletal muscle.

Summary of carbohydrate metabolism

Glucose, whether it is taken up by the cell from the blood or derived from glycogen within the cell itself, is first metabolized in the pathway of glycolysis. Under anaerobic conditions, the pyruvic acid that is produced by glycolysis is converted to lactic acid, which leaves the cell to be either used by other tissues or reconverted to glucose in the liver (Fig. 10.10). Under aerobic conditions, pyruvic acid is fully metabolized to carbon dioxide by the Krebs cycle (Fig. 10.14). Because of the operation of the electron transport chain and oxidative phosphorylation, aerobic metabolism provides a much greater energy yield than does anaerobic metabolism. The aerobic metabolism of carbohydrates to carbon dioxide yields about 4 kcal (kilocalories) of energy for each gram of carbohydrate.

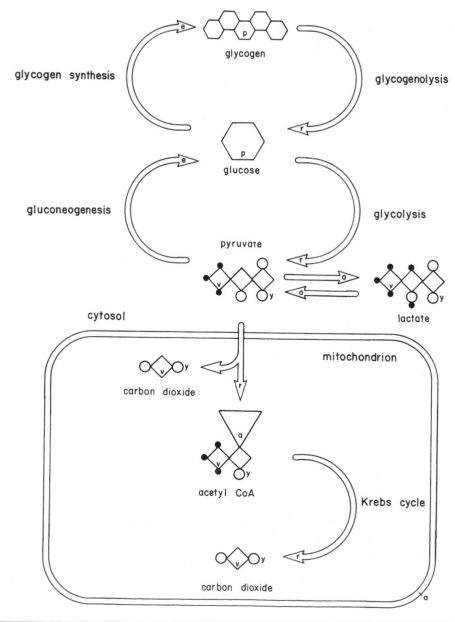

Fig. 10.14 *Overview of carbohydrate metabolism. Begin at the top by coloring the glycogen molecule and continue down the right side, coloring the arrow that indicates glycogenolysis, the glucose molecule produced by this pathway, the arrow indicating glycolysis, and the pyruvate molecule produced by this pathway. Color the molecule of lactate and the arrows that show that it is reversibly synthesized from pyruvate. Continue up the left side, coloring the arrows for gluconeogenesis and glycogen synthesis. Note which pathways are anabolic (green arrows) and which are catabolic (red arrows). Now color the mitochondrial membrane and the one-way arrow from pyruvate showing its entry into the mitochondrion and its irreversible conversion to acetyl CoA and carbon dioxide. Finally, color acetyl CoA and its irreversible breakdown to carbon dioxide in the Krebs cycle, noting that the Krebs cycle takes place in the mitochondrion. Follow the arrows from lactate and pyruvate to make a path to glucose; note that both compounds can be used to make glucose. Note also that there is no path from acetyl CoA to glucose, indicating that acetyl CoA cannot be used to make glucose.*

Metabolism of fat

Fats are found in the blood in the form of triglycerides and as free fatty acids, which are fatty acids that are not incorporated into triglyceride. Circulating triglyc- eride comes both from dietary fat and from fat that is packaged by the liver for export to tissues; free fatty acids come from the breakdown of triglycerides that are stored in adipose tissue (Fig 10.15).

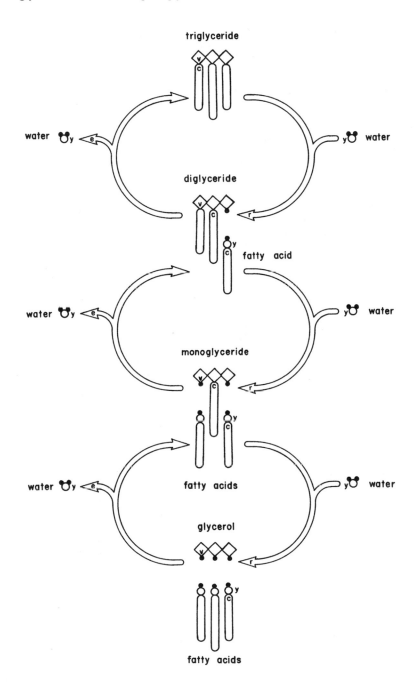

Fig. 10.15 *Metabolism of triglyceride. Begin at the top and color all of the figures that are in the center of the picture. Note how the names of the compounds correspond to the number of fatty acids. Go down the right side and color the arrows that show lipolysis, which is the hydrolysis of triglyceride, along with the water added at each step. Note how many fatty acids remain attached to the glycerol portion at each step. Now go up the left side, coloring the arrows that represent esterification, or condensation of fatty acids with glycerol, and the water molecules that are produced at each step. Note the reversibility of these processes.*

Lipoprotein particles

Since triglycerides are not water-soluble and cannot attach to plasma proteins to remain in solution (as free fatty acids do) they must be surrounded by water-soluble components in order to travel through the blood. The form in which they are packaged is as a lipid and protein-containing particle called a lipoprotein; an example of this, the chylomicron, has been described in chapter 9.

All lipoprotein particles contain triglycerides, phospholipids, cholesterol, cholesterol esters (in which cholesterol forms an ester linkage with a fatty acid), and specific proteins. The size of the particles and relative amounts of these components vary among the different particles (Fig. 10.16).

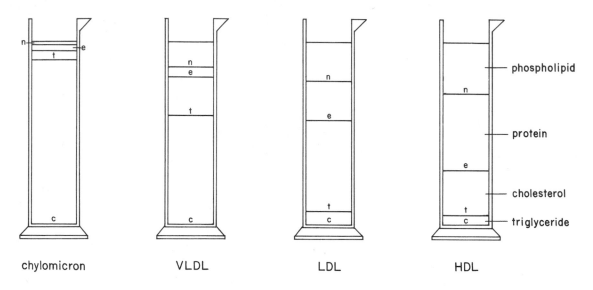

chylomicron   VLDL   LDL   HDL

Fig. 10.16 *Composition of lipoprotein particles. Identify the four graduated cylinders that represent the different lipoprotein particles. Color the bottom layer, representing triglyceride, across the four cylinders and then color each additional layer, going across all cylinders before beginning the next layer. Compare the relative proportions of triglyceride, cholesterol, protein, and phospholipid among the types of lipoprotein particles.*

Chylomicrons

Chylomicrons carry dietary fat and are made in the mucosal cells of the small intestine (Fig. 9.30). They lose their triglyceride, primarily to adipose tissue, through the action of the enzyme lipoprotein lipase, which is released by adipose tissue into the blood (Fig. 10.17). Lipoprotein lipase hydrolyzes the triglyceride in the lipoprotein particle to three fatty acids plus glycerol; the fatty acids then enter adipocytes (fat cells) and the glycerol remains in the blood to be taken up by the liver. The chylomicron becomes smaller as it loses its triglyceride and the resultant remnant is ultimately removed from the blood by the liver.

Triglyceride and other lipids, such as cholesterol, are also carried in the blood by other lipoprotein particles that originate in the liver. These lipoprotein particles include VLDL (very low density lipoprotein), LDL (low density lipoprotein) and HDL (high density lipoprotein) particles.

Very low density lipoprotein particles (VLDL)

VLDL particles contain fat that was either synthesized by the liver (see fatty acid synthesis, below) or derived from the chylomicron remnants. Triglyceride in VLDL particles is taken up by skeletal muscle, cardiac muscle, and adipose tissue. When the VLDL particles become smaller, they pick up cholesterol and specific proteins from other lipoprotein particles in the blood and become LDL particles.

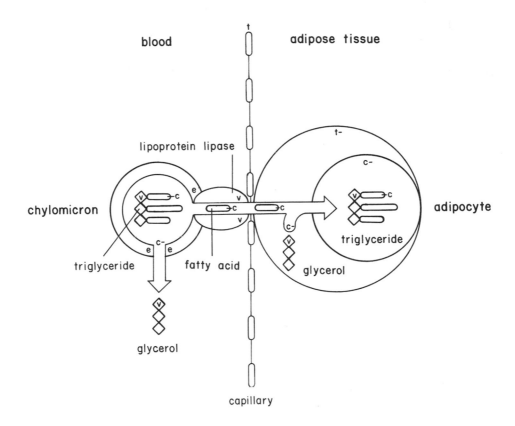

Fig. 10.17 *Storage of dietary fat in adipose tissue. Begin at left by coloring the triglyceride molecule within the chylomicron in the blood. Color the enzyme lipoprotein lipase, noting its location, and color the fatty acid and the glycerol molecules that result from the breakdown of triglyceride. Color the capillary membrane, noting that the fatty acids cross the membrane to enter the adipocyte, while glycerol remains in the blood. Color the adipocyte, the glycerol that it produces, the triglyceride molecule and the fat droplet in which it is stored. Note that triglyceride is formed by combining this glycerol with the incoming fatty acids. Compare this figure with Fig. 9.30.*

Low density lipoprotein particles (LDL)

LDL particles have the highest cholesterol content of the lipoprotein particles (Fig. 10.16). They enter most cells through endocytosis; this process is regulated so that the cell takes up only a limited amount of LDL. Uptake of LDL particles provides cells with lipid materials and thereby decreases the cell's production of cholesterol.

Cells of the immune system, called macrophages, have receptors that are less specific and will take up unlimited amounts of LDL. These cells can contain a large amount of cholesterol, and when they migrate to damaged blood vessel walls, the cholesterol that they deposit contributes to the development of vascular disease (atherosclerosis). Therefore, a high blood level of LDL cholesterol is associated with an increased risk of cardiovascular (heart and blood vessel) disease.

High density lipoprotein particles (HDL)

HDL particles have the lowest lipid content of the lipoprotein particles (Fig. 10.16). They pick up cholesterol from cell membranes and other lipoprotein particles and convert it to cholesterol esters that remain in the HDL particle. When the cholesterol-filled HDL particle is taken up by the liver, the liver decreases its synthesis of cholesterol; HDL particles therefore serve to notify the liver of the level of cholesterol in the body. High blood levels of HDL cholesterol are associated with a decreased risk of cardiovascular disease.

Fatty acid synthesis

Some of the fatty acids in the triglyceride carried in the VLDL particle were synthesized in the liver from glucose, fructose, or ethanol from alcoholic beverages. The pathway of fatty acid synthesis joins acetyl groups (2-carbon units) from acetyl CoA and reduces them (adds

hydrogen atoms); this pathway operates in the liver and consumes energy (Fig. 10.18). In a person who is on a mixed diet (consuming carbohydrate, fat, and protein) and not gaining weight, very little fatty acid synthesis occurs; most of the triglyceride in adipose tissue is derived from dietary fat.

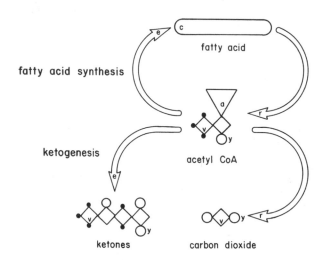

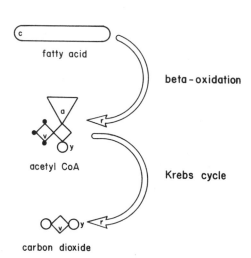

Fig. 10.18 *Metabolism of fatty acids. For both panels, begin at the top by coloring the fatty acid molecules and then go down the right side, coloring the arrows that signify beta-oxidation and the molecules of acetyl CoA that are produced. Continue downward, coloring the arrows representing the Krebs cycle and the molecules of carbon dioxide that are produced. For the left panel, color the two arrows from acetyl CoA, which show that the liver can synthesize fatty acids and ketones (or ketone bodies) from acetyl CoA. Color the ketone molecule, noting its number of carbons and the carboxyl group at one end. Compare the metabolism of fatty acids in the liver and muscle, considering the liver's role in the storage and mobilization of fuel.*

Triglyceride formation

Triglycerides, which are comprised of three fatty acids bound to a 3-carbon glycerol molecule (Fig. 10.15), are stored in adipose tissue. The fatty acids are provided by triglyceride molecules that are carried by chylomicrons and VLDL particles. The fatty acids in the triglyceride in these lipoprotein particles are released by the action of lipoprotein lipase and they enter the adipocyte. Glycerol is synthesized from glucose in the adipocyte. The fatty acids are esterified with glycerol (Fig. 9.26) and the triglyceride that is produced is added to the large lipid droplet that occupies much of the volume of the adipocyte (Fig. 10.17).

Lipolysis

Triglyceride in adipose tissue is hydrolyzed to three fatty acids plus glycerol by the enzyme hormone-sensitive lipase, in a process called lipolysis (Fig. 10.15). Hormone-sensitive lipase is stimulated by epinephrine, which is released by the sympathetic nervous system. Fatty acids and glycerol may leave the adipocyte and be used as fuels by other tissues; fatty acids are the major

fuel of cardiac muscle and resting skeletal muscle. The glycerol that is released by lipolysis may also be converted to glucose by gluconeogenesis in the liver.

When the level of fatty acids in the blood is very high (as occurs in starvation or in diabetes mellitus) the liver converts fatty acids to 4-carbon compounds called ketone bodies (Fig. 10.18). Ketone bodies refer to three compounds: acetoacetic acid, beta-hydroxybutyric acid, and acetone; the first two compounds are acids, also known as ketoacids. These water-soluble compounds may be used by muscle and other tissues as fuel. In contrast to fatty acids, ketone bodies may be used as a fuel by the brain under certain conditions. However, the very high production of ketone bodies that can occur in diabetes mellitus can lead to metabolic acidosis (Fig. 8.32).

Oxidation of fat

Fat, which is a concentrated source of energy that provides 9 kcal of energy for each gram, can only be metabolized in aerobic pathways.

Fatty acids that are taken up by tissues, either from lipoprotein particles or as free fatty acids, are first broken down into 2-carbon acetyl units, each carried by coenzyme A, in the pathway of beta-oxidation (Fig. 10.18). For example, a fatty acid that consists of 18 carbons (Fig. 9.25) will produce 9 units of acetyl CoA. Hydrogen atoms in the fatty acids are removed in beta-oxidation and are carried by the coenzymes NAD+ and FAD to the electron transport chain (Fig. 10.13), where their energy will be stored in ATP; therefore, beta-oxidation is an energy-yielding pathway.

The acetyl CoA that is produced from fatty acids in beta-oxidation can be metabolized in the Krebs cycle (Fig. 10.11), and the hydrogen atoms that are removed from each unit of acetyl CoA are carried to the electron transport chain, where their energy is stored in ATP. Ketone bodies, which are 4-carbon compounds that are derived from fatty acids (Fig. 10.18), are each converted back to 2 units of acetyl CoA, which are also metabolized in the Krebs cycle.

Metabolism of protein

Amino acids that are absorbed from a meal may be used for the synthesis of protein (Fig. 2.8) or as a source of energy (Fig. 10.19). Amino acids can also be obtained by cells from the breakdown of cellular proteins; proteins within cells are constantly being hydrolyzed to their constituent amino acids. The short lifespan of most proteins gives the cell the ability to rapidly adapt to changes in its environment by changing the relative amounts of specific proteins (e.g., enzymes, transport proteins) in the cell. The breakdown of cellular proteins not only provides the raw material for the synthesis of new proteins, it also supplies fuel for either direct use in the same tissue or conversion to glucose by the liver.

Before amino acids can be used as fuel in the Krebs cycle or converted to glucose, they must lose their amino groups (NH_2); the remaining portion of the amino acid is called the carbon skeleton (Fig. 10.19). Some carbon skeletons can enter the Krebs cycle directly; (e.g., the carbon skeleton of the amino acid alanine is pyruvic acid), while other carbon skeletons must be greatly altered before they can enter the Krebs cycle.

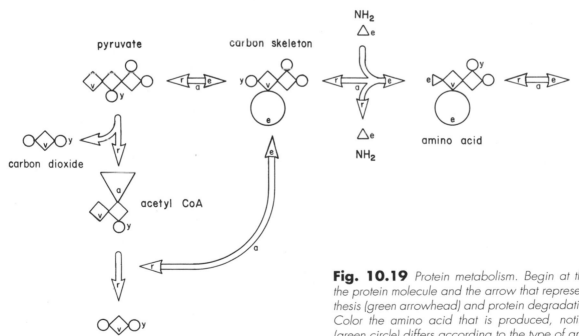

Fig. 10.19 *Protein metabolism. Begin at the right by coloring the protein molecule and the arrow that represents both protein synthesis (green arrowhead) and protein degradation (red arrowhead). Color the amino acid that is produced, noting that its R group (green circle) differs according to the type of amino acid. Color the remaining compounds, noting the step where the amino group (NH_2) is removed to form a carbon skeleton. The amino group will be excreted as part of the compound urea. Note also that the carbon skeleton is ultimately metabolized in the Krebs cycle. Color the arrows, noting which reactions are anabolic (green arrowheads) and which are catabolic (red arrowheads). Note also which portions of the metabolic pathways are reversible.*

The amino group of the amino acid may be reused by the cell to make a new amino acid through its combination with another carbon skeleton that the cell has synthesized. For example, pyruvic acid, which is produced by glycolysis, can combine with NH_2 to form the amino acid alanine. The amino group may also be excreted as part of the compound urea. The urea cycle is the energy-using pathway in which the liver produces urea. Urea that is released into the blood is not used by other tissues and is excreted in the urine (Fig. 7.15). High protein intakes provide an excess of amino acids;

the excess carbon skeletons are processed as fuel and the amino groups are excreted as urea. Therefore, high protein diets lead to a high level of urea production.

Amino acids are also used for a number of anabolic purposes. Portions of amino acids are used for the synthesis of the heme portion of hemoglobin (Fig. 8.10), the production of purines and pyrimidines that form nucleic acids (Figs. 2.3, 2.5), and the formation of neurotransmitters such as norepinephrine and serotonin.

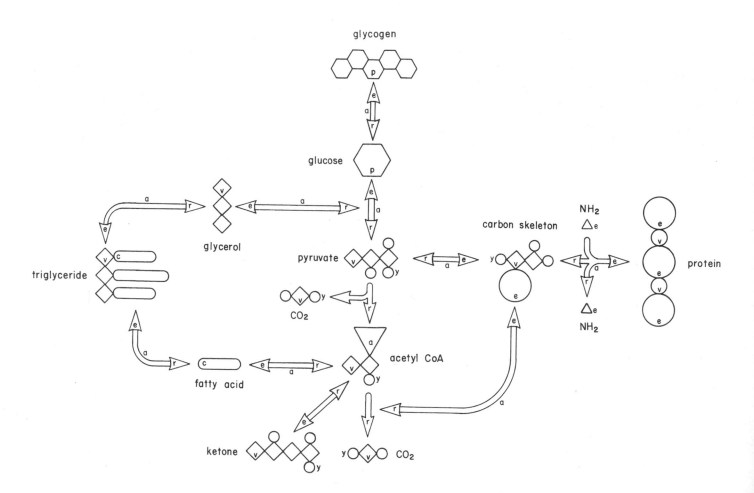

Fig. 10.20 *Overview of metabolism. Begin at the top by coloring the glycogen molecule and continue downward, coloring all compounds and arrows and noting whether the pathway in each direction is anabolic (green arrowhead) or catabolic (red arrowhead). Go to the left side; color the triglyceride molecule and the glycerol and fatty acids that are released during lipolysis; color all compounds and arrows as you go. Color the two-way arrow that indicates the metabolism of glycerol by glycolysis. At the right, color the protein molecule and note that the protein must first be hydrolyzed to amino acids (not shown). Color the amino group that is removed from the amino acid and the carbon skeleton that remains, as well as all arrows. Color the two-way arrows that indicate the conversion of carbon skeletons to pyruvate or compounds within the Krebs cycle. Notice where the subunits of protein, triglyceride, and glycogen enter the catabolic pathways. Trace a path from protein to glycogen. Trace another path, beginning with fatty acids and see whether you can reach glucose; note any one-way steps that block the path. Compare this figure with Figs. 10.14, 10.18, and 10.19.*

Summary of metabolism

Carbohydrates, fats, and proteins provide energy that can be stored in the bonds of ATP. All fuels can ultimately be metabolized in the Krebs cycle, an aerobic pathway that completely oxidizes fuel to carbon dioxide and extracts all of the available energy from the fuel (Fig. 10.20). The electrons that are removed from fuels in the metabolic pathways of glycolysis, beta-oxidation, and the Krebs cycle are carried by the coenzymes NAD+ and FAD to the electron transport chain, where their energy is used to form the high-energy phosphate bonds of ATP. The electrons reunite with protons to form hydrogen atoms, which then combine with oxygen to form water.

Fuels may be stored and released from storage as needed: glucose is stored as glycogen in the liver and muscle while fatty acids are stored as triglyceride in adipose tissue. There is considerable interchange among forms of fuel, so that one type of nutrient may be converted into another (Fig. 10.20). However, not all steps are reversible. For example, since acetyl CoA cannot be converted to pyruvic acid, fatty acids cannot be converted to glucose (Fig. 10.20). This explains why fats cannot be used as a fuel in anaerobic metabolism.

Since metabolism has both anabolic and catabolic pathways, appropriate responses to changes in the availability and need for fuels require that there be control of the metabolic pathways. Catabolic pathways that mobilize fuel from storage are active when availability of fuels is low, as in fasting, or when energy needs are high, as in exercise. On the other hand, anabolic pathways that build compounds are active when fuel availability is high, as occurs following a meal, or when tissue is being added, as occurs during growth. The regulation of metabolism is largely the responsibility of the endocrine system.

chapter **eleven**
endocrine system

The endocrine system regulates metabolic functions by releasing chemical substances called hormones (or endocrines) into the blood.

The endocrine glands

The endocrine system consists of a number of glands, which are organs or tissues that are distinguished by their secretion of a particular product (Fig. 11.1). Each endocrine gland secretes one or more particular hormone.

Hormones act only on those cells that have specific receptors for them in their cell membranes; these cells are called their target cells. Target cells respond to the hormone in a fixed, predictable way. By controlling the behavior of many individual cells, the endocrine system regulates metabolic processes on both a local and a body-wide level.

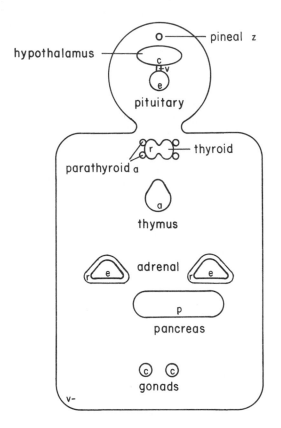

Figure 11.1 *Anatomy of the endocrine system. Color the endocrine glands and notice their locations relative to each other and in the body as a whole.*

Regulation of endocrine gland secretions

The release of hormones by the endocrine glands is regulated by a variety of stimuli, including signals from the autonomic nervous system, the levels of other hormones in the blood, and the levels of blood-borne substances such as glucose or sodium. The hormones that are released travel through the blood and stimulate their target cells, which then induce the biological effects of the hormones. The release of hormones is modulated by feedback loops that relay information related to the effects of the hormone back to the gland (Fig. 11.2).

Mechanisms of hormone action

There are two major mechanisms by which hormones affect their target cells. One mechanism produces effects that have a rapid onset and a short duration; the other mechanism produces effects that have a slow onset and a long duration.

Second messenger mechanism of hormone action

The first type of mechanism, which is employed by the hormones glucagon, which is released by the pancreas, and epinephrine, which is released by the adrenal gland, is called a second messenger system. In this mechanism, the hormone, which is considered to be the first messenger, does not have to enter the cell to have its effect. The hormone binds to a specific receptor protein on the cell membrane and changes the shape of the receptor. This leads to the production of an intracellular substance that acts as a second messenger, stimulating a series of intracellular effects. Since the second mes-

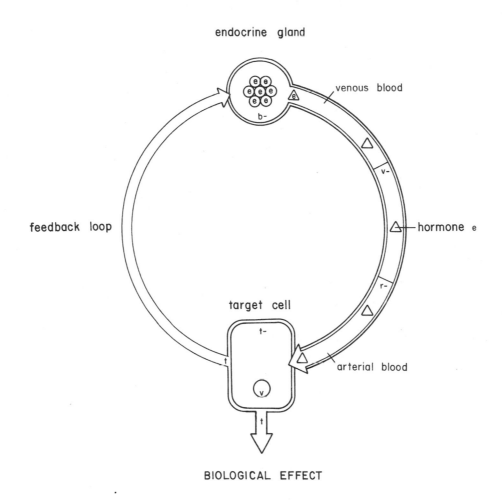

endocrine gland

venous blood

feedback loop

hormone e

target cell

arterial blood

BIOLOGICAL EFFECT

Figure 11.2 *Schematic diagram of hormone action. Color the endocrine gland and its target cell and the arrows that form the connections between them. Note that usually the hormone is released into venous blood, returns to the heart, travels through the lung, and reaches the target organ in its arterial blood supply. Then note that when the target cell has brought about its effect, the endocrine gland will change the rate of its secretion of the hormone. For example, when the pancreatic islets secrete insulin and it travels through the blood to muscle (arrow at right), muscle removes glucose from the blood; the lowering of blood glucose then (arrow at left) signals the islets to decrease their secretion of insulin.*

senger exerts its effect by activating existing enzymes within the cell, the effects of this mechanism are immediate but temporary (minutes).

An example of a second messenger system is the process by which glucagon exerts its effect on the glycogen that is stored in liver cells. Glucagon in the blood binds to a receptor on the liver cell membrane and stimulates the enzyme adenylate cyclase within the cell (Fig. 11.3). Adenylate cyclase catalyzes a reaction in which ATP is converted to cyclic AMP (cAMP) plus pyrophos-

phate, which is made up of two phosphate groups that are linked.

Then cAMP, acting as the second messenger, stimulates an intracellular enzyme that, in turn, stimulates other enzymes that catalyze reactions leading to the breakdown of glycogen into glucose (Fig. 10.7). Since cAMP is rapidly degraded, its effect on glycogen breakdown ends quickly unless another molecule of glucagon occupies a receptor on the cell membrane and stimulates the sequence of events again.

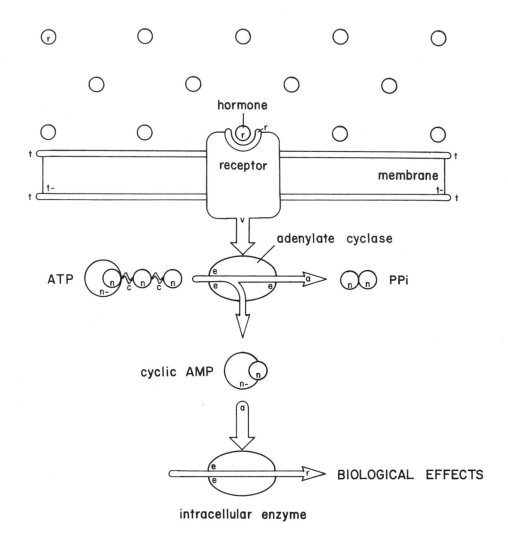

Figure 11.3 *Second messenger mechanism of hormone action. Begin by coloring the hormone molecules outside the cell, including the hormone that is in position to bind to its receptor; color the receptor and the membrane that it traverses. Color the enzyme (adenylate cyclase) that the occupied receptor stimulates, its substrate ATP, and its products; cyclic AMP and pyrophosphate (PPi), as well as the arrows that indicate the reaction. Finally, color the intracellular enzyme that is affected by cyclic AMP and the arrow that indicates the biological effects that this enzyme will ultimately bring about. Note that these effects are usually brought about by a cascade of reactions, through which the effect of a small amount of cyclic AMP is amplified. Note also that the biological effect occurs rapidly but is short-lived, as cyclic AMP is quickly metabolized to another form and its effects within the cell are terminated.*

Mechanism of steroid hormone action

The slower and longer-lasting mechanism of hormone action is employed by steroid hormones (Fig. 11.4), which are produced by the adrenal cortex and the gonads. In this mechanism, the hormone enters the cell where it combines with a specific receptor protein in the nucleus. The hormone-receptor complex then directs the

transcription of a specific portion of a DNA molecule, which leads to the formation of a complementary strand of mRNA (Fig. 2.7). The mRNA strand leaves the nucleus and travels to the ribosome where it directs the synthesis of a specific protein (Fig. 2.8). It is this protein, which could be an enzyme, that is responsible for the biological effect of the hormone.

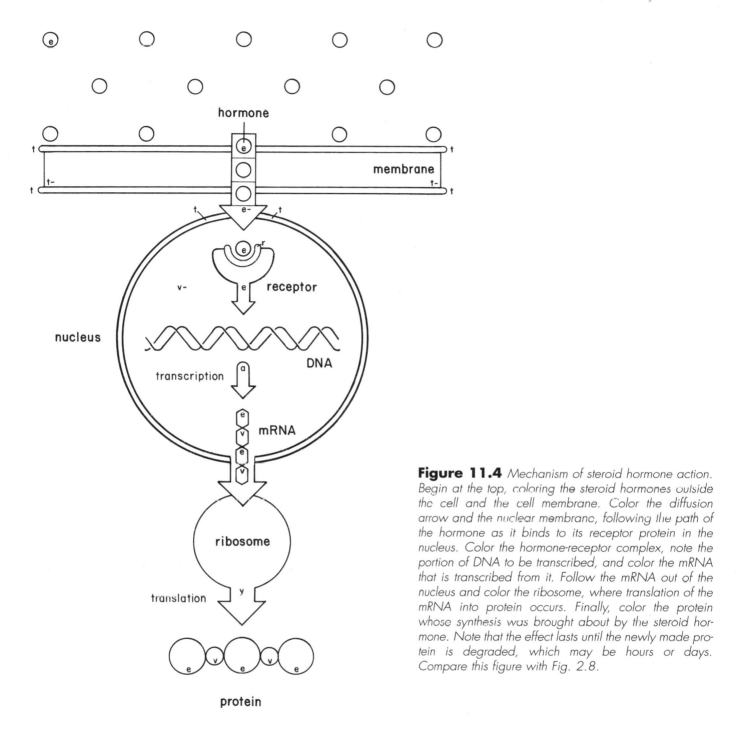

hormone

membrane

receptor

nucleus

DNA

transcription

mRNA

ribosome

translation

protein

Figure 11.4 *Mechanism of steroid hormone action. Begin at the top, coloring the steroid hormones outside the cell and the cell membrane. Color the diffusion arrow and the nuclear membrane, following the path of the hormone as it binds to its receptor protein in the nucleus. Color the hormone-receptor complex, note the portion of DNA to be transcribed, and color the mRNA that is transcribed from it. Follow the mRNA out of the nucleus and color the ribosome, where translation of the mRNA into protein occurs. Finally, color the protein whose synthesis was brought about by the steroid hormone. Note that the effect lasts until the newly made protein is degraded, which may be hours or days. Compare this figure with Fig. 2.8.*

As an example of this mechanism, the hormone cortisol, which is released by the adrenal gland, causes liver cells to produce larger amounts of an enzyme that catalyzes a key reaction in the pathway of gluconeogenesis (Fig. 10.20). In this way, cortisol is able to regulate the activity of this anabolic pathway in the liver. Since the effect of cortisol persists as long as there is more of the key enzyme in the cell, cortisol stimulates gluconeogenesis for a prolonged period of time (hours).

The pituitary gland

The pituitary gland, which is also called the hypophysis, is located adjacent to the brain and functions as an intermediary between the brain and a large number of endocrine glands (Fig. 11.5). It is comprised of an anterior component that is also called the adenohypophysis, and a posterior component that is also called the neurohypophysis.

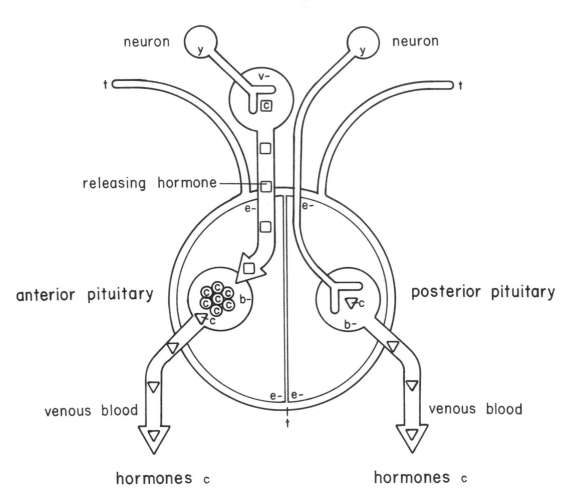

Figure 11.5 *Pituitary gland. Beginning at the top left, color the neuron in the hypothalamus, the portal blood system carrying releasing or inhibiting hormones to the anterior pituitary, and the release of hormones by the anterior pituitary gland into the general circulation. Color the right side of the figure, beginning with the neuron in the hypothalamus and its nerve ending in the posterior pituitary gland, which also releases hormones into the general circulation. Compare the communication between the hypothalamus and each lobe of the pituitary gland.*

Hypothalamic releasing and inhibiting hormones

The anterior pituitary gland receives small compounds, called releasing (RH) or inhibiting (IH) hormones, that are released by nerve cells in the hypothalamus. These hormones, which are itemized in Fig. 11.6, travel from the hypothalamus to the pituitary gland through a system of local blood vessels known as the hypothalamic-pituitary, or the hypothalamic-hypophyseal, portal system.

Each of the releasing and inhibiting hormones regulates the secretion of a particular hormone by the anterior pituitary gland. The anterior pituitary hormones, which are initially released into venous blood, end up in the general circulation (Fig. 11.2). Some anterior pituitary hormones stimulate other endocrine glands to release hormones that act on target cells, while other anterior pituitary hormones act directly on their target cells (Fig. 11.6).

Anterior pituitary hormones

Anterior pituitary hormones that stimulate other endocrine glands include thyroid stimulating hormone (TSH), which acts on the thyroid gland, adrenocorticotropic hormone (ACTH), which acts on the adrenal gland, and follicle-stimulating hormone (FSH) and luteinizing hormone (LH), which act on the gonads (Fig. 11.6).

Anterior pituitary hormones that directly stimulate their target cells are prolactin and growth hormone (GH) (Fig. 11.6). Prolactin stimulates milk production in the mammary gland (see chapter 12) and growth hormone stimulates protein synthesis. Growth hormone also causes the liver to secrete the protein somatomedin, also called insulin-like growth factor (IGF), which increases the rate of bone growth.

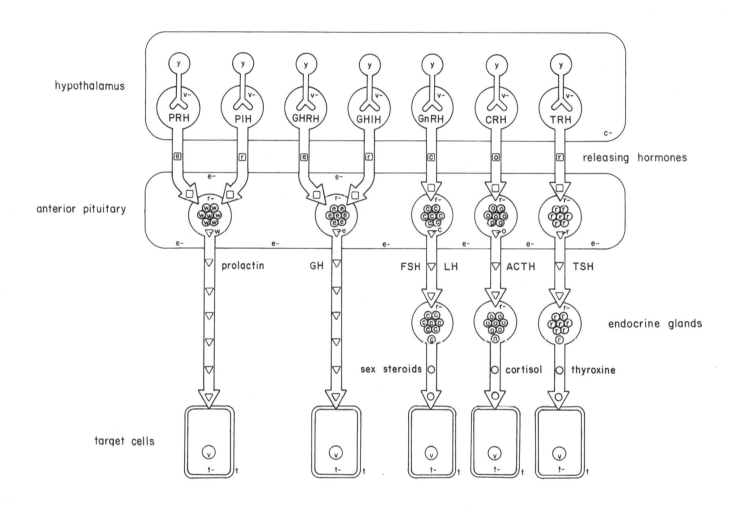

Figure 11.6 Anterior pituitary hormones. Color the hypothalamus and, for each hypothalamic neuron shown, color it and the path of its releasing or inhibiting hormone through the portal blood vessels to the anterior pituitary gland. For prolactin releasing (PRH) and inhibiting (PIH) hormones, color the prolactin secreting cells in the anterior pituitary and the path prolactin takes through the general circulation to the mammary gland, where it increases milk production. For growth hormone releasing (GHRH) and inhibiting hormones (GHIH), color the growth hormone secreting cells and the path of growth hormone to its many target tissues, including liver and muscle. For gonadotropin releasing hormone (GnRH), color the cells that secrete either luteinizing hormone (LH) or follicle-stimulating hormone (FSH) and their path to the ovaries or testes. In the ovaries, LH and FSH stimulate secretion of estrogen and progesterone, which act on the uterus and mammary glands; in the testes LH increases the release of testosterone, which promotes growth and development of sexual characteristics. For corticotropin releasing hormone (CRH), color the cells that secrete ACTH, its path in the blood to the adrenal cortex, the adrenal cells that secrete glucocorticoids, mainly cortisol, and then the path of glucocorticoids to their many target organs, including the liver. Finally, for thyrotropin releasing hormone (TRH), color its path to the anterior pituitary cells that secrete thyroid stimulating hormone (TSH), the path of TSH to the thyroid gland, and then the path of the thyroid hormones, mainly thyroxine, to their many target cells. Note which hormones are directly controlled by hypothalamic releasing or inhibiting hormones and which are controlled by tropic, or stimulating, hormones from the pituitary gland. Compare this figure with Fig. 11.5.

Regulation of anterior pituitary hormones

The secretion of hypothalamic releasing factors and the secretion of anterior pituitary hormones are modulated by multiple negative feedback loops (Fig. 11.7). As an example, high levels of thyroid hormone inhibit the release of TSH by the anterior pituitary gland, and high levels of either thyroid hormone or TSH inhibit the secretion of the releasing hormone TRH by the hypothalamus (Fig. 11.6).

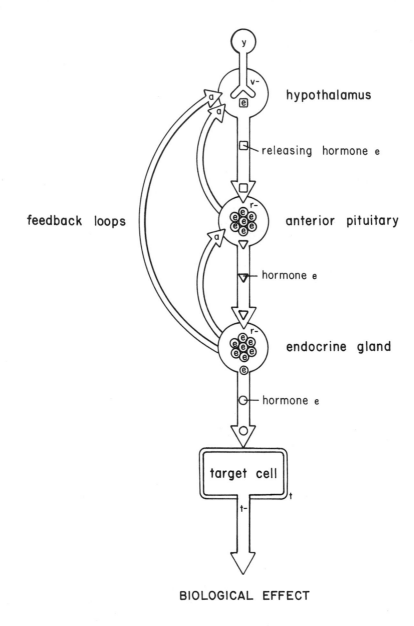

hypothalamus

releasing hormone e

feedback loops

anterior pituitary

hormone e

endocrine gland

hormone e

target cell

BIOLOGICAL EFFECT

Figure 11.7 *Regulation of anterior pituitary hormone secretion. Begin at the top, coloring the neuron in the hypothalamus, then color the path of the hypothalamic releasing hormone through the hypothalamic-pituitary portal system, the release of the pituitary hormone into the general circulation, and its delivery to another endocrine gland by the arterial blood. Color this endocrine gland and the hormone that it secretes in response to the pituitary hormone. Finally, color the arterial blood that brings this hormone to its target cell, as well as the target cell, which will produce the biological effect that was initiated by the hypothalamus. Color the arrows that represent the feedback loops from the endocrine gland and from the anterior pituitary. Compare this figure with Fig. 11.6.*

Posterior pituitary hormones

The posterior pituitary gland contains the nerve terminals of neurons whose cell bodies are located in the hypothalamus (Fig. 11.5). These nerve terminals secrete oxytocin and antidiuretic hormone (ADH), which are classified as neurohormones because they are released by neurons (Fig. 11.8).

Oxytocin stimulates the contraction of smooth muscle, most notably uterine muscle during childbirth, and the muscle in mammary tissue that is involved in milk ejection during lactation. ADH is secreted in response to neural signals from hypothalamic osmoreceptors. It increases the permeability of the distal tubule and collecting duct to water which, in turn, regulates water reabsorption in the kidney and thereby maintains the normal sodium concentration in extracellular fluid (Fig. 7.26).

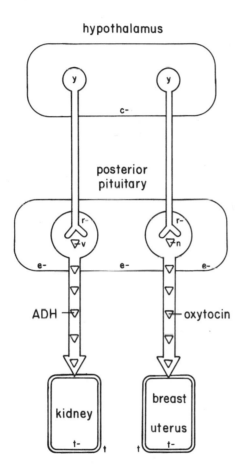

Figure 11.8 *Posterior pituitary hormones. Begin by coloring the hypothalamus and its neurons, which descend to the posterior pituitary gland, and the molecules of ADH and oxytocin that are secreted into the blood; note that each neuron only secretes one of the hormones. Color the rest of the posterior pituitary gland and the target organs; ADH increases water reabsorption in the kidney and thereby regulates the sodium concentration of extracellular fluids, and oxytocin stimulates contraction of uterine smooth muscle during childbirth and contraction of myoepithelium around the ducts of the mammary glands during lactation (Fig. 12.9). Compare this figure with Fig. 1.8.*

Adrenal hormones

The two adrenal glands are located above each kidney (Fig. 11.1); each consists of two functionally different types of tissue: the outer portion of the adrenal glands, which is called the cortex, produces corticosteroids, and the inner portion, which is called the medulla, produces epinephrine and norepinephrine, collectively referred to as catecholamines (Fig. 11.9). The adrenal cortex is divided into an outer region called the zona glomeru-

losa, a middle region called the zona fasciculata, and an inner region called the zona reticularis.

The corticosteroids are synthesized from cholesterol. They are categorized as mineralocorticoids (made in the zona glomerulosa), glucocorticoids (made in the zona fasciculata), and adrenal androgens (made in the zona reticularis) (Fig. 11.9).

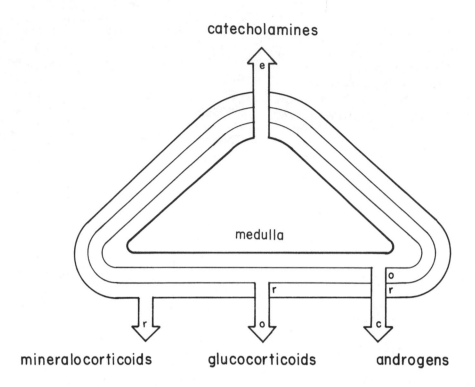

Figure 11.9 *Adrenal gland. Color the inside portion, or medulla, and the arrow representing its secretion of the catecholamines, primarily epinephrine. Next, color the outer portion, or cortex, and the arrows representing the hormones it secretes: mineralocorticoids (primarily aldosterone), glucocorticoids (mainly cortisol), and androgens.*

Mineralocorticoids

Mineralocorticoids maintain normal concentrations of sodium and potassium in the extracellular fluid. Aldosterone is the major mineralocorticoid in humans. Its release is stimulated by a high potassium concentration in extracellular fluid, increased activation of the renin-angiotensin system (Fig. 7.14), a low sodium concentration in extracellular fluid, or an increased level of ACTH in the blood (Fig. 11.6).

Aldosterone causes the sodium-potassium pump in the kidney tubules to secrete more potassium in the urine and thereby maintain the normal potassium concentration in extracellular fluid (Fig. 7.27).

Glucocorticoids

Glucocorticoids affect the metabolism of carbohydrate, fat, and protein. Cortisol is the major glucocorticoid in humans; its release is stimulated by ACTH (Fig. 11.6). The release of ACTH is regulated by corticotropin releasing hormone (CRH), which is released by the hypothalamus in response to physical and/or emotional stress. For example, trauma, starvation, or profound anxiety can lead to the release of glucocorticoids.

Increased levels of glucocorticoids in the blood cause: 1) skeletal muscle to break down its protein and release amino acids into the blood; 2) adipose tissue to break down its stored triglycerides and release fatty acids and glycerol into the blood; and 3) the liver to increase glucose production through gluconeogenesis, using the amino acids and glycerol that have been released (Fig. 10.20).

These fuel-mobilizing effects of glucocorticoids are long-lasting (hours) since some of them involve the synthesis of enzymes that regulate metabolic pathways (Fig. 11.3), and not just temporary activation of existing enzymes (Fig. 11.2).

Adrenal androgens

The androgens, also called male sex hormones, that are produced and released by the adrenal cortex of both males and females, are much less potent than the androgen testosterone, which is produced by the testes in males. Although the adrenal androgens have little effect on the development of sexual characteristics, they do affect sexual behavior and act as raw material for the synthesis of steroid hormones by other tissues.

Catecholamines

The adrenal medulla is functionally part of the sympathetic nervous system. It releases epinephrine and, to a lesser extent, norepinephrine, into the blood when it is stimulated by sympathetic nerve fibers.

The catecholamines are derivatives of the amino acid tyrosine, and their effects are similar to those of the neurotransmitters of the sympathetic nervous system. For example, catecholamines increase heart rate and myocardial contractility (Fig. 6.27), and stimulate lipolysis in adipose tissue (Fig. 10.15). Catecholamines act on many tissues by raising the level of cAMP, which quickly acts as a second messenger and initiates a series of intracellular events (Fig. 11.3).

Thyroid hormones

Thyroid stimulating hormone (TSH) regulates the secretion of hormones from the thyroid gland (Fig. 11.6). The release of TSH is controlled by TRH, which is released by the hypothalamus in response to changes in the external environment. For example, exposure to a cold environment can lead to an increase in the release of thyroid hormones.

The thyroid hormones are triiodothyronine (T_3) and thyroxine (T_4); T_3 contains three iodine atoms and T_4 contains four (Fig. 11.10). Within the target cell, T_4 is converted to T_3, which is the active form of the hormone. Both hormones are synthesized within the thyroid follicle (Fig. 11.11), where dietary iodine is incorporated into units of tyrosine which, themselves, are part of the large protein called thyroglobulin (Fig. 11.12).

These tyrosine units are modified to form the hormones T_3 and T_4 while they are still part of thyroglobulin. TSH stimulates the thyroid follicle to hydrolyze thyroglobulin and release T_3 and T_4, which pass through the thyroid cells and into the blood.

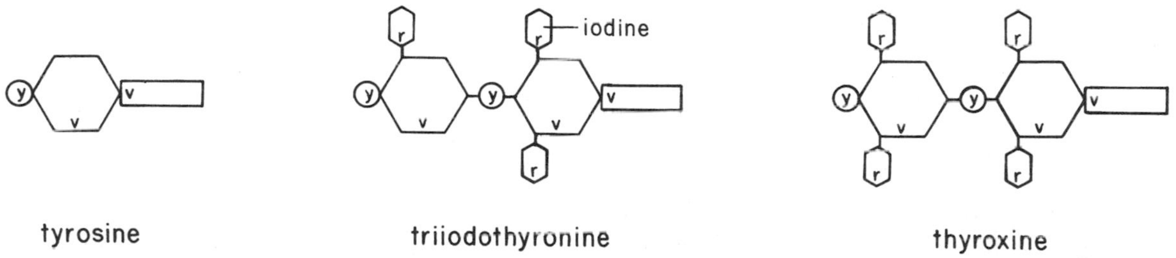

tyrosine   triiodothyronine   thyroxine

Figure 11.10 *Thyroid hormones. Color the tyrosine molecule, noting the 6-sided ring and the portion to the right that represents the alpha-carbon, amino group, and carboxyl group that are found in all amino acids (Fig. 9.31). Next color the thyroid hormones, triiodothyronine (T_3) and thyroxine (T_4); count the iodine atoms in each. Compare the structures of the thyroid hormones with that of tyrosine, from which they were formed.*

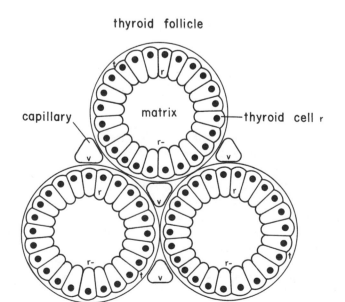

thyroid follicle

capillary   matrix   thyroid cell r

Figure 11.11 *Thyroid gland. Color the cross-sections of follicles that comprise the thyroid gland, as well as the capillaries that are outside of them. Note that the lumen of each follicle contains a gel-like matrix into which thyroid cells secrete iodine obtained from the blood. Note also that the thyroid hormones, which are secreted by the thyroid cells, enter the nearby capillaries to reach their target cells by way of the circulation.*

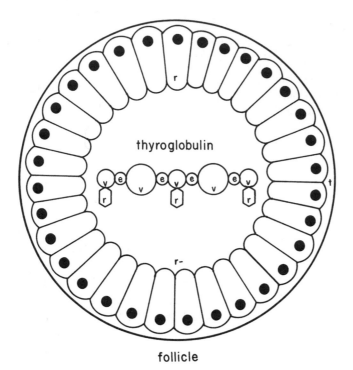

thyroglobulin

follicle

Figure 11.12 *Thyroglobulin. Color the cross section of the thyroid follicle, the gel-like matrix inside of it, and the protein molecule, thyroglobulin, in the matrix. Note that the thyroid hormones, shown as violet and red structures, are part of thyroglobulin and are linked by peptide bonds with the other amino acids (Fig. 9.32). When thyroglobulin is hydrolyzed, the thyroid hormones are released from the protein and pass through the thyroid cells to enter the capillaries outside of the follicle (Fig. 11.11).*

Action of thyroid hormones

Thyroid hormones are necessary for growth and development, especially before birth. Prenatal deficiency of thyroid hormones causes the retardation of physical and mental development known as cretinism. Thyroid hormones also increase metabolic rate, probably through their ability to increase the size and activity of mitochondria. Abnormalities in thyroid function can cause an elevated (hyperthyroid) or a depressed (hypothyroid) metabolic rate.

The thyroid gland also produces the hormone calcitonin; its role in the regulation of blood levels of calcium is described below.

Control of blood levels of calcium

The maintenance of the normal concentration of calcium in the extracellular fluid is essential for the function of nerve, muscle, endocrine, and other excitable cells. The two hormones that are responsible for regulating blood calcium levels are parathyroid hormone (PTH), which is produced by the parathyroid glands, and calcitonin, which is produced by the thyroid gland. The parathyroid glands are located on both sides of the thyroid gland (Fig. 11.1).

The parathyroid glands release PTH whenever blood levels of calcium are low. PTH causes: 1) the conversion of vitamin D into its most active form, calcitriol, by the kidney; 2) a decrease in the excretion of calcium in the urine; and 3) the breakdown of bone mineral, which is rich in calcium, and its release into the blood (Fig. 11.13). The latter two actions produce a rapid rise in blood calcium levels. Calcitriol increases the efficiency of calcium absorption by the intestine, thereby replacing the bone mineral over a prolonged period of time (days).

In contrast to PTH, calcitonin is released by the thyroid gland in response to a long-term elevation in blood calcium concentration. Calcitonin inhibits the breakdown of bone mineral, thereby preventing the entry of calcium from bone into the blood.

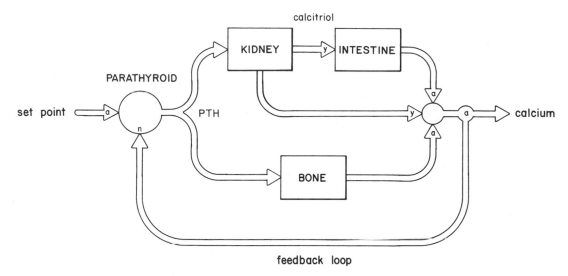

Figure 11.13 *Block diagram of a calcium control system. Begin at the parathyroid gland, coloring it and the arrows indicating the secretion of parathyroid hormone (PTH). Next color its target organs, bone and kidney, noting that: 1) bone releases calcium into the blood; 2) the kidney conserves blood calcium by decreasing the amount of calcium that is excreted in the urine, and 3) the kidney puts vitamin D in its most active form, calcitriol. Calcitriol, released by the kidney into the blood, stimulates calcium absorption by the mucosal cells of the small intestine. All of these actions add calcium to the blood. Finally, color the feedback loop that notifies the parathyroid gland of the actual calcium level of the blood and the set point arrow that represents the desired level of blood calcium. Compare this figure with Fig. 1.7.*

Pancreatic hormones

The pancreas is both an exocrine gland (secreting to the outside of the body, Fig. 9.12) and an endocrine gland (secreting into the blood). The endocrine tissue constitutes a small portion of the organ (< 5%). It consists of clusters of 100-1000 cells that make up what are called the islets of Langerhans; these are dispersed throughout the organ (Fig. 11.14). Among the islet cells are alpha cells, which secrete the hormone glucagon, and beta cells, which secrete the hormone insulin into the blood.

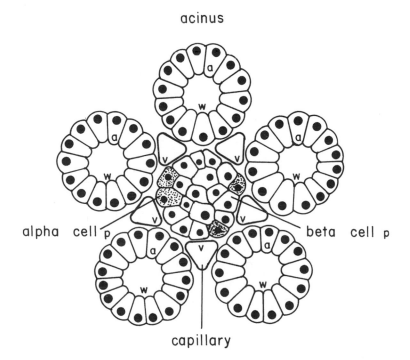

Figure 11.14 *Islet of Langerhans. Color the cross-sections of the exocrine pancreatic cells arranged in acini (Fig 9.12), noting the lumens into which they secrete digestive enzymes. Next, color the alpha cells, which produce glucagon, and the beta cells, which produce insulin, within the islet. Finally, color the cross-sections of capillaries that insulin and glucagon will enter in order to reach the general circulation.*

Insulin

Insulin is the primary anabolic hormone in the body; it promotes the storage of glucose and fat and the synthesis of protein. It is secreted by the beta cells of the pancreas in response to: 1) an increase in the level of blood glucose (Fig. 11.15) or amino acids; 2) parasympathetic stimulation (Fig. 9.3); and 3) hormones released by the gastrointestinal tract, such as cholecys-

tokinin (Fig. 9.13).

Insulin removes glucose from the blood by stimulating its transport by facilitated diffusion into skeletal muscle and adipose tissue, and by increasing its storage as glycogen and its utilization as a fuel (Fig. 11.16). Insulin also increases the storage of fat as triglyceride in adipose tissue (Fig. 10. 17).

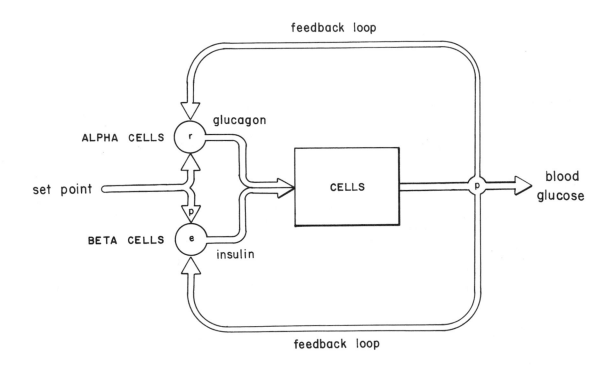

Figure 11.15 *Block diagram of a glucose control system. Begin at the left, coloring the alpha cells and the arrow signifying glucagon release, and then the beta cells and the arrow signifying insulin release. Next, color the arrows representing their effect on blood glucose concentration: glucagon causes the liver to release glucose into the blood, thereby raising blood glucose concentration, and insulin causes liver, muscle, and adipose tissue to remove glucose from the blood, thereby lowering blood glucose concentration (Fig. 11.16). Finally, color the feedback loops to the alpha and beta cells as well as the glucose set point, to which actual blood glucose levels are compared. When actual blood glucose levels are higher than the set point, more insulin is secreted; when actual blood glucose levels are lower than the set point, more glucagon is secreted. Compare this figure with Fig. 1.7.*

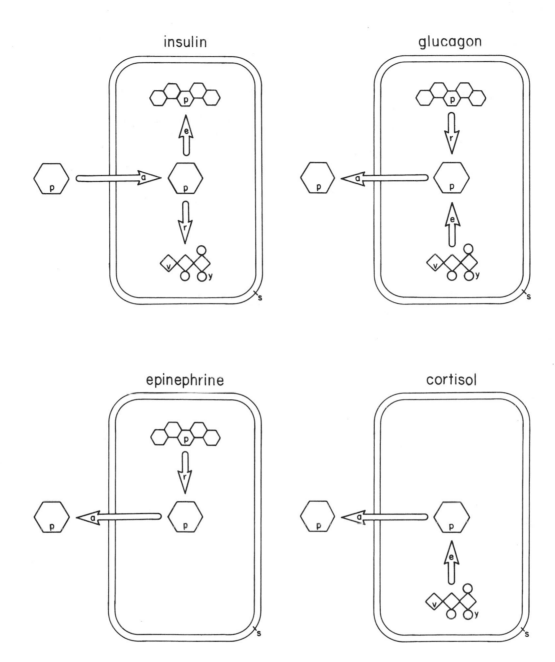

Figure 11.16 *Metabolic hormones. For each panel, color the cell membrane and the molecules of glycogen, glucose, and pyruvate within the cell, and the molecule of glucose outside of the cell. Color the arrows within the cell, noting which reactions are anabolic and which ones are catabolic (Fig. 10.14). Color the arrows that show glucose entering or leaving the cell. Examine each panel to see what effect each hormone has on blood glucose level and how it produces this effect. Although this figure shows the effect that these hormones have on the liver, the top left panel also applies to skeletal muscle.*

Glucagon

Glucagon causes the breakdown of glycogen into glucose (Fig. 11.16) through a second messenger mechanism (Fig. 11.2). It also increases the process of gluconeogenesis, which can utilize amino acids, glycerol, or lactate (Fig. 10.20). Through these actions, glucagon raises the level of blood glucose (Fig. 11.15). Glucagon is secreted by the alpha cells of the pancreas in response to sympathetic stimulation or low levels of blood glucose.

Regulation of metabolism

The endocrine and nervous systems regulate metabolic pathways in order to assure that: 1) blood levels of glucose are maintained to meet the needs of the nervous system; 2) catabolic pathways operate at a rate that produces adequate amounts of ATP; and 3) fuels will be mobilized or stored as needed.

Fuel flux in the fed state

Following the ingestion of food, insulin is released by the beta cells of the pancreatic islets in response to three factors: 1) stimulation by the parasympathetic nervous system, 2) endocrine signals from the gastrointestinal tract, and 3) increased levels of glucose and amino acids in the blood. Since insulin is released by the pancreas into the portal vein (Fig. 9.20), the liver is directly exposed both to the highest levels of insulin and the highest levels of glucose and amino acids coming from the G.I. tract. The liver is therefore in an ideal position to remove much of the absorbed glucose from the blood (Fig.11.16).

Insulin stimulates the facilitated diffusion of glucose into skeletal muscle and adipose tissue and increases glycogen synthesis in liver and muscle (Fig. 11.17). Both of these actions lower blood glucose levels.

Insulin stimulates the activity of the enzyme lipoprotein lipase, which increases the uptake of fatty acids from lipoprotein particles into adipocytes (Fig. 10.17). Since glycerol is produced in the adipocytes from glucose, and since glucose uptake by the adipocytes is stimulated by insulin, insulin increases the availability of both the fatty acids and glycerol that are needed for triglyceride synthesis. For these reasons, insulin also increases the storage of triglyceride in adipose tissue (Fig. 11.17).

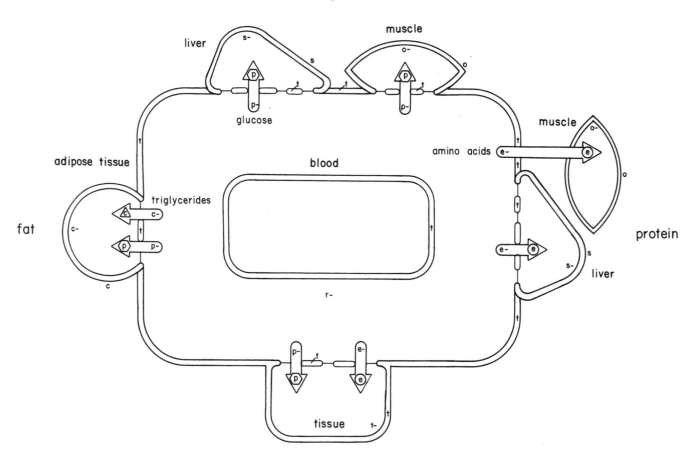

Figure 11.17 *Fuel flux in the fed state. Color the outline of the system, noting that sienna signifies liver, orange signifies muscle, canary signifies adipose tissue and tan signifies all other tissues and membranes. Note that they are situated relative to the general circulation from which they receive, and to which they contribute, various forms of carbohydrate (top of figure), fat (left side of figure) and protein (right side of figure) that are used as fuels. This picture represents the period a few hours after consuming a meal, when insulin levels are high. Color the molecules of glucose, triglyceride, and amino acids and the arrows representing their entry into tissues. Finish the picture by coloring the blood and the interiors of the tissues and organs. Note which tissues take up which fuels, and consider the way in which each substance may be stored.*

Insulin increases the transport of amino acids into tissues, as well as their incorporation into protein (Fig. 11.17). Insulin is also necessary in order for other hormones, such as growth hormone, to exert their anabolic effects.

Therefore, in the fed state, the storage of fuels as glycogen and triglyceride and the growth of tissue through protein synthesis is promoted both by the availability of nutrients and the elevation of insulin levels.

Fuel flux in the food-deprived state

Once nutrients from the meal have been cleared from the blood, the body must rely on its stored fuel to meet its energy needs. This requires a shift from a fuel storage mode to a fuel mobilization mode.

The means by which fuel is mobilized changes with time. A few hours after a meal, glycogen stores in liver and muscle begin to be broken down (Fig. 11.18); when a person begins to consume the next meal glycogen breakdown is curtailed. If the next meal does not commence at this point, as occurs overnight, glycogen breakdown is accompanied by the mobilization of additional fuels: triglycerides in adipose tissue are hydrolyzed and their component fatty acids and glycerol enter the blood, and proteins are degraded and their amino acids also enter the blood. The amino acids and glycerol that are released can be converted to glucose by the liver, through gluconeogenesis (Fig. 11.18).

If no food is consumed, glycogen stores will be exhausted in less than a day and gluconeogenesis will become

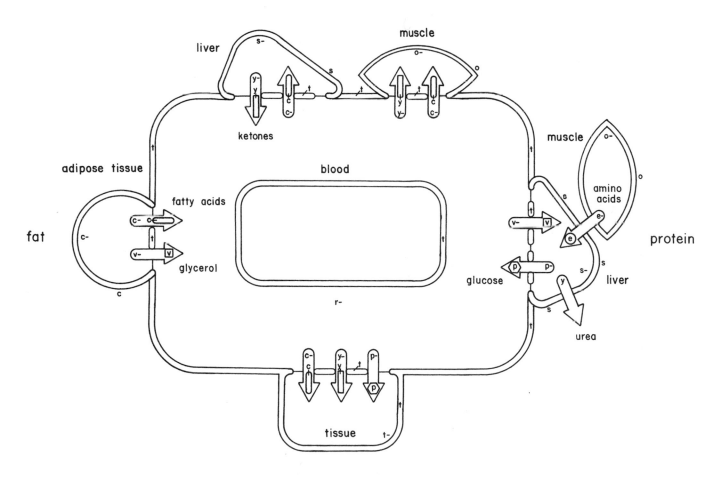

Figure 11.18 *Fuel flux in the food-deprived state. Color the outline as you did in Fig. 11.17. This picture represents a period of no food intake (a fast) or insufficient food intake (starvation) when insulin levels are low but glucagon and cortisol levels are high. Color the molecules of glucose, fatty acids, glycerol, ketones, and amino acids and the arrows representing the movement of substances into and out of each tissue. Note that urea produced by the liver is not taken up by other tissues. Finish the picture by coloring the blood and the interiors of the tissues and organs. Note which fuel each tissue is using and which tissues are contributing fuel to the blood. How does the liver interact with muscle and adipose tissue to provide glucose and ketones to the circulation?*

the major source of blood glucose. Since amino acids, which are derived from tissue proteins, are a major substrate for gluconeogenesis, blood glucose levels will be maintained at the expense of tissue proteins. Tissues that are losing protein (e.g. skeletal muscle, pancreas, heart, intestine) will show a decline in function with prolonged (weeks) starvation.

After a few days of starvation, the brain begins to utilize another fuel besides glucose, thereby sparing protein from breakdown; this is an important survival mechanism. The fuel it uses is called ketone bodies (Fig. 10.18); this fuel is made from fatty acids by the liver. Blood levels of ketone bodies become elevated early in a fast, as fatty acids released from the breakdown of triglycerides in adipose tissue become available to the liver (Fig. 11.18).

The brain must undergo a few days of exposure to high levels of ketone bodies before it can metabolize them. Once the brain is no longer totally reliant on glucose (it can satisfy about half of its energy needs with ketone bodies), it has a large fuel reservoir to draw upon, namely adipose tissue, and does not remove as much glucose from the blood. This adaptation spares body protein and prolongs survival, since production of glucose from amino acids in gluconeogenesis is reduced. Furthermore, most other tissues can use ketone bodies as well as free fatty acids as fuel (Fig. 11.18).

Once adipose tissue stores are depleted, the body must revert to using protein as a source of fuel. Since this breakdown of protein undermines the function of vital organs, survival is short once adipose tissue is depleted.

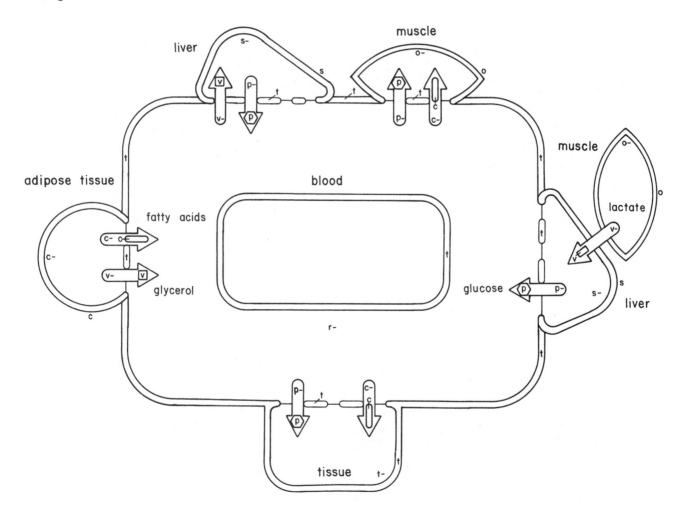

Figure 11.19 *Fuel flux in exercise. Color the outline as you did in Fig. 11.17. This picture represents moderate-to-strenuous exercise. Color the molecules of glucose, fatty acids, glycerol and lactate, as well as the arrows that represent the movement of substances into or out of each tissue. Finish the picture by coloring the blood and the interiors of the tissues and organs. Note which fuels muscle is using and the sources of these fuels. Identify the Cori cycle.*

Endocrine responses to the food-deprived state

The state of fuel mobilization that occurs when no food is consumed for a long period is due to a lack of available nutrients, to low levels of insulin, and to elevated levels of the catabolic hormones glucagon, epinephrine, and cortisol (Fig. 11.16).

Because insulin levels are low, the storage of glucose, fat, and amino acids is decreased and the breakdown of their storage forms by glycogenolysis, lipolysis, and proteolysis is increased.

Glucagon promotes glycogenolysis and gluconeogenesis in the liver, as well as lipolysis in adipose tissue. Epinephrine stimulates lipolysis in adipose tissue and glycogenolysis in muscle and liver. Cortisol promotes protein breakdown in muscle and abdominal organs, gluconeogenesis in liver, and lipolysis in adipose tissue (Figs. 11.16, 11.18).

Exercise

During exercise, the fuel needs of skeletal and cardiac muscle increase markedly. Blood levels of the hormones glucagon, epinephrine and, eventually, cortisol rise, while the blood level of insulin falls.

Skeletal muscle draws on its own stores of glycogen by increasing the rate of glycogenolysis. Glycogenolysis in muscle is stimulated by the release of intracellular calcium, which causes muscle contraction (Fig. 5.8), and by elevated levels of epinephrine in the blood (Fig. 11.16). Glucose is also made available to muscle and other tissues by the liver (Fig. 10.7); glycogenolysis and gluconeogenesis are stimulated by glucagon, and gluconeogenesis is further stimulated by cortisol if the exercise is prolonged or strenuous (Fig. 11.19).

Lipolysis in adipose tissue, which is stimulated by epinephrine, glucagon, and cortisol, provides tissues with a supply of fatty acids (Fig. 11.19). Muscle is an avid user of fatty acids during aerobic exercise, deriving a progressively larger portion of its fuel from fatty acids as the duration of exercise increases.

Muscle also metabolizes glucose anaerobically when the intensity of exercise is high. Anaerobic metabolism leads to the production of lactic acid (Fig. 10.14), which is released into the blood. Some of this lactic acid is converted back to glucose by the liver through the Cori cycle (Fig. 10.10). This energy-consuming pathway is important in maintaining blood glucose levels so that

brain function is not compromised by the high amounts of glucose used by exercising muscle (Fig. 11.19).

Summary of control of blood glucose level

The concentration of glucose in the blood is maintained at about 80 mg/dL; the glucose that is absorbed from a meal raises the level of blood glucose, insulin release is stimulated, and glucose is quickly removed from the blood (Fig. 11.15).

During a period in which a person abstains from eating, or during a period of exercise, blood levels of glucose decline until glucose is supplied to the blood by the pathways of glycogenolysis and gluconeogenesis in the liver. These glucose-producing actions of the liver are stimulated by the increased release of glucagon (Fig. 11.15), epinephrine, and cortisol (Fig. 11.16).

Hypoglycemia

The normal blood glucose level supplies glucose-dependent tissues, primarily the central nervous system, with an adequate supply of fuel. Hypoglycemia, which is a lower than normal blood level of glucose, is detected by receptors in the hypothalamus. These receptors stimulate the sympathetic nervous system to release catecholamines, which suppress insulin release and stimulate glucagon release, which causes glycogen breakdown. These actions raise the level of blood glucose; if blood glucose had continued to fall, coma and death would result.

Hyperglycemia

A low production of insulin or a failure of tissues to respond to insulin, both of which occur in the disease diabetes mellitus, cause hyperglycemia, which is a higher than normal blood level of glucose. If the rise in blood glucose after a meal is not checked by insulin, plasma glucose levels may exceed the kidney's ability to reabsorb it and glucose will appear in the urine (Fig. 7.16).

The excretion of glucose in the urine creates an osmotic pull on water that increases urine output, which can lead to dehydration. Other long-term consequences of hyperglycemia are due to damage to proteins that is caused by the spontaneous addition of glucose to them; a process called glycosylation. Pathological consequences of glycosylation include renal disease, retinopathy, which leads to blindness, and cardiovascular disease; these are the major complications of diabetes mellitus.

Glucose tolerance test

An individual's ability to regulate blood glucose levels can be assessed through a glucose tolerance test (Fig. 11.20). After an overnight fast, a baseline blood sample is taken; then a glucose load (e.g. 75 grams of glucose) is ingested and blood samples are taken 30, 60, and 120 minutes after the load.

The concentration of glucose in all of the blood samples is measured and compared with normal standards to judge whether or not blood glucose is brought back to the baseline level within a normal period of time; individuals with diabetes mellitus show both an elevated baseline level of glucose and a much slower return to baseline following the ingestion of an oral glucose load (Fig. 11.20).

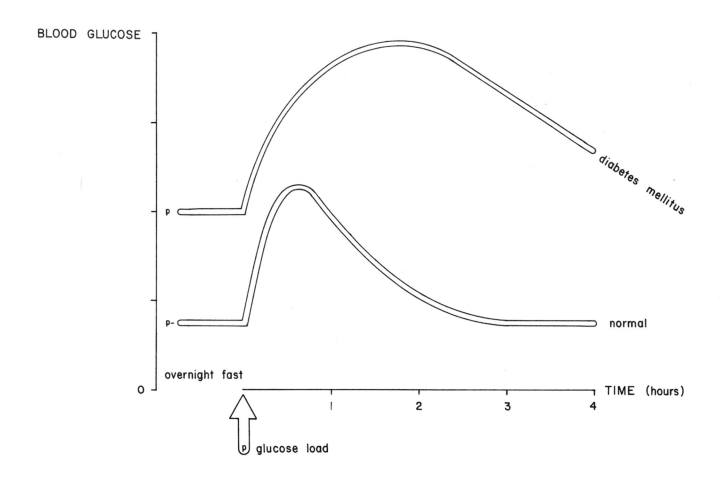

Figure 11.20 *Glucose tolerance test. Begin at the left by coloring the baseline levels of glucose for both conditions. Color the arrow indicating the glucose load and the subsequent changes in blood glucose that occur. Note that individuals with diabetes mellitus show an elevated baseline level of glucose and a much slower return to baseline following an oral glucose load.*

chapter **twelve**
reproduction

Reproduction is the process through which organisms produce their offspring.

The process of reproduction

The process of reproduction includes: 1) the formation of gametes, or mature germ cells, 2) fertilization, in which the male and female gametes combine to form a zygote; 3) the development of the organism during gestation, which is the period between fertilization and birth; 4) parturition, which is the delivery of the baby and the placenta, and 5) lactation, or milk production, which provides for the early survival of the offspring.

Formation of gametes

Gametes are the mature germ cells of each sex; the sperm is the male gamete and the ovum, or egg, is the female gamete. Gamete production involves the formation of cells that have only half of the normal complement of chromosomes (Fig. 12.1). Somatic cells, which are cells other than gametes, have one set of chromosomes from each parent; therefore, they each have two sets of genes. In humans somatic cells have 23 pairs of chromosomes, for a total of 46 chromosomes.

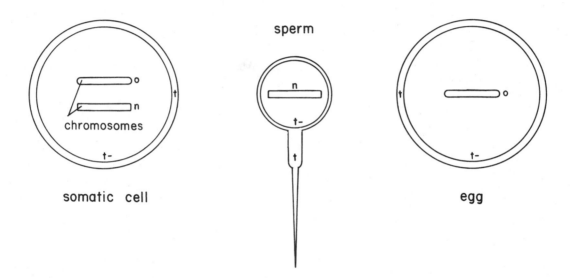

Figure 12.1 *Somatic cells and gametes. Color the cell membranes and cytoplasm of each of the cells shown. Color the chromosomes of the somatic cell, the sperm, and the egg or ovum. Note that somatic cells contain a double set of chromosomes, which is 46 chromosomes in humans, whereas gametes contain only a single set, or 23 chromosomes.*

Homologous chromosomes

Each gene codes for a specific protein, but there may be different versions of a gene and, therefore, different proteins that it codes for. These different versions of the same gene are called alleles. The pair of chromosomes that contain the same genes, but may have different alleles, are called homologous chromosomes (Fig. 12.2). The allele on one homologous chromosome may dominate the allele on another and cause its version of the protein to be synthesized by the cell. Since each new organism receives only one chromosome from each homologous pair of its parents, each gamete (sperm and ovum) must contain only a single set of chromosomes.

Cell division

Cell division consists of two parts; division of the nucleus and division of the cytoplasm. The two types of cell division are called mitosis and meiosis, and they differ in the way in which they divide the nucleus. In mitosis, one cell divides into two new cells, each of which has two sets of chromosomes, as is normal for somatic cells. In meiosis, one cell divides into two new cells, each of which has only one set of chromosomes, as is normal for gametes (Fig. 12.1).

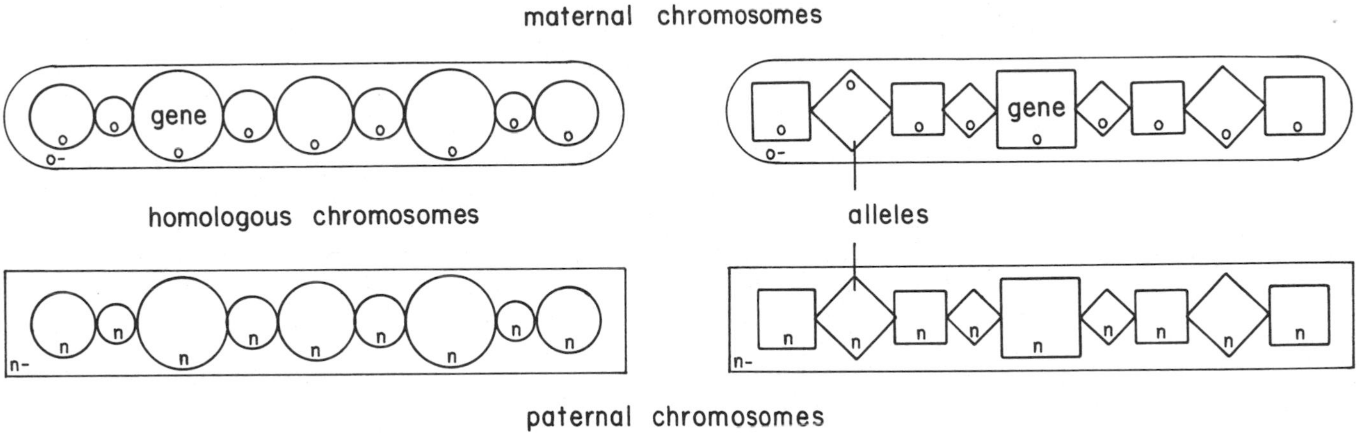

maternal chromosomes

homologous chromosomes

alleles

paternal chromosomes

Figure 12.2 *Homologous chromosomes. Color the string of genes in each chromosome; note that each homologous pair consists of a maternal chromosome that came from the mother and a paternal chromosome that came from the father. Identify the alleles for each gene in the homologous pairs.*

Organelles used in cell division

Mitosis and meiosis both utilize cellular organelles to sort and move the chromosomes, and split the cytoplasm into two new membrane-surrounded portions that each contain a nucleus. The organelles used in cell division are the centrioles and the spindle fibers. The pairs of centrioles, which each consist of two cylindrical structures that are positioned at right angles to each other, move to opposite sides of the cell during cell division. The centrioles organize the spindle fibers and are transformed into asters, which define the opposite poles of the dividing cell. The spindle fibers are comprised of microtubules, which are tubular structures made of protein. Spindle fibers that pull the chromatids apart in mitosis (see below), or pull the chromosomes apart in meiosis (see below) are connected to an aster at only one end. Other spindle fibers that elongate the dividing cell are connected to asters at both ends.

DNA duplication

Cell division begins with the duplication of all the DNA in all of the chromosomes. Since each molecule of DNA is comprised of two complementary strands that form a double helix, duplication of DNA requires that the strands separate and that each strand is duplicated (Fig. 2.4). This process utilizes a number of enzymes, including DNA polymerase, which creates the bond between the nucleotides that make up each DNA strand. Duplication of DNA occurs during the period between cell divisions, or interphase; each chromosome that has been duplicated is now in the form of pair of chromatids, linked together at a point called the centromere, or kinetochore. Therefore, each pair of homologous chromosomes becomes two pairs of identical chromatids.

Mitosis

Cell division is organized into the following phases. In prophase, the spindle fibers are assembled from microtubule segments in the cytoplasm; spindle fibers that are connected at their ends to the centrioles push the centrioles apart when the fibers lengthen. Tubules grow radially from each centriole, and the new structure is called an aster. In prometaphase, the nuclear membrane disintegrates and other spindle fibers, which are connected at one end to an aster, become connected at their other end to a chromatid near its kinetochore. In this way, one chromatid from each pair is connected by spindle fibers to an opposite aster. In metaphase, the chromosomes line up along a plane that bisects the cell between the asters; this is called the equatorial plate. In anaphase, all 46 pairs of chromatids are separated, with one set going toward each aster. Since each chromatid ends up in a new cell, the chromosomes of the daughter cells are identical to those of the original parent cell (Fig. 12.3). Finally, in telophase, a new nuclear membrane develops around each set of chromosomes and the cell pinches into two daughter cells, each with its own nucleus.

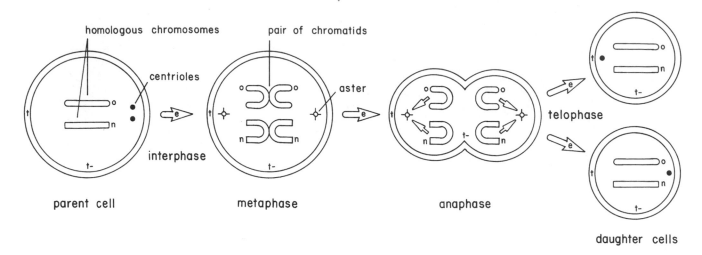

Figure 12.3 *Mitosis. Begin with the parent cell at left and, for each stage of mitosis, color the cell membranes, cytoplasm, chromosomes, chromatids, and arrows. Examine each cell, noting that in interphase, each chromosome doubles to become a pair of chromatids, and that the centrioles migrate to opposite poles and become asters; in metaphase the chromatid pairs that make up each chromosome line up at the equatorial plate; in anaphase the chromatid pairs separate; and in telophase the cell pinches into two daughter cells.*

Meiosis

Meiosis consists of a sequence of two cell divisions. The first meiotic division occurs after all of the DNA is duplicated in interphase. During prophase, homologous chromosomes, each consisting of a pair of chromatids, line up so that corresponding genes, or alleles (Fig. 12.2), lie next to each other. Portions of the chromosomes, consisting of a number of genes, are exchanged between the homologous pairs; this cross-over produces a new combination of alleles in each of the chromosomes (Fig. 12.4). The 23 pairs of homologous chromosomes then line up at the equatorial plate at metaphase. In anaphase, the spindle fibers pull the chromosome pairs apart so that one chromosome from each homologous pair moves toward its aster. In telophase the cytoplasm divides and the resulting daughter cells each have only one chromosome from each homologous pair (Fig. 12.5).

The second meiotic division then proceeds without any replication of DNA. The chromosomes, which still consist of a pair of chromatids, line up at the equatorial plate during metaphase. The chromatids are separated during anaphase, each being pulled to the opposite aster (Fig. 12.4). After the cytoplasm divides in telophase, each daughter cell has one chromatid from only one chromosome of each homologous pair. In this way, meiosis produces gametes that have half the amount of DNA of somatic cells (Fig. 12.3). Male gametes are formed in a process called spermatogenesis and female gametes are formed in a process called oogenesis.

Spermatogenesis

In the male, many immature, undifferentiated germ cells are found in the seminiferous tubules of the testes and these cells continue to proliferate by mitosis throughout life. Each germ cell undergoes meiosis to form four sperm cells; this is the process of spermatogenesis (Fig. 12.4). Spermatogenesis begins at puberty, the onset of adult sexual function, and continues throughout life in the male. The anterior pituitary gland secretes follicle stimulating hormone (FSH), which promotes sperm development, and luteinizing hormone (LH), which stimulates the Leydig cells of the testes to secrete testosterone, which is also necessary for spermatogenesis (Fig. 11.6).

Oogenesis

In the female, all of the undifferentiated germ cells (about 2 million) are already formed in the ovaries before birth and will not proliferate further by mitosis. Since they begin but do not complete the first meiotic division, they remain in the form of primary oocytes until they individually mature during adulthood. Completion of oogenesis (both meiotic divisions, Fig 12.4), or the formation of a mature egg, occurs only for those eggs that are fertilized by a sperm cell. In contrast to the four functional gametes that are formed by each germ cell in the male, each undifferentiated germ cell in the female gives rise to only one functional gamete.

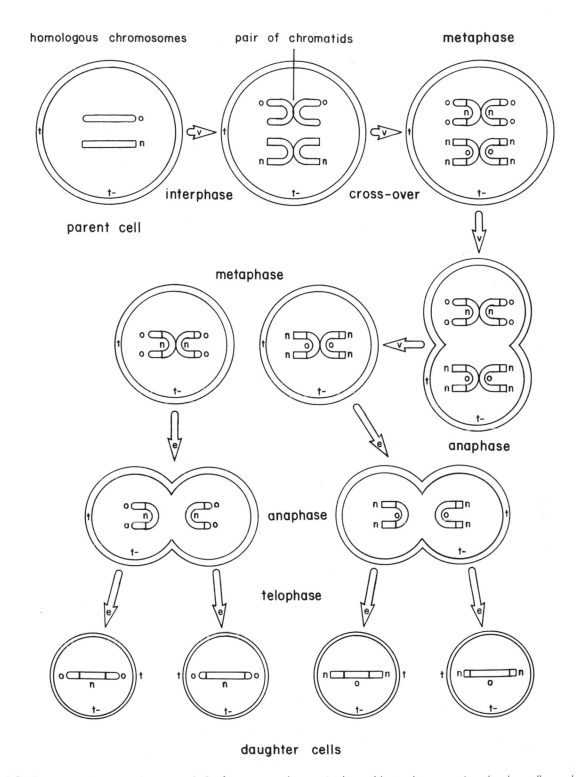

homologous chromosomes · pair of chromatids · metaphase

parent cell · interphase · cross-over

metaphase · anaphase

anaphase · telophase

daughter cells

Figure 12.4 *Meiosis. Begin at the top with the first meiotic division (indicated by violet arrows); color the cell membranes, cytoplasm, chromosomes and chromatids up to the first cell division. Compare the chromosomes before and after the cross-over. Note that during the first metaphase, pairs of homologous chromosomes line up across from each other at the equatorial plate and in the first anaphase the chromosomes of this pair are separated. Color the daughter cells in the first meiotic division and note that each cell contains both chromatids from each chromosome that it receives. Now color all of the structures in the second meiotic division (indicated by green arrows). Note that there is no replication of genetic material between the two divisions. Note also that in the second metaphase, the chromatids belonging to each chromosome line up across from each other at the equatorial plate and are separated in the second anaphase. Compare the four daughter cells with the original parent cell and those shown in Fig. 12.3.*

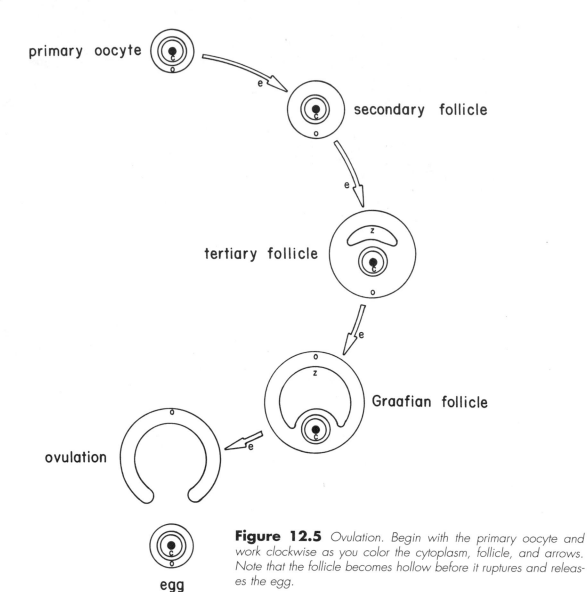

primary oocyte

secondary follicle

tertiary follicle

Graafian follicle

ovulation

egg

Figure 12.5 *Ovulation. Begin with the primary oocyte and work clockwise as you color the cytoplasm, follicle, and arrows. Note that the follicle becomes hollow before it ruptures and releases the egg.*

Ovulation

Beginning at puberty, secretion of FSH by the anterior pituitary gland (Fig. 11.6) causes one primary oocyte to complete the first meiotic division each month. Primary oocytes are encased in a cellular shell called a follicle, and FSH causes the follicle to mature and produce the hormone estrogen; LH causes the follicle to rupture, releasing the egg; this is the process of ovulation (Fig. 12.5).

Menstrual cycle

The pattern of secretion of FSH and LH has a monthly cycle, which accounts for the monthly occurrence of ovulation (Fig. 12.6). The follicle that remains after ovulation forms a yellow cluster of cells called the corpus luteum, which secretes the hormones progesterone and estrogen. After the egg is released, it travels through a fallopian, or uterine, tube that is located near each ovary. If the egg is not fertilized by fusion with a sperm at this point, the egg and corpus luteum will degenerate.

Menstruation

Concomitant with these events in the ovary are changes in the endometrium, which is the cellular lining of the uterus. When estrogen production by the ovaries is high, endometrial cells proliferate; when progesterone production by the corpus luteum is also high (Fig. 12.6), the blood vessels in the endometrium increase in number. When the corpus luteum degenerates, as occurs in the absence of a signal from the fertilized egg, progesterone and estrogen levels drop, and the newly developed cells slough off and menstrual bleeding occurs (menstruation).

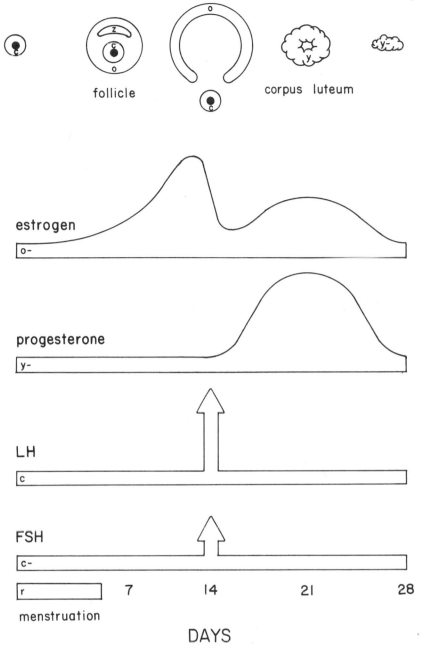

Figure 12.6 *Menstrual cycle. At the top, color the egg, mature follicle, ruptured follicle, and corpus luteum during one turn of the menstrual cycle. Below it, color the graphs for estrogen, progesterone, FSH, LH, and menstruation. Note that a surge in FSH and LH occurs just before ovulation, and that the mature follicle produces estrogen, whereas the corpus luteum produces both estrogen and progesterone. Menstruation occurs when levels of estrogen and progesterone decline.*

Fertilization

If the egg is fertilized, it produces a hormone called chorionic gonadotropin that stimulates the corpus luteum to continue to secrete progesterone and estrogen until tissue derived from the fertilized egg can take over the role of producing these hormones. The high levels of estrogen and progesterone prevent menstruation, and are also instrumental in the development of adaptations that support the growth of the new organism.

The fertilized egg completes the second stage of meiosis to become a mature gamete, with only one set of chromosomes. Then the nuclei of sperm and egg fuse; the new nucleus contains two sets of 23 chromosomes and the cell that is formed is called the zygote (Fig. 12.7).

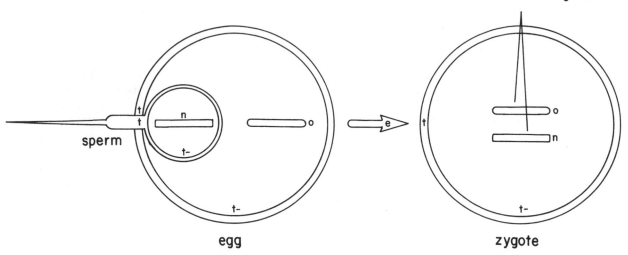

Figure 12.7 *Fertilization. Color the cell membranes, cytoplasm and chromosomes of the sperm and egg; note that the chromosome in each represents a single set of chromosomes (23 chromosomes in humans). Next, color the fertilized egg, or zygote, that results. Note that it has two sets of chromosomes (46 in humans), and that they consist of pairs of homologous chromosomes. Compare this figure with Fig. 12.1.*

Implantation

The zygote enters the uterus where it undergoes a series of mitotic divisions and begins to change shape. It is during this early period of development that attachment to the uterine wall, or implantation, occurs. The outer cell layers of the zygote invade the endometrium, and this anchors the zygote. Implantation also ruptures maternal blood vessels, thereby establishing communication with maternal tissues. Inner cell layers of the zygote differentiate to form the embryo and the outer cell layers differentiate to form the placenta. It is the embryo that will develop into the fetus.

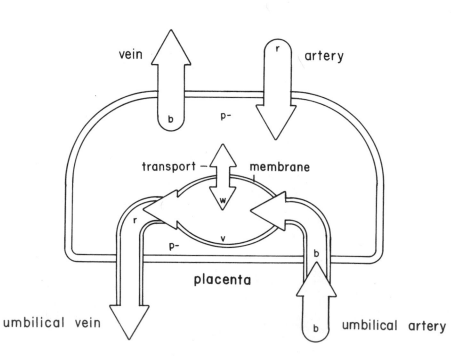

Figure 12.8 *Placental circulation. Color the umbilical artery, capillary bed and vein. Note that the placental membrane, which consists of several layers of cells, separates the fetal circulation from the maternal circulation. Next, color the maternal blood flowing from the uterine artery, the blood that pools outside of the placental membrane, and the blood returning to the maternal circulation by way of the uterine vein. Note that fetal and maternal blood do not mix. Note also that substances are transported in both directions across the placental membrane.*

Placenta

Since the placenta develops from the zygote it contains the same DNA as the fetus. Because of their identical DNA, samples of the placenta are used in prenatal testing for genetic abnormalities in the fetus.

The function of the placenta is to the provide for the exchange of materials between fetal and maternal blood, while keeping the two circulatory systems separate (Fig. 12.8). The placental blood, which is the same as the fetal blood, travels through an umbilical vein, which carries oxygenated blood from the placenta to the fetus, and two umbilical arteries, which carry deoxygenated blood from the fetus to the placenta; these vessels comprise the umbilical cord.

Transport of substances between the maternal and fetal circulations

There is net transfer of needed substances such as oxygen, glucose, amino acids, water, vitamins, and minerals from mother to fetus, and net transfer of waste products such as carbon dioxide and urea from fetus to mother. This exchange is accomplished by the transport mechanisms of passive diffusion, facilitated diffusion, and active transport (Fig. 12.8). There are other mechanisms that regulate the exchange of substances between the maternal and fetal circulations. For example, there are transport proteins in the fetal circulation that have higher affinities for certain vitamins than those of the comparable maternal proteins.

The placental membrane forms structures called chorionic villi, which are similar to intestinal villi (Fig. 9.19) and are embedded in the uterine walls; these provide a large surface area for exchange of substances between maternal and fetal blood. On the maternal side, the ruptured blood vessels create pools of slow-moving blood and on the fetal side there is an extensive capillary network. Materials are transferred between the two blood supplies by crossing the placental membrane (Fig. 12.8). Although maternal antibodies and viruses can cross this membrane, bacteria and many hormones cannot.

Endocrine function of the placenta

Throughout the pregnancy, the placenta also functions as an endocrine gland, producing estrogen and progesterone, which promote maternal adaptation to the pregnancy. The adaptations include an increase in the maternal blood supply, suppression of maternal immunologic response to the fetus, and maintenance of elevated maternal plasma glucose levels in order to supply glucose to the fetus.

Gestation

The period of development from fertilization to birth is known as gestation. The average length of human gestation is 38 weeks. During gestation, the embryo, which is called a fetus after week 8, increases in size through cell division and develops different types of cells that form organs with specific functions; this second process is called differentiation. The growth and differentiation of cells and of the organism as a whole are guided by the information in its DNA, and are influenced by the environment within the uterus, including the adequacy of the oxygen and nutrient supply and the presence of toxic substances.

Parturition

At parturition, or birth, both fetus and placenta are delivered from the mother. Parturition involves the dilation of the cervix, which is the lower part of the uterus that opens into the vaginal canal, and forceful contraction of uterine muscle. Once the umbilical cord is cut, the lungs, kidneys and gastrointestinal tract of the baby must perform all of the functions that were formerly carried out by the placenta.

Lactation

Lactation is the production and secretion of milk by the mammary glands. The milk of each type of mammal differs in composition and suits the stage of physiologic development of the newborn of that species. Human milk provides appropriate nutrition and immune protection for infants.

The mammary glands consist of a highly branched duct system with exocrine cells arranged around the lumen, thereby forming acini that are similar to those of other organs (Fig. 9.12). The mammary cells produce and secrete milk. Myoepithelium, which consists of contractile cells, surrounds the exocrine cells and the part of the duct into which they secrete (Fig. 12.9).

During pregnancy, estrogen promotes the proliferation of the duct system of the mammary glands; the hormones prolactin, which is secreted by the anterior pituitary gland, and progesterone, which is secreted by the ovaries (Fig. 11.6), promote the growth of the mammary gland as well as the production of a secretory fluid called colostrum. Colostrum has a higher protein but lower fat and carbohydrate content than mature milk; it also has a higher concentration of antibodies to microorganisms. Colostrum collects in the mammary ducts before parturition and is released during the first few days after birth in response to suckling by the infant.

The main stimulant of milk synthesis is prolactin; although elevated blood levels of prolactin during pregnancy promote growth of the mammary gland, the high levels of estrogen that also occur during pregnancy inhibit the production of milk. At parturition, however, estrogen levels abruptly decline as the placenta is delivered, and prolactin can then exert its stimulatory effect on milk production.

Let-down reflex

Milk production and ejection from the mammary gland are largely controlled by the infant's suckling (Fig. 12.9). During each feeding, neural signals from the nipple to the hypothalamus cause the latter to send pro-lactin releasing hormone (PRH) to the anterior pituitary gland, which then releases prolactin (Fig. 11.6). Therefore, longer and more frequent feedings will cause more milk to be produced.

The actual ejection of milk, which is called the let-down reflex, is initiated by impulses generated at the nipple during suckling that travel along afferent nerve pathways to the hypothalamus. These excitatory impulses stimulate the posterior pituitary gland to release the hormone oxytocin (Fig. 11.8). Oxytocin stimulates contraction of the myoepithelial cells that surround the terminus, or end, of the milk duct, thereby pushing the milk that had already been released by the exocrine cells down toward the nipple (Fig. 12.9).

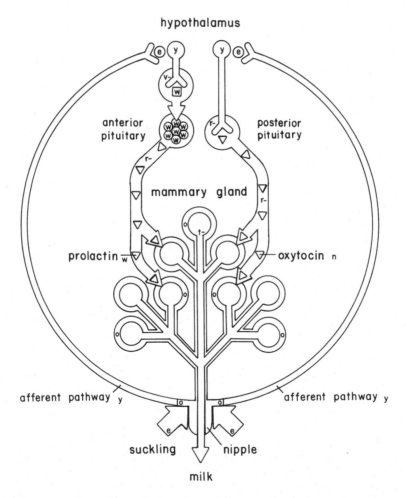

Figure 12.9 *Let-down reflex. Begin by coloring the nipple and the arrows representing suckling by the infant. Color the afferent neuron on the left side, and the excitatory neurotransmitter that it releases at the synapse in the hypothalamus; color the molecule of prolactin releasing hormone (PRH) secreted by the hypothalamus, the anterior pituitary gland, and the prolactin released into the general circulation. Note that prolactin acts on mammary cells to increase their production of milk. Now return to the nipple and color the neuron on the right, its excitatory neurotransmitter and the hypothalamic neuron that releases oxytocin in the posterior pituitary gland. Color the gland and the oxytocin molecules that travel through the general circulation and stimulate the myoepithelium in the mammary ducts to contract, thereby pushing the milk that collects in the duct down toward the nipple. Finally, color the mammary ducts, acini, and the lumen, which is filled with milk. Note that both ejection, or let-down, of milk and synthesis of milk are stimulated when the infant suckles. Compare this figure with Figs. 1.9, 1.10, and 11.6.*

chapter **thirteen**
index

About the Authors

Dr. Kenneth Axen is an Associate Professor of Rehabilitation Medicine at New York University Medical Center. Since receiving his Ph.D. in Biomedical Engineering from New York University, Dr. Axen has been conducting basic research on respiratory perception in humans, regulation of breathing in neuromuscular disorders, and rehabilitation of people with respiratory impairments. His numerous research articles in the Journal of Applied Physiology have earned him international recognition in the area of respiratory control. He also has many years of experience teaching physiology to physical therapy students and health science majors. Dr. Axen is the co-editor of Pulmonary Therapy and Rehabilitation: Principles and Practice, and the illustrator of The Essential Asthma Book and The Chronic Bronchitis and Emphysema Handbook.

Dr. Kathleen Vermitsky Axen is a Professor in the Department of Health and Nutrition Sciences at Brooklyn College of the City University of New York where she teaches undergraduate and graduate courses in nutrition and metabolism. Dr. Axen received her Ph.D. in Nutritional Biochemistry from Columbia University, New York. She trained as a postdoctoral fellow in Endocrinology at the Albert Einstein College of Medicine, New York. Dr. Axen's research on the regulation of insulin secretion and on the development and treatment of diabetes mellitus in animal models of the disease has been published in the American Journal of Physiology and the Journal of Clinical Investigation.

Free!

Did you know that The Microsoft Network gives you one free month?

Call us at 1-800-FREE MSN. We'll send you a free CD to get you going.

Then, you can explore the World Wide Web for one month, free. Exchange e-mail with your family and friends. Play games, book airline tickets, handle finances, go car shopping, explore old hobbies and discover new ones. There's one big, useful online world out there. And for one month, it's a free world.

Call **1-800-FREE MSN,** Dept. 3197, for offer details or visit us at **www.msn.com**. Some restrictions apply.

Microsoft® Where do you want to go today?®

FIND US...

International

Hong Kong
4/F Sun Hung Kai Centre
30 Harbour Road, Wan Chai,
Hong Kong
Tel: (011)85-2-517-3016

Japan
Fuji Building 40, 15-14
Sakuragaokacho, Shibuya Ku,
Tokyo 150, Japan
Tel: (011)81-3-3463-1343

Korea
Tae Young Bldg, 944-24,
Daechi- Dong, Kangnam-Ku
The Princeton Review- ANC
Seoul, Korea 135-280,
South Korea
Tel: (011)82-2-554-7763

Mexico City
PR Mex S De RL De Cv
Guanajuato 228 Col. Roma
06700 Mexico D.F., Mexico
Tel: 525-564-9468

Montreal
666 Sherbrooke St.
West, Suite 202
Montreal, QC H3A 1E7 Canada
Tel: (514) 499-0870

Pakistan
1 Bawa Park - 90 Upper Mall
Lahore, Pakistan
Tel: (011)92-42-571-2315

Spain
Pza. Castilla, 3 - 5° A, 28046
Madrid, Spain
Tel: (011)341-323-4212

Taiwan
155 Chung Hsiao East Road
Section 4 - 4th Floor,
Taipei R.O.C., Taiwan
Tel: (011)886-2-751-1243

Thailand
Building One, 99 Wireless Road
Bangkok, Thailand 10330
Tel: (662) 256-7080

Toronto
1240 Bay Street, Suite 300
Toronto M5R 2A7 Canada
Tel: (800) 495-7737
Tel: (716) 839-4391

Vancouver
4212 University Way NE,
Suite 204
Seattle, WA 98105
Tel: (206) 548-1100

National (U.S.)
We have over 60 offices around the U.S. and run courses in over 400 sites. For courses and locations within the U.S. call 1 (800) 2/Review and you will be routed to the nearest office.

More expert advice from The Princeton Review

CRACKING THE MCAT WITH
PRACTICE QUESTIONS ON CD-ROM
0-375-76352-X • $59.95

PRACTICE MCATS
0-375-76456-9 • $22.95

CRACKING THE NCLEX-RN
7TH EDITION
0-375-76316-3 • $25.00

CRACKING THE NCLEX-RN
WITH SAMPLE TESTS ON CD-ROM
7TH EDITION
0-375-76302-3 • $34.95
WIN/MAC COMPATIBLE

ANATOMY COLORING WORKBOOK
2ND EDITION
0-375-76342-2 • $19.00

BIOLOGY COLORING WORKBOOK
0-679-77884-5 • $18.00

HUMAN BRAIN
COLORING WORKBOOK
0-679-77885-3 • $17.00

PHYSIOLOGY
COLORING WORKBOOK
0-679-77850-0 • $18.00

BEST 162 MEDICAL SCHOOLS
0-375-76420-8 • $22.95

GUIDE TO CAREERS IN THE
HEALTH PROFESSIONS
0-375-76158-6 • $24.95

If you want to give yourself the best chance for getting into the medical school of your choice, we can help you get the highest test scores, make the most informed choices, and make the most of your experience once you get there. Whether you want to be an M.D., a nurse, or any other kind of health care professional, we can even help you ace the tests and make a career move that will let you use your skills and education to their best advantage.